'Driberg was the original William Hickey of the *Daily Express* and there has never been another to approach him'
Terence Lancaster, *Daily Mirror*

'Driberg wants readers to know about his private life so they may better understand what made him the politician he was: and I think he succeeds'
Robert Skidelsky, *New Society*

'But there's no doubt how seriously to take the homosexuality. This was *the* ruling passion of Driberg's life . . . Everything relating to this is brilliantly and, I would judge, honestly written . . . He recollects best what is most personal'
Paul Barker, *The Times*

'There is no great bitterness in what Tom Driberg has written. The story is unfolded in that scalding prose style for which he was renowned, with wit, with much dramatic incident, and with a strange dignity'
Michael Mason, *Gay News*

RULING PASSIONS

Ω_____

TOM DRIBERG
Postscript by Michael Foot
QUARTET BOOKS
LONDON MELBOURNE NEW YORK

Published by Quartet Books Limited 1978
A member of the Namara Group
27 Goodge Street, London W1P 1FD
First published in Great Britain by Jonathan Cape Limited,
London, 1977

ISBN 0 7043 3223 X

Printed and bound in Great Britain by
Hazell Watson & Viney Ltd,
Aylesbury, Bucks

Contents

Foreword by David Higham   ix

1   Born out of due time   1
2   Piety and puberty   10
3   Family ties   17
4   Grace and disgrace   44
5   Oxford 1   54
6   Oxford 2: Vacations   74
7   Down and out, and in   87
8   Hickey at large   107
9   Against the law   129
10   Phoney war and real bombs   149
11   American journey   166
12   Going to Westminster   178
13   War correspondent   204
14   Russian escapades   228

Postscript by Michael Foot   251
Note   256
Index   257

Illustrations

Illustrations between pages 132 and 133

1   Tom Driberg as a young man
2   The Sixth Form at Lancing, 1921
3   (*Right*) Alan Jones, 'the exaggeratedly Welsh' night news
     editor of the *Daily Express*
4   (*Below*) At a Mayfair fashion show, April 1933
     (*Radio Times Hulton Picture Library*)
5   Guy Burgess and Tolya in Moscow
6   On television with Dame Edith Sitwell, November 1962
     (*BBC*)
7   'William Hickey fights a by-election.' Campaigning as an
     Independent in Maldon, 1943 (*Radio Times Hulton
     Picture Library*)
8   With Harold Wilson at the 1955 Labour Party Conference in
     Margate (*Radio Times Hulton Picture Library*)
9   Leaving for the 1963 Scarborough Conference with
     Jennie Lee and Anthony Wedgwood Benn
     (*Keystone Press Agency*)
10   With Pandit Nehru
11   With King Hussein of Jordan (*Keystone Press Agency*)
12   With Pope Paul VI
13   Talking to Barbara Castle at the Labour Party Conference,
     1971
14   Tom Driberg's home for many years, Bradwell Lodge, Essex

Foreword
by David Higham

I learnt only from his will that Tom had made me his Special Trustee — and so literary editor — for his memoirs, though we had met and discussed the work only a month or so before he so suddenly died. He was sure then that he wouldn't live very long and after our talk I had made proposals to his publishers founded on the fairly short lease he expected and even felt he could guarantee. Meanwhile he set out to finish the book as quickly as he could, for his own satisfaction as well as to lodge it with his publishers as full security against the bargain he wanted to make.

The question of a bargain arose because he had shown part of what he had written to two of his friends, both, like himself, in the House of Lords, and they had told him that if he published what they had read, attendance at the Lords would in practice be impossible. Tom had been delighted with his peerage not, I think, so much for the honour as for the chance of a return to active politics. The advice of his friends — and they *were* and would remain friends — dejected him, but his response was typical. He wouldn't publish in his lifetime — but he wouldn't alter.

So what is now printed is what Tom wrote, amended only to fill in a few missing names and dates or to correct a rare mistake of fact and to exclude risks of libel, risks which turned out to be slight. What had bothered his friends, and what Tom was determined not to modify, was the defiant — you could call it crusading — exposition and defence of homosexuality: its pleasures, its dangers, its right to be practised, its case against discrimination.

Tom left a manuscript, typed fair and corrected in his own hand, of book length but not complete. No notes could be found from which any further episodes might be added, even if there were anyone to match his style. In two or three places the words 'More to come' appear; only one note, 'War in Korea', indicates what is missing. But the book doesn't go beyond the middle 1950s. That apart, he had written nothing of his beautiful house at Bradwell (from which he took his title as a peer): and, more importantly, nothing of his long and active career as a Labour M.P. and a member – chairman eventually – of the Party Executive. His publishers and I both felt it essential that this aspect of his life – its public culmination – should be covered: and Michael Foot, his friend and close associate in the Commons, willingly agreed to deal with it. His account supplies the postscript to the book.

Acknowledgments

Acknowledgment is due to the following for permission to quote the copyright material on the pages mentioned. The Estate of W. H. Auden (p. 62); Robert Graves (pp. 64, 65); the *Daily Express* (pp. 116–28, 151, 155–6, 158–61, 170–6, 185); the *Evening Standard* (pp. 105–6); Eric Walter White (pp. 69–70); Cassell & Co., Ltd, and Houghton Mifflin Company for *The Second World War* by Winston S. Churchill (p. 184); Faber and Faber, Ltd, and Farrar, Straus and Giroux, Inc, for 'This be the verse' from *High Windows* by Philip Larkin (p. 17); the Estate of Constant Lambert (pp. 163, 164); and the Co-operative Press, Ltd (pp. 205–8, 210–13, 218–22, 240–5).

I

Born out of due time

When I have taken a sleeping pill (Mogadon) and woken at 3.30 or 5.30 a.m., peed, taken two paracetamols to boost the pill, and slept for two or three hours more, the dreams on which I then wake are a complex jumble of phenomena, often brightly coloured and, briefly, memorable. The person most often present in them is my mother.

She is looking small, frail and wounded, as I remember seeing her standing alone at Victoria Station, one morning in the 1930s, when I had promised to meet her on her arrival from the country and was late because of a hangover.

It seems odd that this woman, who died in 1939 at the age of seventy-three, should still be featuring in my morning dream routine in the 1970s. I do not know what, if anything, it 'means'. There is no sexual content in this dream encounter (as there is in so many others); but it does, perhaps, suggest a somewhat obsessive filial relationship of the kind from which Freud constructed his theory of the Oedipus complex. My father, however, does not appear in these dreams, nor do I, even symbolically, kill him (unless a parricidal urge is expressed simply by his absence). It would, in fact, be surprising if he were to be visible to my dream eye, for I have only a shadowy, two-dimensional memory of him in his lifetime. I was born in 1905: he was born in 1840, and died in 1919. So I remember him only as an old and sick man, with a beard like Edward VII's and a monocle. The monocle was constantly falling out, sometimes – to my embarrassment, if guests were present – into the soup. He also wore a glass eye, which I have in a drawer. I remember being irritated by him and, once, hitting him: I remember not one word that he ever spoke to me.

One phrase often used in accounts of family relations – the term 'very close' – seems to me detestable, in its suffocating cosiness. Despite the apparent fixation already mentioned, my feelings for my mother were not of that cloyingly sweet, adulatory kind so familiar in descriptions of the lives of celebrated actors such as Ivor Novello. My childhood life at home was blank and lonely, and became more and more boring as I grew into adolescence. I was 'very close' to nobody. There were these parents, one aged, the other aging. (My mother was born in 1866, and so was thirty-nine when I was born.) There were two elder brothers, young men of twenty and twenty-two by the time I was five years old, and even before that mostly away at school. There were seaside holidays with cousins with whom I never felt at ease: used to my solitude, I was uncouth when thrown into the easy, joky company of the (I think) eleven children of my mother's brother, my uncle Herbert ('Bertie') Irving Bell.

I must not exaggerate, or seem to whine. There were agreeable passages – hours spent alone, reading, in a comfortable seat I had contrived on the bough of a tree in the garden; driving in a dog-cart, with my mother and a maid or nanny, to picnic on the edge of Ashdown Forest, at a secluded spot called Greenwood Gate. I grew up, too, in fair material comfort and, by the mid-Victorian bourgeois standards of my parents, was well looked after and educated. Much as I have sometimes regretted the mess that my life has largely been – and some of this must be attributable to the circumstances of my childhood – it would not be reasonable to blame my parents for behaving according to the customs, obsolescent even then, of their age and class. It is I who was 'born out of due time'.

But why 'go on so' about it? Why not skip straight to the 1940s, the war, the political battles ... ? For two reasons: first, no one who sets out to write an autobiography need apologise to the reader (who *is* free to skip) for dwelling for as long as he wants to on any part of the story; but second – and this is, arguably, more important – in so far as anybody who has been a Member of Parliament and a widely read journalist may have had some impact, however infinitesimal, on public affairs and public attitudes, it may be worth considering what it was that made him what he is, what influences of heredity and early or later environment may have shaped his motives. There is, further, no point in writing such a book unless it is as completely candid as the laws of libel allow it to be; in particular, though it may distress the writer to cause distress to some of his friends, he must not exclude relevant material merely because its inclusion may make him vulnerable to ridicule and contempt.

I have never bothered to trace my ancestry on my father's side, but I was told as a child that his forefather had come from Holland a couple of centuries earlier. His father was an Anglican missionary clergyman in India. My father was sent home to school at Lancing, then newly founded to promote the principles of the Oxford Movement, or Catholic ('Tractarian') revival in the Church of England.[1] The fact that he was sent to Lancing suggests that his clergyman father was a supporter of this movement. My father's entire career was spent in India—for a short while in the Army, then, until his retirement in the early 1890s, in the Indian Civil Service. In this service he seems to have achieved a respectable position: he became Chief of Police and Inspector of Jails for the Province of Assam. Two of his junior colleagues—Sir Robert Neil Campbell and Sir Edward Gait, who was to become Governor of Bihar and Orissa—were my godfathers. But it was not until he was nearing retirement, in 1887, that my parents were married, and I was not born until they had retired and settled down at home.

By ironic chance or because of some instinctive drive, there are several correspondences between the career of this father, whom I hardly knew and did not much care for, and some of the interests that I have pursued in political life. I have spent a good deal of time in the promotion of penal reform and in visits to friends and constituents in prison; and it is pleasing to note, in the printed reports painstakingly compiled by my father, that he was taking a reasonably liberal line on prison conditions—opposing, for instance, the chaining and the shaving of the heads of women prisoners.

[1] This movement began with Keble's Assize sermon in 1833. It is not to be confused with the 'Oxford' Group (M.R.A.) of Dr Frank Buchman.

Since such modest comfort as my family enjoyed was due to the existence of the Raj, it was almost inevitable that I should feel, not at first consciously, some sense of guilt and that one element in my political outlook should be strong opposition to Imperialism; and in the years after the Second World War I was glad to be one of the few M.P.s who campaigned in Parliament for Burmese, as well as for Indian, independence. It may be conceded, however, that people like my father built the Indian Civil Service into a service worthy of those to whom it was bequeathed. I do not know personally if it is now as corrupt as it is said to be; but I think that many older people in India retain some regard for their former exploiters. Two of my father's clerks, Bireswir Sen and Raj Chandra, went on writing to my mother, inquiring about the welfare of her children, long after my father's death; and at an official reception in New Delhi in 1950 a senior civil servant introduced himself to me as the son of one of these two clerks.

Strangest of the echoes of my father's career in my life occurs, most unexpectedly, on the drug scene. Some years ago Allen Ginsberg, the American poet and propagandist for marihuana, asked me to look up for him the report of the East India Hemp Commission of the Eighteen Eighties and there, in the library of the House of Commons, I found that my father had given evidence before this Commission, putting forward strongly the view that people living in a damp, cold climate needed the traditional consolation of *ganja*, as the stuff was called there. The climate referred to was that of Assam rather than England; but I felt that it was almost an act of filial piety to sign a full-page advertisement in *The Times* calling for a liberalisation of the law on pot. This advertisement was signed by a number of artists and writers but by only two M.P.s, Brian Walden and myself, and one would-be candidate, Jonathan Aitken. The advertisement was paid for by one or more of the Beatles, and caused considerable controversy: signing it was the only thing I did which provoked overt hostility among some of my political supporters in Barking.

When my parents came home from India, as the nineteenth century was dying, they knew nothing of the the new ideas that were stirring in the arts and in politics: they brought with them the prejudices formed in my father's youth. They looked for somewhere to live which had to fulfil two conditions: it should be more than 600 feet above sea-level (this was then thought to be a safeguard against malaria, which my father had suffered in India); and, for the benefit of my brothers and in due course of myself, it should have 'good' schools — that is, examples of the worst possible kind of school, the independent fee-paying boys' preparatory school. They found what they wanted at Crowborough, Sussex, a place which (with one important exception) I can never revisit, or think of, without a feeling of sick horror, a place which John Betjeman would love — would love, that is, to write a poem about, not to live in. It is like his 'conifer county of Surrey' and used to be advertised on railway platforms (when there was a railway there) as 'Scotland in Sussex': pine, gorse and heather, eroded more and more by what the house-agents call 'desirable residences', houses-in-their-own-grounds (not one of them old or, architecturally, worth a glance) smothering the 800-feet-up Beacon hill. The air was always described as 'bracing'.

But, though childhood in such surroundings gave me a permanent dislike of the conifer type of landscape, the fauna housed in these premises were far worse than the flora about them. For this is, and was already beginning to be, in the stockbroker belt — inhabited by prosperous middle-class commuters and 'retired people' like my parents. Since they were all solidly Conservative voters, it was not necessary to mention politics. The foci of their leisure hours (ample, since most of them had servants) were the bridge-table and the golf links; and when the husbands were away in the City, the wives, day after day, had afternoon bridge-parties in each others' houses. No doubt there were extra-marital sexual activities also, but these I would not have heard of from my puritanical mother.

Nor were my parents entirely involved in this vacuous social existence: my father was old and had trouble with his eyes and his kidneys; while India and a Presbyterian upbringing in Scotland had given my mother some sense of public duty. (She was descended collaterally from Helen of Kirkconnel, heroine of an ancient Border ballad, and from William Jardine, the villainous founder of the great Far Eastern capitalist firm of Jardine Matheson. Though her relatives were mostly in Dumfriesshire, she was born in Mauritius, her father having gone with her mother to live there because he had been advised that a hot, damp climate would be best for his tuberculosis. He soon died, and my grand-mother brought the children home to Lockerbie.) Most of my mother's Crowborough friends, though not intellectual, were relatively serious-minded spinsters and widows, engaged in 'charities' and apt to be religious. After my father's death she took, with passionate intensity, to bee-keeping: she became president of the local apiculturists' association, held gatherings of them in our garden, and even (a thing she would never have presumed to do when my father was alive) contributed little articles to their journal. One of these described a method she had devised (and believed to be new) of introducing an alien queen to an existing stock. She read, avidly, Fabre, Maeterlinck and the Reverend Tickner Edwardes (*The Lore of the Honey-bee*). She installed an observation hive in her bedroom: though I found her enthusiasm fairly ludicrous, I took a mild interest for a time in removing the green baize covers from the glass sides of this hive and watching the bees busy within – their heads, as my mother showed me, always pointing in the direction of the queen.

I suspect that my mother, though conventionally pious, did superstitiously 'tell the bees' of events in her uneventful life. Except in the dream which I have described, I remember her best wearing a wide-brimmed hat, with her black bee-keeper's veil. During her terminal illness, leukaemia, she could see to the hive in her bedroom, but the hives in the garden, though still populated, were neglected. When she died, we were within a few weeks of the Second World War. We had a hurried sale of most of the contents of the house: a few of the Indian 'curios' went to museums; most were sold, for practically nothing; I wish I had kept more of them – for instance, a Tibetan prayer-wheel.

The house was at once taken over by the Army, and a section of (I expect) anti-aircraft gunners put into it. By arrangement with the military authorities, the beehives were left for a time in the garden. Perhaps the soldiers were drunk, perhaps they were inquisitive and got stung: at any rate, they kicked and smashed the hives to pieces, and burned the remains.

Several years later I was, for some reason, travelling on top of a bus to Crowborough from the nearest town, Tunbridge Wells. Two women sitting behind me were talking about 'her'. One said: 'She was always very kind ... It was a shame what those soldiers did to her bees.' It was evident that they were talking about my mother, but I did not dare to interrupt. Then one of the women said: 'They say she's been *seen* ... quite often ... in her black veil – at the end of the lawn, where they bees used to be.'

My mother left a few thousand pounds to each of my brothers and me. She would have left a good deal more had not the manager of the local branch of the Westminster Bank, perhaps with good intentions, induced her, a year or two earlier, to invest a substantial sum in the purchase of an annuity. Shortly after my mother's death, this plausible adviser was sent to prison for some financial misdeed. As my mother's fatal illness had already begun when she bought the annuity, it seemed worth suing the Westminster Bank. I still have the Opinion in which learned Counsel advised against this course.

Since bee-keeping was the most exciting domestic activity of my boyhood – though I must not forget the set of meteorological instruments which my father kept in the garden and told us about at luncheon daily – and since Crowborough was as I have described it, I became conscious, fairly early on, of a considerable sense of *ennui*.

My brothers sought to relieve this by giving me, on my tenth or eleventh birthday, a handsome set of golf-clubs, and paying for a course of lessons by the local professional, Mr Macey. But I was never any good at outdoor games or at *aiming*: I often missed the ball completely, however neatly it was teed up (just as at O.T.C. rifle practice I was to miss the target by a wide margin and – even more humiliating – when a prefect at Lancing, was to miss the bottom of some delinquent boy whom I was required to cane). So Mr Macey gave me up, with unconcealed disgust; I felt (unfairly) that my brothers had played a mean trick by pressuring me, under the guise of generosity, into learning a game I could never play; and the golf-clubs gathered dust in a corner of the attic, eventually to be swept off to one of my mother's charities – perhaps to be sent to under-nourished children in central Africa, where one of her favourite missions operated.

In a situation of such tedium, the thoughts of any decently instructed child would have turned to sex. But I was not decently instructed: the most that my mother had said to me about it was: 'You must never let anybody touch your private parts' – which

left me wanting a lot more information. Some of this I got from
my second brother's medical text-books (he was a surgeon): I
found these one day in a high cupboard, and was startled and
repelled (why?) by diagrams of the foetus curled up in the womb.
There was also much half-informed speculation on the processes
of sex and parturition at the prep school to which I went at the
age of eight. But some sexual impulses had made themselves felt
at a much earlier age. I was crawling about on the carpet in my
father's study (called the smoking-room), and cannot therefore
have been more than two or three, when I found myself between
the flannel-trousered legs of my eldest brother, who was standing
in the middle of the room talking. Looking up towards the crotch,
I perceived a small hole—some stitches loose in the seam. Gently
I inserted a finger—so gently that I don't think my brother
noticed—and, though I did not quite touch flesh, I experienced
what I clearly recall as the first authentic sexual thrill of my life.

The next incident that comes to mind brought no satisfaction:
it was merely a remark, made by me, and I have never understood
why I made it in the circumstances in which it was made. At the
age of five I was sent to a kindergarten, conducted by two elderly
sisters, the Misses Hooker, in a house named Hookstead. Each day
I was walked there by our gardener, a middle-aged man with a
drooping greyish-ginger moustache, named Hemsley. One
morning, on our way to Hookstead in the main Beacon Road, I
stopped, looked up at him and said: 'Hemsley, will you please take
down your trousers?' I cannot remember his reply: I suppose that
it was dismissive. But the whole episode, brief as it was, is incom-
prehensible. Had I, a five-year-old, been making a serious pass at a
married forty-year-old gardener (not, intrinsically, a probable
initiative), I should have chosen some less public and more
romantic setting for the proposal—a far corner of the kitchen-
garden, say, or, better still, the potting-shed.

Equally mysterious was my inspection, frequent in extreme
youth, of some figurines of Indians of various callings and types,
six or eight inches tall, which were disposed about the smoking-
room. These were modelled in plaster and realistically coloured,
and their clothing was of some actual textile. It used to excite me
to lift up a kind of apron worn by some of the men—to find, alas,
nothing there but a slight bump. I transferred my infantile

affection to the face of a smiling young man on a tin of Mackin-tosh's Toffee de Luxe, kissing the shiny surface as one sees Indian peasants in Mexico kissing the glass that covers the relics of some saint.

It must have been about now that my parents arranged to supplement the academically meagre curriculum of the Misses Hooker by getting me private tuition – and with a little girl. (Had Hemsley grassed?) Her name was Dorothy Osborne, and she lived in a house rather grander than ours. I remember nothing about these lessons or who gave them, or what Dorothy looked like. I only remember two appalling scenes in which she, I, and my mother were involved. Some friend of my mother's had given us two small toy animals, a donkey and an elephant, one for each of the children. I desperately wanted one of them – I think the donkey, though the elephant seems more likely – but my mother said that Dorothy must have first choice. She chose the one I wanted, and I took my defeat badly, bursting into screams of frustrated rage.

The other scene was even more traumatic – perhaps lastingly so. Dorothy and I had spent the afternoon playing in the nursery at my home. We had had a good tea, and were tired of games. Suddenly she stood still in the middle of the room, began to cry, and pissed on the floor. As the rippling pool spread over the linoleum, she ran out of the room, and out of my life; for I, also in tears – tears of shocked horror – swore that I hated her, and I think my parents felt that she was not, after all, a suitable companion.

2

Piety and puberty

Against this background of social mediocrity and a dull life at home — where, because my brothers were so far my senior, I was in effect the only child of old parents who kept on voicing their inexplicable nostalgia for India, my mother calling her store-room a *go-down* and the laundry the *dhobi*, my father mumbling about *chota hazri* and *chota-peg* — against such a background there now arose a concatenation of menaces which must be attributed partly to sheer bad luck and not only to my parents' ignorance.

The 'good' school to which they had chosen to send me was called the Grange. The headmaster was a notable former county cricketer and practising sadist named Frank Gresson. Because he or his wife was a distant relative of one of my parents, and because the school was only five minutes' walk from my home, I was allowed to go there as a day-boy. But this was the reverse of a privilege — for I was the only day-boy in the school. Possibly this was, for my parents, a measure of economy: my mother never tired of telling me how she and my father had denied themselves and saved in order to be able to give 'you boys' a 'good education'; and we were expected to be grateful for this. They did not have enough imagination to realise that, by putting me in this peculiar status at school, at the age of eight, they were cutting me off entirely from the general life of the school, from the dormitory fun, from everything except the lessons and the games, which included such sporting activities as going to a meet of the local Hunt and trying to follow the hounds on foot (the headmaster's

wife baying 'Come on, Tom, you duffer ... Don't lag behind!')·
So I was, compulsorily, a loner.

Worse: I was soon to be an enemy loner. The First World War
had broken out shortly after I had gone to the Grange. In that war
there was far more xenophobic hysteria than in the second:
London shops with names like Appenrodt were wrecked; the
papers were full of stories of atrocities committed by the 'Huns'.
And I had a German-sounding name ...

Probably I could have got away with it had I had a different,
more care-free disposition, had I been more of an extrovert and,
above all, good at games. But I was shy and timid and—the best
word is *gawky*: fat, plain, myopic (rather like Piggy in *Lord of the
Flies*), an obvious butt and scapegoat. Inevitably, I became not
only 'fat Tom' but 'Kaiser Tom', and was duly bullied in accordance with the canons of English private education. Then, every
night I had to walk home through a dark wood in which, terrify-
ingly, I often lost my way.

Such a boy may sometimes compensate for his unathletic
lumpishness, and acquire a little esteem, by quickness of wit
(though the pack will see through his motives and not hesitate to
exploit them if he slips). Thus I took care each morning to study
my father's newspaper at home, so that I could come to school
primed with the latest and most sensational war news. Again, such
a boy can earn cheap laughter and applause by playing smart
tricks on the teaching staff. Such daring has its dangers, and once
I went too far, by drawing a caricature of a master on a blackboard
in his classroom.

I have said that the headmaster, Gresson, was a sadist. None of
us had any doubt at all that he enjoyed the beatings he frequently
inflicted on boys whom he disliked (or, perhaps, liked?); these
beatings were delivered not on the bottom but on the hand; and
by some chance Gresson would often manage to hit not the hand
but the wrist, at a tender spot. I recall seeing boys emerge from his
study, weeping in agony, one hand clutching the other wrist, on
which a weal was darkening.

It so happened that I never qualified for a beating. Instead, on
the occasion of my exercise in blackboard art, I was subjected to
the most severe penalty available—a school mobbing. This
punishment was only rarely awarded. It was carried out at the

mid-morning break. The offender had to stand in the middle of a concrete squash court, with his back to the wall. The entire school — about a hundred boys — would be drawn up in a semi-circle before him. Then, as a silence fell, the headmaster would bark 'Go for him!' and the whole crowd would rush at the miscreant, knock him down, pummel and kick him, until the headmaster, reluctantly, called them off.

When this happened to me, I was shaken and bruised, and my clothes were covered with dirt, but I had so little *rapport* with my parents that I would not have dreamed of mentioning the incident to them that evening, still less of complaining of the punishment. However, the headmaster sent round a note telling them of my disgrace — though not of the nature of the punishment, of which I do not believe that they would have approved — and I had to suffer my mother's anxious reproaches. I do not think it fanciful to find in this kind of experience, both at this school and at my (much better) public school, the roots of a hatred, maturing much later in life, not only of corporal punishment, but of all kinds of disciplinarian cruelty.

After two or three years at the Grange I must have acquired some slight popularity or charm, for by the age of ten or eleven I was indulging fairly regularly in sexual play (though it was still too early for full consummation). This had begun when I was in the lowest form, and the war had swept into the Forces all the masters who were even half-competent. We were in the care of a silly old thing called Rice, who used surreptitiously to eat sweets in class, raising the lid of his desk in an attempt to prevent us from seeing him do so. Meanwhile, all the little boys in the back row, hardly more surreptitiously, would bring out and compare and fondle their tiny, wriggling white worms of penises.

One rather older and better-endowed boy, Derek P., excited me more teasingly. Once I was showing him round our garden: taking advantage of the quiet place and inflamed by the heat of the day, I offered to give him a new pencil if he would unbutton his trousers and produce his member. He consented readily.

But there was another Derek, Derek G., a boy with dark hair and a sunburnt oval face, a scar on one cheek, with whom I had, for the first time, what can be called a serious love-affair (no emission of semen, however, occurring as yet). He and I would repair to the lavatory, lock ourselves in one of the W.C.s, and engage in such oral and manual caresses as occurred to us to be worthy of experiment. There was a row of half-a-dozen of these W.C.s. Each boy in the school was allocated to one of them, and a list was posted showing the order in which boys had to 'go', as soon as possible after breakfast, the headmaster's wife prowling and sniffing ('Have you done your business yet, Tom?'). This procedure was apt to cause psychological or even rebelliously deliberate constipation: the seat was always warm, the smell of strong disinfectant competed with the smell of shit; yet this disgusting place would also be, later in the day, the scene of embraces with Derek as intensely passionate (even if in a junior league) as those of Héloïse and Abélard. Probably I can trace back to this period of my schooling a chronic, lifelong, love-hate relationship with lavatories.

It is also a quaint illustration of the complete lack of sex education at such a school that — though we knew vaguely that the sex act had something to do with parenthood and that a baby came 'out of' the woman — we half-toyed with the fantasy that the pangs of constipation might mean that one of us was about to give birth. At any rate, my love for Derek seemed to be (and therefore was) deep and sincere. I remember saying to him: 'Wouldn't it be awful if they ever separated us?' Soon we were separated, by the fate which separates schoolboys: he, a year or two the older, left the school. I missed him for a while, but we did not correspond and I have never seen him again.

I am sure that I should have known more of the 'facts of life' had I been friendly with any of the working-class boys in 'the village' (the street where my mother went shopping) or on the farms which must have existed within a mile or two of the residential highland (strange to grow up in 'the country' and yet to see and know nothing of the processes of agriculture); for working-class children were always better-informed on such matters, earlier in life, than those more sheltered from reality. But I knew no working-class boys: I don't think I was 'forbidden to mix with them'; the occasion simply didn't arise. Ever since adolescence, I have found males of the working class infinitely more desirable than those with bourgeois backgrounds and accents. Meanwhile, Derek G. and Derek P. and one or two others were the best playmates I had. Besides being himself personable, Derek P. had another asset in his mother — an elegant and beautiful war-widow with a grand car. 'Parents' Day' used to aggravate my inferiority complex, for my parents looked so much older and shabbier than the others.

Of course I was not fully aware that, even in those days and by the standards of the Grange and Crowborough, my parents were distinctly old-fashioned. I doubt whether many other households kept up, as we did (until my father became more or less permanently bed-ridden), the Victorian custom of family prayers. These took place before breakfast, at or just before eight o'clock, in the smoking-room: the sons of the house, whatever our ages, were expected to attend, the maids rustled in demurely, my father officiated. Apart from the Collect for the day, the ritual was formal and unvarying (the great fault also of the State prayers in the House of Commons, though extempore inspiration, as in Congress, could be worse). We began with a psalm — always, so far as I remember, Psalm 45 in the Book of Common Prayer translation, and splendidly sonorous it is:

> My heart is inditing of a good matter ...
> My tongue is the pen of a ready writer ...
> Thou art fairer than the children of men:
> full of grace are thy lips, because God hath
> blessed thee for ever.
> Gird thee with thy sword upon thy thigh,
> O thou most mighty, according to thy worship
> and renown ...
> On thy right hand did stand the queen in a
> vesture of gold, wrought about with divers colours.
> All her garments smell of myrrh, aloes, and
> cassia: out of the ivory palaces whereby they
> have made thee glad.

Though I can recite only fragments of this psalm now, and though I wondered at the time what 'divers colours' were, for I had seen pictures of Indian boys diving for pearls, the beauty of the words seemed to sink into my being, by osmosis rather than by intelligent appreciation. The same may be even truer of the prayers which followed. (At this point we all had to turn and kneel with our elbows on our chairs, presenting to God a row of bottoms big and small, in black dresses or grey shorts.) For several centuries, before the era of universal literacy and general illiteracy, good writers, consciously or unconsciously, echoed in their prose the rhythms of the Prayer-book. I cannot claim so much for my own writing, but some of those cadences — from, for instance, the Collects for Advent and for Trinity, the General Thanksgiving, and the prayer for 'the good estate of the Catholic Church' — at the slightest prompting roll round majestically in my head. That is the best I can say for family prayers, which in childhood I found one of the most disagreeable features of life at home.

By the time I was twelve, puberty was setting in. The first long, straggling pubic hair was a source of amazement to me. So were the erections, which I did not yet know what to do with. (Nor did I have any wet dreams.) Within a year I had learned: my juvenile lust was so importunate that an old tramp was induced to masturbate me in an underground lavatory at Tunbridge Wells. He did it rather roughly, with a mechanical action, and, since I did not understand what was happening, the moment of ejaculation was as agonising as it was exquisite. Throughout adolescence, during holidays from school, I used to cycle into Tunbridge Wells or Brighton and haunt the various public lavatories for hours on end, especially the one in which I had lost what I can hardly call my virtue. This gents' convenience (in an alley just opposite a railway station) had one feature which was both a safeguard against snoopers and a spur to tumescence: there was quite a long flight of steps down to it, so that one could hear a newcomer, and guess what he was like, before seeing him. If he was quick and light of step and turned out to be a randy soldier or a rosy errand-boy — best of all, if he was ready and willing, but sometimes even if he was not — the impatient sperm would not be contained and the coming was a good deal hotter and faster than that of the Magi.

During these vigils, I hardly ever failed to score, except when the prospects were scared of having so young a boy. So far as their ages went, my taste was more catholic than it later became: I found middle-aged men as exciting as boys of my own age. I have often thought how wrong it is (as also, I believe, in the case of girls) to assume that the senior partner must be the seducer. I remember an agreeable session when I was at Lancing, lying on top of the Sussex downs with a man of about fifty. At the time I was in quarantine after a bout of measles and had been allowed out for a walk from the school sanatorium: I only hope he didn't catch anything. The pleasure was mutual: the fault, if there were one, mine.

These lavatory sojourns would alternate with, or be followed by, visits to various churches — in Tunbridge Wells, St Barnabas' (red-brick Gothic and 'high') and St Augustine's (R.C.); for this period of intense erotic activity occurred just when my interest in a newly discovered religious cult was also at its keenest. Puberty is a state of mental and emotional confusion, and so many excitements were merging or overlapping that it is difficult now to be sure of the exact sequence and timing of events; but, whichever order they occurred in, the most moving experiences — the first emission, just mentioned, the first High Mass (at St Andrew's, Worthing, with lashings of incense, burnished brass, and the hymn 'Lord, Enthroned in Heavenly Splendour', to the 1861 *Ancient and Modern* tune) — stand out in my memory with absolute and equal clarity.

Most schizophrenes, no doubt, have two conflicting compulsions banging about inside them: from the start of puberty I had these two, and within a few years was to have three — all, it seemed, mutually irreconcilable, yet each, in its different way, expressing rebellion against the values of my home: 'deviant' sex, 'exotic' religion — and Left-wing politics.

3

Family ties

But what made me such an odd child? How distribute the causes between heredity and environment, which are by no means mutually exclusive? Philip Larkin, in a poem 'This be the verse' in *High Windows*,[1] says:

> They fuck you up, your mum and dad.
>   They may not mean to, but they do.
> They fill you with the faults they had
>   And add some extra, just for you.
>
> But they were fucked up in their turn
>   By fools in old-style hats and coats,
> Who half the time were soppy-stern
>   And half at one another's throats ...

There are eccentrics in every family, but mine seems, especially in recent generations, to have produced an unusually high proportion of the vicious and/or dotty. As I have said, I know very little of the ancestry of my father, John James Street Driberg. I know of no namesake of mine in Britain; there are some in Ceylon and in Australia. One R. H. Driberg White emigrated to Australia from Stroud, Gloucestershire, in 1838; his grandfather had been a Colonel Van Driberg, which tends to confirm a Dutch origin. More than thirty years ago, however, I corresponded with an Australian namesake: he had traced the line a little further back, to an estate in Hanover from which some of the family came to England, perhaps via Holland, in about 1714.

[1] Faber & Faber, London, 1974.

My mother's known ancestry goes much further back. She belonged to the enormous Bell clan of Dumfriesshire, her parents being Herbert and Margaret Irving Bell. She was christened Amy Mary. In an old album I have a picture of Bell Tower, one of the peel-towers which the Scots built along the Border as a defence against English aggression: this one was built by William Bell 'of the lands of Kirkconnel', whose charter was granted in 1424. In 1483 there was a threat of English invasion: a garrison, maintained at the charge of the Scottish Crown (a tax being raised for the purpose), was ordered to 'lie' in this tower. Above the gate of the tower were 'cut in freestone in a scutcheon three bells, and for a crest a hand holding a dagger paleways proper'. The motto was 'I BEIR THE BEL'. My mother told me that our branch of the clan were the Bells of Neuke, but that we were descended collaterally from Helen of Kirkconnel, defunct heroine of a Border ballad: I am not sure how or why Helen died, but the Chief of the clan, according to the epitaph on his tomb, slew her,

> Burnt the Lochwood, tower, & hall,
> And dang the ladye ower the wall.

A sixteenth-century John Bell was Chief Baron of the Exchequer for Dumfriesshire. William 'the Redcloak' (c. 1586) was 'a famous Reiver' (cattle-raider). Was he the same as Willie o' the Neuke (1585)? A later John Bell of Blackethouse 'stood firm to King Charles I in all his troubles. Being Governor of Carlisle, he refused to yield the city for some days, for which the tower of Blackethouse was entirely burnt ... Notwithstanding of that, he, at the head of a flying party, cut off the stragglers of Cromwell's army.'

A strange and, at first sight, ambiguous epitaph, on Jockie Bell of Brackenburn is, or was, to be found in Kirkbankhead church-yard:

> Here lies Jockie Bell of Brackenburn under this stane,
> Five of my ain sons laid it on my wame.
> Man for my meat and master for my wife
> Lived all my days without sturt or strife.
> If thou be better in thy days than I have been in mine,
> Take the stane off my wame and lay it on thine.

But I suppose that my first predecessor as the misfit of the family may have been the cause of a plea by Sybella Bell — who, in 1762, petitioned the Duchess of Queensberry for the return of the land of Neuke, her husband's grandfather 'having with his own hand (then suffering from melancholy) brought himself to an untimely end, by which, according to the rigour of the Scots law, his lands became escheat to the family of Queensberry, the superiors thereof, but as never any instance occurred hitherto where such law was put to its utmost stretch, therefore' — and so forth: I have not found out what response there was to this petition; but for a time this branch of the Bells were described as 'in' not 'of' Neuke.

This petitioner, by the way, was 'a large and powerful virago', who smuggled brandy in from the Isle of Man and could drink a bottle of it (holding 'a Scotch pint') at a sitting.

A later relative not to be proud of was William Jardine, that villainous founder of the firm of Jardine Matheson, whose fortune was originally built on the sale of opium to the Chinese: he looted the finest jade in Peking — and in the 1950s his descendant, Sir Jock Buchanan-Jardine, sold most of it for another fortune.

Enough of such atavistic ramblings: I cite these family data (which indeed go back much further, to Norman times) merely because they may throw some light on one curious circumstance attending my parents' marriage in 1887: this is that it was bitterly opposed by my mother's mother. The ostensible reason for this was the disparity in age: my father was twenty-five years older than my mother (and she was always sensitive about this — for instance, when he died she omitted the years of his birth and death from his gravestone). But could it not also be that my grandmother felt my father, besides being of foreign ancestry, to be socially inferior to her family? It is impossible to prove this, but letters from her to my mother which survive show a continuing prejudice against my father. Thus, on June 25th, 1914, in a letter in which she offered to join my mother and me in a holiday at the seaside, she included an irrelevant passage about a marriage that had just taken place:

An old friend of ours (yr. Aunt M. and myself) married the other day one of his young servants, he is *83*, she *24*, perhaps

you may have seen it in the papers, Sir Francis Powell, an
artist, he is said to be 80 in the papers but he is more, when
your Aunt M. and I were at school he came of age and we
were allowed to go to the festivities, it was a great treat to us.[1]
The ball was grand. His first wife was plain-looking and some
years older, they had no children, so perhaps he thinks he
may still have an heir to his large estate. I have not seen him
for more than 59 years ...

Why did my grandmother include this gossip in a letter about a
prospective holiday? Surely to get in an implied dig on a sore
subject on which she had been nagging my parents for years. My
mother may have taken it as such, for in her reply she did not
refer to my grandmother's offer to join us on holiday. Instantly
came another letter from my grandmother:

You don't take the least notice of what I thought was a kind
offer, it certainly was not made for my own pleasure, but from
the desire to help you ... Evidently you can afford to do all
you wish to do without my help, but it would only have been
ordinary politeness to say whether you accepted or not. I see
you prefer to go with Tom alone so that is settled ...

This was unfair. In her previous letter my grandmother had
said nothing about helping to pay for our holiday—merely 'I
might also go for a couple of weeks'. But my mother should not
have ignored the suggestion: I think she was incapable of even the
slight dishonesty of a stalling excuse. Presumably memories of
innumerable rows inhibited her from a directly negative answer.
But in the next sentence grannie's letter gathers steam:

It is a pity you should copy Jack [my father] in rudeness as
well as in other things. Since he made the unseemly remark
to me, that I shld leave my best jewellery to you, as you had
always been a good daughter and I told him I wd do what *I*
thought best, there has been a change in the conduct of both
of you. You were a good daughter before you married, but he
soon altered that. I don't forget your behaviour to me when I
visited you in India, nor when Nora was to have visited you
in the north of Scotland, nor after Laurie's death, when your

[1] She rarely used a stronger stop than a comma.

duty as a daughter was exhibited in a most disgraceful way but it is no use going into further details, you are simply hypnotised and always have been by the stronger will of a very selfish man. Mrs Stenson Hooker has spent today with me, now it is late and I must close, but I cd not sleep without telling you to be a little more courteous in the future.

Yr affectionate mother,
M. I. BELL.

Obstinately quarrelsome as this letter is, there may be something in what my grandmother says about my father's 'stronger will'. Mrs Jeannie Hunt—who was in our household when I was a child and still happily survives—recalls that when my father went out for a walk alone, she used to watch for his return and warn my mother, who might be resting. Lying down in the daytime was disapproved of, 'If you are ill,' my father would say, 'send for the doctor. If you are not ill, there is no need to lie down.' Is Larkin right? 'They fill you with the faults they had.' I hope I have not inherited this one—but I have inherited (if it be a fault) some of my father's obsessive punctuality. He kept all the clocks in the house five minutes fast: this I always thought absurd. I was also, for some reason, enraged by my parents' habit of never cutting the string from round a parcel. Every piece of string was painstakingly unknotted, neatly rolled and kept in an old cigar-box. 'Why not buy a ball of string?' I used to protest—to which my mother would reply with some such sedative aphorism as 'Waste not, want not.'

I must explain my grandmother's references in these letters to Aunt M., Nora, and Laurie. 'Aunt M.' was her sister, my great-aunt Mary Whitaker, née Richardson. She had married into a Shropshire family and lived in a large, late-Georgian house called Broadclough Hall, at Bacup, Lancashire. She was an aged widow when I first stayed with her as a small boy: this was also my first intimation of the existence of industrial workers, for when I woke I could hear the mill-girls going to work, their clogs clattering on the cobbled streets; and in the evenings I was allowed to run out of the long drive and down the street to a stall where chips, vinegar-sprinkled, were sold in twists of newspaper. Aunt Mary had a sly Welsh maid named Morgan, who robbed her and encouraged her to drink, so that the old lady was sometimes found prostrate on the dining-room floor, clutching an empty bottle. I think she liked my mother and me. Because of the Shropshire connection, she happened to have a first edition (uncut, unopened, unread) of Housman's *A Shropshire Lad*. On one visit, when I was just old enough to know that this had some value, I drew her attention to it and she gave it to me. Next time I was broke in London, I sold it to a well-known antiquarian book-dealer. He gave me four guineas for it. A few months later I saw it in his catalogue, priced £50. When Aunt Mary died, aged eighty-five, in 1923, she left my mother some good seventeenth-century oak furniture.

Nora was my mother's younger sister. She had a kind of puckered face and had once been pretty. On the ship returning from a visit to India, she had a mild flirtation with a young man, another passenger. My grandmother disapproved of this. Nora was suffering from nervous depression, following an attack of erysipelas. Grandmother bullied her: Nora got worse. Grandmother got a doctor who was in some way under her influence to certify Nora insane. (At that time only one doctor was required to certify insanity.) Aunt Nora was put away for the rest of her life in a large private mental hospital, Camberwell House. When my mother went to visit her, she used to take me with her. At first, when very young, I did not understand what was the matter with Aunt Nora, why she sometimes had a bloodstained bandage round her head, or why I could hear the nurse saying in a low voice to my mother: 'She's been naughty again – tearing up her bed-linen ... ' By the time I understood that my aunt was simply what people in those days called 'a raving lunatic', there was some apparent improvement in her condition, possibly due to the development of modern tranquillising drugs. At any rate, the hospital superintendent, Dr Norman – a man who (as I happened to learn later from a bookseller friend, Eric Bligh) had one of the world's finest collections of pornographic books – told my mother that we could take Aunt Nora out for occasional drives, even to tea. We took her out to tea several times, usually to Whiteley's in Bayswater, where we would see nobody we knew. She was fairly presentable, though apt to be audibly querulous if advised against more than three or four iced cakes; and my mother sometimes had to pull her hat well down to hide the places where she had been scratching her head. I suppose it was an educative experience for me. I am not sure that my mother was wise to expose me to it, but perhaps she found it distressing to be alone with her sister.

A more difficult test confronted us after my grandmother died, in 1922; for she left a sum of money in trust, to be administered by my mother, not only to cover the mental hospital fees, but to provide various amenities for Aunt Nora. It was hard to know how to spend this money. It was no good buying her clothes or pretty ornaments: in one of her manic moods she would destroy them. After much thought, and consultation with Dr Norman, we decided to take a considerable risk: we would hire a chauffeur-driven Daimler car—that should cost quite a bit—and take my aunt to stay for a few days at an hotel that was then, as now, thought of as expensive and luxurious: Gleneagles, in Perthshire. We stopped a night on the way: even so, the second day's drive was tiring to my aunt; she was becoming fretful when we arrived in the hotel—as luck would have it, just as the other customers were coming down to dinner, all in evening dress. By contrast, we looked the more bedraggled—particularly my aunt, who was talking rapidly to herself, with wisps of grey hair straggling from under the hat that had slipped to one side. However, we somehow got her up to our suite, had dinner in the sitting-room, and retired early to bed. I had just got to sleep when I was woken by some horrifying shrieks: I am not sure whether they came from my aunt or from some guest or maid whom she had frightened; but there she was, in the corridor, in her nightdress, uttering a stream of gibberish, of which I remember only the words 'Heaven and earth must be turned into Hell'. I do not think we stayed at Gleneagles long; and I do not recall in what state we got back to London. The Daimler bill was satisfactorily heavy. We did not risk so ambitious an outing again: but Aunt Nora's closing years were brightened by a mildly Lesbian friendship with another elderly patient in the hospital, known as 'the Marquise'.

Aunt Nora died in 1929. As my mother was ill, and I was by now on the *Daily Express*, it fell to me to arrange for her cremation and to transport her ashes to the family vault at Lockerbie. After the dreary service, I collected from the crematorium a square, warm brown-paper parcel, alleged to contain the ashes of my aunt. Before catching the night train to Scotland, I took the parcel to the

Express office, and deposited it on my desk while I wrote a piece. Some people are easily shocked — for instance, a tall, gentlemanly reporter who happened to come into my room, when I said 'I don't think you knew my aunt?' and introduced him to the parcel.

The third relative mentioned in those letters from my grandmother was 'Laurie'. Two of my mother's brothers were Laurence and Maurice. I know very little about them, except that one of them had tuberculosis and one was homosexual (or so I was told by a second cousin, Colonel James Richardson, who commanded the 13th Hussars) and died in a brawl in a male brothel in Paris. Laurence died aged twenty-seven, Maurice aged thirty-five. In some cupboard I still have a brass clock on which an inscription states that it was the Ellen Potts memorial gymnastic prize, awarded to M. D. Bell at Fettes College, in Scotland, in 1888.

I do not know whether people of that generation actually enjoyed quarrelling with their kin, but, as the echoes reached me, life seemed to be one long unmerry-go-round of furious scenes, with abusive letters flying in all directions. My elders were always, in Larkin's phrase, 'at one another's throats'. (Nowadays it would be done by telephone.) In 1915, when I was ten, my grandmother came to stay at Crowborough: within two days, after a series of rows, she had left the house, but, instead of returning to London, where she lived in a flat in Kensington, she went to stay at a local hotel, no doubt in order to embarrass my parents. It took my mother nearly five years to get around to writing to her to say 'I regret having spoken as I did' — adding 'whatever provocation I received'. This merely excited a fresh tirade:

> You say you regret ... but there is no real feeling or contrition expressed, perhaps you forget that after a volley of abuse you denounced me to your husband as 'that woman's a devil and has ruined all her children'. The fact is you had been harbouring evil thoughts of me for a very long time wh culminated in words & temper terrible to witness, I never saw anything like it, I don't think you knew what you were saying & were probably obsessed by an evil spirit, therefore not responsible, on that account I long ago forgave you, but your sin of vindictiveness in causing your sons to discard me is a sin that

needs repentance ... Little Tom I loved & to return me the
present I sent him at Xmas was an additional cruelty, of
course the child cd not help himself ...

Your affecte mother,

M. I. BELL.

Despite what might have been taken as a conclusive breach, in
1922, a little more than two years after my father's death, my
mother wrote and invited my grandmother to come and spend her
remaining years with her at Crowborough. For once missing a
golden opportunity for prolonged disputation, my grandmother
refused, for her, quite mildly:

A few years ago it might have been, but not now. I have
become accustomed to the neglect of my family ... and just
wait patiently for God's time for my departure from this
world. My only anxiety is poor Nora ...

As we have seen, her bequest to 'poor Nora' was perhaps my
grandmother's last and sharpest stab in the long vendetta that she
and my mother waged against each other. 'God's time' for her
came only a few months later – she was eighty-seven – but it was
not an easy death. This may have been, as my mother thought,
because my grandmother had 'dabbled' in exotic cults. When I
was a baby, she had caused the celebrated (or notorious) Bishop
Leadbeater – with Annie Besant the co-sponsor of Krishnamurti
and the founder of his Order of the Star in the East – to lay his
hand on my head. Now, when the doctors said she was 'just
going' and 'won't last the night', some apparently demonic force
kept her alive day after day, lying rigid on her bed and staring
fixedly at the ceiling with what looked like intense malignancy.
Eventually my mother, having consulted the clergy of St Alban's
Church, Holborn, sent for a monk from the Anglican Community
of the Resurrection at Mirfield, Father Edmund Seyzinger, a
stout and rosy-faced man. He went into my grandmother's room,
locked the door, and stayed there for over an hour. When he
came out he was sweating and looked paler and somehow shrunken,
as if he had been engaged in desperate hand-to-hand combat.
My grandmother also looked quite different, but much more
relaxed: she died peacefully in half-an-hour.

But the most ferocious (on paper) of my relatives, as well as the wealthiest, was my mother's eldest brother, my Uncle Bertie Irving Bell. Here the main *casus belli* was Spiritualism, to which he and his wife, my Aunt Birdie, were ardent converts. Neither their Spiritualism nor my mother's more conventional Christianity ever seemed to suggest to either party that there was any virtue in mutual tolerance: like Ulster Orangemen and Papists, they were spoiling for a fight – though they may merely, under the cover of religious controversy, have been rationalising the 'malice, hatred, and all uncharitableness' that permeate so much of family life.

At any rate, on July 13th, 1912, Aunt Birdie wrote to my mother, starting her letter abruptly:

My dear Amy,

I have been writing 'verses' lately – I who never wrote a verse in my life before last month – and now I write or rather 'receive' them through my hand every day. Bertie and I call them 'inspirational', for we believe in communion with 'the other side', though the gift of being able to communicate is only given to the few. However you and Jack must judge yourselves of the quality and character of the verses ...

And there is a postscript by my uncle certifying that his wife's claims are 'the literal truth'. The 'quality and character of the verses' may be assessed from brief quotation (for Birdie had actually had some *printed*, printed in mauve type, and enclosed them). One is called 'The Angel's Story' and runs, in part:

> Outside the wind is howling,
>   Inside a mother cries,
> She weeps, she says, for her baby,
>   Who, toss'd in fever, lies ...
>
> Can I help in this stricken household?
>   Anyhow, friend, I will try;
> I lay my hand on her shoulder,
>   And whisper, 'Dear, don't cry' ...
>
> So I soothe her painful sobbing,
>   And I tell her of all that is bright,
> How her boy longs to be playing
>   In the Summerland of Light ...

One quality my dear mother was certainly lacking in was tact. On the day that these effusions arrived, she wrote back to Birdie:

The poems are pretty and the ideas nice, some of the lines do not scan but no doubt you will improve in that respect with practice. You know that many women in your condition [the menopause?] are often subject to hallucinations, but so long as they are good for yourself and your household so much the better, and in the years to come no doubt you will look back with interest to this period of your life and to the poems you have written ...

Back, inevitably, came a furious eight-page letter, written by Birdie but signed by Bertie, taking strong exception to the word 'hallucinations', applying by inference, as it did, to him as well as to Birdie — 'and that, you should know, I am not likely to take lightly'. Then a general apologia for Spiritualism, on which my father was 'an absolute ignoramus'. And 'our children' — all eleven of them? — 'are at one with us in that, and will be pioneers and carry on the "mission", as we like to call it ... *I* know the truth, and *you* will know it one of these days ... ' Then the letter switches to another topic:

I have been very outspoken with *mother* [my grandmother, then aged seventy-seven] on the subject of 'drink'. I have pointed out the curse that this has been to her and her sister [Aunt M.] all their lives, and she knows now that she will never enter my house again, nor will I nor my children set foot in hers, nor have any intercourse with her, until every whisky and brandy bottle is out of her house, and she has given us a promise that she will not touch alcohol in any shape or form again. The curse has ruined her morally and shattered her nerves, and I will not let my children run the risk of seeing her in the dazed and fuddled condition (as I described it to her) which is characteristic of her after her potations. If our father were alive he would look to *me* to remonstrate with her and put pressure on her — and *as my father's eldest son and the head of the family* I shall insist on my wishes being listened to and *respected*, for I will take no refusal. If you and Jack did your duty, you would also refuse, with me, to enter her

house ... If you don't take that step, there will be a measure
of responsibility on your shoulders for which you will have to
account afterwards ...

Although this letter was written in the comparatively recent reign
of George V, it seems to me, in its patriarchal arrogance, an
epitome of the attitudes manifested by all the heavy fathers of
Victorian fiction, from *The Way of All Flesh* to *Vice Versa*.

The ding-dong battle went on daily. My mother replied at once:
'I received your wife's letter, and a more self-righteous impudent
letter I have never received' — and six pages more, with corrections
by my father. (I should explain that, as we all should, my mother
kept copies of the letters she sent.) Back came a seven-page blast:
my mother's letter was 'a cowardly one', since she must have known
that the previous letter was from Bertie, though 'copied' by his
wife from his pencilled draft; and for her and my father's cowardice
'I will expect full reparation before you ever come near me or mine
again.' Then:

> As regards my mother, she wrote me an atrocious letter
> endeavouring in her old pernicious way to sow discord
> between my wife and myself ... She knows that until that
> letter is withdrawn and her guarantees given on the question
> of drink (for I will take no refusal) my house is closed to
> her ... From this day forth we cut the fetters of all relation-
> ships, which have been too long irksome — you and yours
> never enter our house again ...

Three years later, in 1915, my mother wrote trying to reopen
communications, and was smartly rebuffed. In 1920, surprisingly,
there seems to have been a reconciliation. No letters survive to
account for this; possibly it was a consequence of my father's
death in 1919. At any rate, Uncle Bertie sent my mother £150
towards the cost of my education — I was by now at Lancing — and
promised the same amount each year till I was twenty-one. (She
never told me about this: I learned of it only when, years after her
death, I went through these letters.) 'I am very comfortably off,'
he wrote. 'I have enough and to spare.' And he ends, 'Ever your
affectionate brother'. I suppose he meant it, and I am, belatedly,
grateful for his generosity. Possibly among the Victorians — which

my uncle and my parents were—the sense of obligation to kindred, of blood ties, prevailed even where there was mutual dislike. But could all those bitter exchanges of the past be so easily forgotten? I wish at this stage that I had kept in touch with some of this polyphiloprogenitive uncle's children: surely they cannot all have acquiesced meekly in his tyranny? Or was he different at home? He died in 1938, a year before my mother's death.

The people of my grandparents' and parents' generations were great haters, and the hatred was concentrated most intensely within the family. Official Christians, and most Conservatives, speak of the family as the essential basic unit of society and the foundation of happiness. From, naturally, my own experience alone (but it cannot be entirely atypical?) I would describe the family as, for the most part, an institution destructive of true affection, a nexus of possessiveness, vindictiveness and jealousy. To the strains of family life may perhaps be attributed many of the large numbers of breakdowns whose victims crowd the mental wards and psychiatrists' consulting-rooms of the West, at any rate in our northern Protestant culture; while, for most of the young people whose problems I know, and have known during twenty-eight years as a Member of Parliament, happiness consists in getting away from parents and 'in-laws', with only brief and occasional visits to the old home.

I must wind up this melancholy chapter with some account of my two brothers, Jack Herbert and James Douglas Driberg. Having been born in 1888 and 1890, they were, as I have said, much older than I. Both were distinguished in their professions, but at crucial points in both their lives something went wrong—through their own faults or not, I cannot tell—and they suffered humiliation and even disgrace. Both were heterosexual (though I have heard that towards the end of the Second World War, in Cairo, Jack began casting lascivious eyes on the Arab boys); both were married, both divorced, both childless (though Jack, again, once told me that he had an 'illegitimate' child in France).

I remember them, when I was a very small boy, as cheerful young men, teasing me sometimes until I wept. This they did by asking me silly catch-questions which were then in vogue—perhaps music-hall jokes. One was 'HAYPF?' which stood for 'How are your poor feet?' Another was: 'How much wood would a wood-chuck chuck if a woodchuck could chuck wood?' They also taught me slang words like 'twig' ('understand') and pop songs of the day ('Alexander's Ragtime Band' and 'Hitchy-coo' were favourites) and tried to correct any tendency to effeminacy which they may already have detected in me. I don't know how much they under-stood such things, but on discovering that (like many homosexuals) I could not whistle, they persisted in trying to make me master this primitive form of music. They also reproved me for striking a match, on the edge of the box, *away* from me: that was the woman's way, they said, men always struck matches *towards* them. In my first days at prep school, at the age of eight, I was pestered with trick questions containing words that I had never heard, such as 'Can you shit?' I said I didn't know and the boys squealed with brutish laughter but wouldn't explain what they meant. So at luncheon at home that weekend, with mother, father and brothers, I naturally asked 'What does "shit" mean?', and it was my brothers' turn to choke with suppressed laughter.

The eldest, Jack, went to Hertford College, Oxford – he played rugger and boxed as a heavyweight for the University – and then into the Colonial Civil Service and to Uganda. This was in 1912, and colonial administrators were not then trained in anthropology; but my brother was fascinated by the culture of the tribe he got to know best, the Lango, and wrote a remarkably comprehensive book about their social structure, religion, customs and language. In 1921 he was transferred to the Sudan Political Service, to administer a district, till then unadministered, in the remote south-east of the Sudan, a cockpit of warring cattle tribes and raiders from Abyssinia. Several years after his death, in 1951, I visited his old hill-station at Nagichot and found growing there rose-trees which I remembered his taking as cuttings from my mother's garden in Sussex; and an old man who had been one of my brother's police orderlies walked ten miles and climbed the hill to pay his respects to me.

But this was where the trouble occurred that, in 1925, ended Jack's career in Africa. He knew his tribe, the Didinga, as well as he had known the Lango. One day a signal came from Khartoum, the capital, to say that His Excellency the Governor would be visiting Jack's district on a certain day and instructing him to gather all the tribal chiefs and village headmen at a central spot on that day, to pay homage to H.E. Now, Jack knew that the appointed day happened to be a day of great local importance, a day when rain-making ceremonies had to be performed, to ensure a good harvest, and the headmen could not be away from their villages. Jack put this urgently to the bureaucrats in Khartoum. No, they said, H.E.'s schedule could not be altered. There must be a full attendance for him. As Jack had foreseen, many headmen stayed away – and he was now ordered to conduct a punitive expedition against the absentees and burn down their villages. He would do no such thing: instead, he drafted and sent to Khartoum a vivid but purely imaginary report on the punitive expedition they wanted. When the truth came out, of course he had to resign 'on medical grounds'.

This is what I remember of the story as he told it to me, many years ago. I may have one or two details wrong, but it is broadly correct, and I know from others that Jack's 'war that never was' became a legend in the Service.

He was indeed a legendary figure. Unlike most Europeans in Africa, he went about clad only in a khaki kilt; and – long before Mountbatten and the troops in Burma discovered that headgear was unnecessary in a tropical climate – he never wore a hat. This was after his had been shot off by an arrow at noon during a battle; the battle had gone on all day, and he had felt no ill-effects. He became expert in spear-throwing, and would settle a dispute by challenging a local chief to a spear-throwing contest. He was a blood-member of his tribe and had to undergo the various initiation rites: these included training in sexual endurance which later enhanced his standing (in every sense) with some of the women of Bloomsbury. He also told me how, on at least two occasions, he had had to eat human flesh: one was a purely ritual occasion and the meat was stringy, an elderly female witch having been killed because she had failed to ensure a good harvest; but the other involved the cooking and eating of a young baby, killed in his honour. He said that the flesh was 'rather like *poussin* in the average London restaurant – a bit tasteless.' He emphasised that cannibalism itself was not illegal in any country in the world.

When he left the Service, Jack became an academic anthropologist, first at the London School of Economics, then, in 1934, as a university lecturer at Cambridge—a post he was well-qualified to fill, having done his field-work first, on the spot. One who told me that he had studied under Jack, and learned much from him, is Jomo Kenyatta. Jack wrote a number of books popularising anthropology, but his most delightful book was called *Engato: the Lion Cub*—a simple account of a pet lion he had at one time in Africa. He also wrote a book attempting to codify the laws of poker, of which he was a good player. He was also a remarkable linguist: he knew eleven African languages or dialects and could speak Arabic in the accents of Cairo or Jerusalem or Damascus. No doubt it was this aptitude which led to his being sent, on some secret mission, to the Middle East, during the Second World War. Before going, he disposed of all his personal effects, gave me his books, and told me nothing except that, as part of what must have been a very thorough disguise, he was required to have all the fillings removed from his teeth and replaced with crude substitutes by a semi-skilled Arab dentist.

Towards the end of his life, Jack (who had been baptised a Christian in infancy, confirmed at Lancing, and grown up a normal unbelieving Anglican) was converted to a liberal Muslim sect. When he died in 1946, after a stupid accident, in the hospital of SS. John & Elizabeth, St John's Wood, I had to arrange a funeral at the Muslim cemetery at Woking, with an *imam* from Regent's Park to conduct it. There was a *contretemps*: the undertakers, despite my careful instructions, had laid on a standard, i.e. Christian, coffin, and as it was removed from the hearse at the graveside, we were shocked to see on the top of it a large brass cross. The *imam* seemed distressed: we hastily hid the cross with flowers. This would have amused my brother a good deal.

In an obituary in *Man*, the journal of the Royal Anthropological Institute, Professor E. E. Evans-Pritchard—whose family, by a coincidence, had been friends of ours at Crowborough in my childhood—wrote of Jack that he was:

gay, versatile, lovable, and adventurous—an Elizabethan. His was a rare spirit and his weaknesses were consistent with the heroic in his personality and further endeared him to his friends ... [His] romantic figure made him a great success at Cambridge. Students felt at once that here was something outside the ordinary academic run ... To him is largely due the continued development of the Cambridge Department into a flourishing school ... For the time it was written (1923), *The Lango* is rightly regarded as an outstanding piece of research, and it will always remain one of the few classical accounts of an African people before the lives of Africans were strongly influenced by European rule and commerce ... Had he been harder-hearted and more of a politician, his talents might have brought him higher preferment ... He gambled with life and did not always win.

My brother Jim's career was more dramatic, in its ups and especially its downs, than Jack's. Jim was the best-looking of the three brothers, and throughout his life had a considerable success with women, thanks also to an air of old-fashioned gallantry which in the end became only slightly blurred by alcohol. Instead of going to university he studied medicine at the London Hospital in Whitechapel and was newly qualified, at the age of twenty-four, when the First World War broke out. He did not at once join the Army, but went to Belgium as the surgeon of an unusual amateur ambulance unit organised by Miss Nellie Hozier, a sister of Mrs Winston Churchill. The unit did good work during the retreat from Mons, but was captured by the Germans. For some time they were allowed to go on working: they set up a 'hospital' in a house and had fifty-three British wounded soldiers in their care, under the general supervision of a German doctor. Among my mother's papers are a number of letters from Lady Manners, whose daughter Angela was with the unit. Through her an occasional brief message from my brother reached us. They are anxious letters, and the later ones are in black-edged envelopes, for Lady Manners's son had just been killed in action. Since this unit consisted of civilians, they were repatriated, through Denmark, as a result of intervention by the American Ambassador to Belgium (the United States not yet being in the war). After this adventure, my brother decided that it was more sensible to practise his skill as a surgeon in a more conventional way and obtained a commission in the R.A.M.C. He went through the terrible battle of Loos and other battles in that bloodiest of modern wars, and won the Military Cross and a mention in dispatches. On one leave, I remember, he spent much of his time sleeping in an easy chair in front of the smoking-room fire – and his sleep was restless, punctuated, as a dog's sometimes is, by twitching of the limbs and faint moaning sounds. My mother put these phenomena down, no doubt correctly, to the nervous strain of his experiences at the Front, and when, later on, his career ended in disaster, she still blamed all his misfortunes on the war. He was, I think, her favourite son. I, after all, as she told me early in my childhood, was 'meant to be a little girl' – to provide company for my parents in their old age. No post-Freudian mother would dare to make this remark to a son, but my mother was innocent of all such knowledge, and I don't suppose it made much difference, anyway.

Jim was a generous son and brother, and spent his pay lavishly on us when he was on home leave. Once he took my mother and me to stay for a few days at the Savoy Hotel, where we watched a *thé dansant*. (My father would by now have been too infirm for such an outing.) He took us to several shows, too, one at the Adelphi Theatre – I can't remember what the show was, but I think it had in it the song 'Winnie the Window-cleaner'. Nor can I recall whether he took me or I went on my own to the first revue I ever saw – *5064 Gerrard* at the Alhambra: the title of the show was the telephone-number of the theatre, and Teddie Gerard was in the show, with Phyllis Monkman and other glamorous creatures. This gave me plenty to boast about at school.

On the last morning of one of Jim's leaves, my mother, realising that he might be returning to the Front to be killed, told me to go into his room – he was still in bed – and kiss him goodbye. I demurred, in acute embarrassment. I can still see this scene vividly: her pleading face, her soft clear voice – 'Do, darling ... ' – and then my unwilling entry to his room and the clumsy kiss. He may have been as embarrassed as I was. I was not entirely without affection for him, but I hated being pressed to show it in this way. Yet it surely would have been a natural enough demonstration, in any less inhibiting and constrictive society or by any 'normal' boy? I must have been eleven or twelve years old, and at school had already exchanged passionate kisses with Derek G.

After the war, Jim returned to the staff of the London Hospital and set up in practice as a consultant. He specialised in orthopaedic surgery, and drew on his experiences at the Front to write for the *Lancet* a paper on new methods of treatment of fractures of the femur. While I was at Lancing, he got married. Apart from a few dinner-parties at his flat, during which I sat, frozen silent with shyness, listening to conversation that I did not know how to join in, I saw and heard little of him at this time – but then everything seemed to go wrong almost simultaneously (and of course, in the stupid old-fashioned way with the young, it was all 'kept from' me). His marriage ended in divorce. He was earning a large income, but this was somehow dissipated – partly, it was hinted to me, in gambling losses at White's – and debts piled up until he was forced into bankruptcy. This meant that even the tools of his trade – his surgical instruments – were seized. For some reason – I don't suppose I shall ever know the full story – he emigrated to Brazil, and there from time to time scraped a meagre livelihood trekking over the Andes and treating Indian peasants' ailments in exchange for a meal or a night's lodging.

He spent some years in Brazil, years during which my mother – always a great worrier – worried constantly about his welfare, longed to see him again, and cannot have been reassured by whatever letters he wrote home (though she wrote to a friend: 'I get cheery letters from the doctor son, he is in much better health now'). Suddenly in 1937, two years before her death and when she was seventy years old and far from well, she took a bold decision: she would go by boat to Rio de Janeiro, see Jim, and – no doubt this was the unspoken thought – by some miracle 'rescue' him. She went on a cruising liner, the *Arlanza*, and sent me a series of ten postcards, all duly numbered, from the various ports of call. Of what happened when she got to Rio – and indeed of the general tenor of my brother's life there – I know only from correspondence which I had at the time with a Rio journalist, Mr H. E. Walker, who – possibly at my request, for I was myself established in Fleet Street by then – most kindly met my mother, booked her a room in a respectable hotel, and helped her in many ways.

It seems surprising – and was a great disappointment to my mother – that, when she was making so great an effort to see my brother, he should not have met her at the dock. Mr Walker saw her 'almost every day,' he wrote, 'until your brother finally arrived from the interior, after she had sent him the money'.

Apparently Jim wanted my mother to go to him in Belo Horizonte. Mr Walker discouraged this: 'it is a train journey of about eighteen hours, in the hottest season of the year'. The background is clearly indicated in a confidential letter which Mr Walker wrote to me after my mother's departure for home:

It was hard work to get your brother to Rio, even after your mother had phoned him several times. She first sent him two pounds to pay his rail expenses; this he returned saying he needed at least twenty-five pounds, and that the money should be telephoned and not sent by check. I arranged this for your mother. Even then he wanted her to go to Belo Horizonte and I finally wrote him myself (I never told your mother this and I don't think he did) urging him to put personal considerations aside as to avoidance of meeting Rio people and come to meet his mother. He must have needed this twenty-five pounds to pay up accounts in B.H.

I know your mother gave him seventy-five pounds later to settle with people who kept coming to the hotel to see him; whether she gave him other money for past accounts I do not know, but I did advise her (at her request) about putting up several hundred pounds to set him up to practice in B.H. when, and if, he is licensed; I advised that she should consult you two brothers in England before she took such a step, as she said she would have to use her capital.

I found your brother very charming but he seems to be very weak in character from a financial standpoint. He owes considerable money to various persons and firms in Rio; your mother paid his entire expenses while she was here. I only had a drink with him the first night I met him because I knew he was spending the mother's money. He used to spend hours at a neighbouring hotel with English people whom he knew before, sitting around a bar table; this happened almost daily but *your mother never knew it*. I'm not criticising except from the point that it wasn't his own money he was drinking up. Your mother told me that she thought he was not as black as he is painted, but she thought he could not stand liquor because just a little affected him; all she understood was what he took with her.

I have no desire to judge anyone; I have been in the news-paper game for more than a quarter of a century in North and South America, Europe and the Far East, but for the life of me I cannot understand how a man forty-six years old and as brilliant as is your brother in his profession can expect his mother to come to his aid whenever he is in financial trouble. If a man of his age cannot stand on his own feet financially then he is never going to be able to do so. The letter your brother wrote to your mother from Belo Horizonte about the money was not the tone of a letter to one's mother; I know it hurt her very much, and I told her my straight opinion when she showed it to me. That night she phoned him in B.H. and told him in so many words 'you can come to Rio and see me or I shall take the next boat to England and you can rot in Brazil' — those are her own words in telling of her message the next day.

She told me once he did not seem to understand that she was making financial sacrifices even in coming out to see him, let alone paying his expenses. She wanted to study him, and stayed several weeks longer than she anticipated for this purpose. I think she is satisfied now; she is a very clever woman as you know, but I am afraid her position as a mother blinds her somewhat in this case.

The reason for this screed is to give you the low-down and in accordance with the request in your first letter months ago, and, of course, is not for your mother's eyes.

Yours,

H.E.W.

This is the letter of a sensible and decent man. He was surely right in thinking that my mother was to some extent blinded by maternal devotion: was he right in calling her 'a very clever woman'? She was impulsive, yet patient and persistent: her bursts of anger were very rare, and I am astonished that she should have used the phrase 'you can rot in Brazil' to the son for love of whom she had crossed the Atlantic. (Perhaps, knowing Mr Walker's view of the situation, she exaggerated to him what she had said: otherwise, there is almost an echo here of the old flare-ups with her mother and brother.)

She was worried about money because she wanted to be fair to all her sons. She was not rich: she was living on whatever an Indian Civil Service widow's pension was, and a small investment income. Possibly my brother's depredations, which did not begin or end with her visit, led her to consider the annuity which I have mentioned. But I think that both Jack and I had our fair shares at various times. A year after her visit to Rio, she made a will in which, to compensate me for what she had given or 'lent' to the others, she left me £2,000 in addition to one-third of the residue. Why, in any case, should we have been 'entitled' to anything at all? Money, and quarrels about money, are the most sordid aspect of the whole family complex.

There was to be one recovery, and a final decline, in my brother Jim's fortunes. When the Second World War broke out, he made what must have been an enormous effort, came back to England, and went to the War Office. They looked up his record in the first war and again granted him a commission in the R.A.M.C. (Despite his bankruptcy, he had never been 'struck off': his name stayed in the Medical Directory, and he was still an F.R.C.S. and an L.R.C.P.) He ended up this war with the rank of colonel, in command of a military hospital in Chittagong, in Lower Bengal. When I was in Singapore in 1945,[1] I mentioned this to Mountbatten: he sent me up to Chittagong in a small aircraft, an Expediter, to spend a night at Jim's hospital. It was a fascinating, sometimes alarming, flight: we bumped and slid our way through spectacular monsoon weather, the pilot ingeniously skirting the worst of the heavy clouds. It was a fortunate coincidence that enabled me to see Jim; for he was leaving the hospital next day (the war being just over) and this was his farewell evening. So there were convivial visits to officers' and sergeants' messes, and toasts to be drunk with matron, sisters and nurses. I could see that my brother — now fifty-five years old — still had a way with women: the staff seemed genuinely fond of him. On this special night I could not, of course, judge fairly if he was habitually drinking too much; but it was late when we turned in, pretty well canned.

After Jim's demobilisation, a dilemma faced him and me. He had no home in England, no regular job, and no money once his gratuity was spent. Although we 'got on' superficially well, we

[1] See p. 217.

did not really care for each other much. But this maddening obligation of 'blood ties' came into operation; he had, after all, been kind to me when I was a small boy and had made a creditable effort to recover from the degradation of Brazil; so it was natural that he should come to stay semi-permanently at my Essex home, Bradwell Lodge. Here he was reasonably well-liked by the village people: despite an inner loneliness, of which he gave only an occasional hint, he could still put on a front of hearty geniality. He could not, of course, return to his profession at the level at which he had left it; but he was glad (and so was I) when he managed to get an occasional job as a ship's surgeon. Such doctors are, I believe, much in demand by shipping lines, since no ship above a certain tonnage can sail without one on board.

One day a report in the *Evening News* showed that my brother had not lost his skill. A ship's fireman, thirty-year-old Denis Buckley, of Custom House, was recovering in the Seamen's Hospital at Greenwich from an operation for appendicitis performed successfully at sea, in the Blue Star liner *Stuartstar*, homeward bound from Buenos Aires, 'although the ship was then ploughing its way through the Bay of Biscay, rolling in the heavy seas and a wind blowing with gale force ... there was no operating table with powerful lights, no supply of running fresh water, and no one on board who had acted as a surgeon's assistant ... Dr Driberg, the ship's doctor, operated ... helped by the Chief Officer and second steward.'

This was, in a sense, the last flicker of hope for Jim. It may have reminded him of what he had been and might still have been. He returned to Bradwell and was soon, every day at opening time, making his way unsteadily over to the King's Head opposite, shuffling back even more unsteadily, often with assistance, when the pub closed for the afternoon.

Then he was taken seriously ill. I went to see him in hospital and we had the first and last really intimate talk we had in the whole of our lives. We discussed our parents, his failed marriage, my homosexuality. There was some risk of his dying. As he had, like all of us, been through the establishment routine of baptism and confirmation, I asked him if he would like to see a priest. No, he said, he had managed without that all these years: it would be cheating to try it now. I did not press the point.

But he recovered, and seemed as if he might be, as they say, 'good for' another ten years. It would have been hypocritical in either of us to welcome the prospect. His drinking (for most of which, incidentally, I was paying, since he ordered bottles of whisky at the pub on my account) became even more obsessive. One weekend I was away, staying with Lord Beaverbrook at Cherkley, when the housekeeper at Bradwell telephoned to say that my brother had had a severe bout of D.T.s and had defecated all over his bedroom floor. This was unbearable, and dangerous (he was in the sixteenth-century timber-framed part of the house); to put it cynically, it was difficult to get and to keep good servants. With the connivance of the local doctor, it was put to him that the east coast was too cold for a man in his condition, used to hot climates; and a room was found for him at a guest-house in Devon. Here, not long afterwards, he was found dead in bed. He had gone to sleep with a very hot bottle against his leg, and there was a severe burn. The medical certificate gave morphine poisoning as one of the causes of death. Apparently, in addition to alcohol, he had been taking morphia for some time, possibly as a sleeping drug. I had not known this.

I had to go to Exeter to identify him. I had performed the same melancholy office for my brother Jack, but had not been in a municipal mortuary before. I arrived after dark, but the big refrigerated room was brightly lit. The dead were in dozens of drawers, end-on, like the drawers of a filing-cabinet. The friendly, business-like attendant slid open a drawer. It contained a baby. 'No, no, let's see ... ' he said. 'Ah yes' — and he slid open another. This was the right one. It was brother Jim all right. I tried to feel pity and regret, but felt no emotion whatever. I put a finger on the cold forehead. It — not 'he' — felt like a Tussaud figure. Perhaps twenty seconds had passed; I must not waste the attendant's time; he was waiting to push the drawer back, stooping over it. He looked up at me and said, briskly and cheerily, 'All right, sir?' I nodded, and the drawer slid back and clicked shut. I spent a comfortable night at the hotel in the Close, and in the morning looked at the cathedral, ran into the Bishop of Crediton (who promised to remember my brother at Mass), and bought a pair of old lacemakers' lamps at an antique shop. It was a tidy finish to a largely unsatisfactory life and a cool fraternal relationship.

So all three brothers have been, more or less, failures: Jack, for his quixotry (which I admire) in championing his tribesmen; Jim, as just described; I, a journalist when I might have been a poet, and a backbench M.P. – the lowest form of parliamentary life – with no hope, under the prevailing heterosexual dictatorship, of ministerial office.

Though it occurred before my brothers' deaths, I may round off the chronicle by mentioning my mother's death also. Here again I was not conscious of the deep emotion that one is supposed to feel, but I felt some remorse for having spent less time with her, in her last months, than I could have. A few weekends before her death, I had to choose between going to stay with her and going to my new home at Bradwell, which I was only just moving into and having done up. There was plenty to see to, but it was not really essential that I should be there. But I wanted to go to Bradwell, and went there. (I should and could have done both, for I had a car and a driver, Bert Westlake, of whom, as novelists say, more anon.) I also spent a long, sunny day at Brighton, where I met a most beautiful Persian student: we made a tentative date, but my mother's death, occurring a few days later, upset all such arrangements, and I never saw him again.

She had by now been moved into a private nursing-home at Crowborough. One day, as I stood at the foot of her bed, she asked me the direct question: 'Do they say I'm going to get better, or not?' As happens in cases of leukaemia, her spleen was enormously swollen; I think she must have guessed that the illness was incurable. The Vicar of St John's had called and anointed her. (She had been in hospital on and off for some months, choosing the London Hospital because it was Jim's old one.) Of course I should have told her the truth: I shirked doing so in the most cowardly way, turning the question aside with a mock-cheerful 'Of course you're going to get better!' If only we could have had a real 'heart-to-heart' talk then ... but I had always responded with an embarrassed lack of warmth to her displays of affection and to any attempt by her to achieve intimacy or to pry into my life. This, I think, was the main cause of my subsequent remorse, and perhaps of her continuing presence in my dreams.

On the night of her death, my mother had been in a coma for

some time. My brother Jack and I stayed at the nursing-home till fairly late and then went home, about ten minutes' walk away, played cards, had a drink, and went to bed. We had left the faithful Jeannie Hunt at my mother's bedside; the nurses said they would telephone us if necessary. The call came in the small hours; she was dead when we got there. At one point she had seemed to regain consciousness and had muttered a few words — her 'last words'. They were: 'All men are liars.' At first Mrs Hunt misheard the word 'liars' as 'flowers', and said 'Yes, they are lovely, aren't they — I'll bring some more tomorrow'; but then she and the nurse, disentangling the syllables, recognised the quotation from the Psalms. What was my mother referring to? To my brother Jim's many lies to her? To my false reassurances, a few weeks before?

The funeral was at St John's. A Mass of Requiem was sung. The Vicar, Father Olive, whom she had liked, celebrated the Mass; a previous Vicar, Father Charlton, whom she had also liked (and so did I, rather enviously: he had two virile, blond, adolescent boys living with him), performed the Absolutions, circumambulating the catafalque to cense it and sprinkle it with holy water, to the shocked horror of some old friends of my parents, firm Protestants, who had turned up. I took pleasure in handing them unbleached candles to hold, and lighting these at the correct places in the service. I got a friend from *Life* magazine to come and take photographs of the funeral and also, at the undertaker's beforehand, of my mother in her coffin. In these pictures the swollen spleen is perceptible. At the undertaker's and in the church — where also, fortunately, there was the fragrance of incense of a fairly expensive brand (I think from Buckfast) — the scent of flowers mingled with, but could not disguise, a slight whiff, already just noticeable, of carnal decay.

The clearing-out of our old home was an appalling task. (*Vide* Emily Dickinson: 'The bustle in a house/The morning after death ... ') My father's smoking-room had been full of 'curios' — objects grotesque or beautiful that he had brought home from Assam, spears, Naga costumes, a Buddhist prayer-wheel. I had so often in my childhood heard my father expatiating on these to visitors that I had become bored with them. My mother's will expressed a hope that they should go to museums. Only a few were good enough for this. The rest were sold, with most of the other contents of the house, for practically nothing. I wish I had some of them today. The better furniture, inherited from great-aunt Mary, I took to Bradwell and still have. There were also gruesome problems about minor personal effects: what was to be done with my mother's spare set of false teeth? But it all had to be settled in a rush: my brother and I were both busy, and the Second World War was only a few weeks away.

We differed over only one item. My mother had a fairly good fur coat, made of a skin called kolinsky. Jack wanted it for his current girl-friend. I, more selfishly, thought it would make a good lining for a winter overcoat for myself. He won.

This, then, was my immediate family. We have seen that the record contains insanity, religious eccentricity of various kinds, broken marriages, homosexuality, drug-addiction, and several cases of alcoholism. I repeat the question I asked at the beginning of this chapter: what made me such an odd child? To what extent, if it had not been for the conventional ties of family life, *could* I have escaped from such genetic influences and the childhood environment described earlier?

I am sometimes disposed to think that it might have been better if I had been dumped anonymously on the doorstep of a prosperous, childless widower.

4

Grace and disgrace

There was one religious exercise which I found even more trying, because longer, than family prayers: this was being taken to church on Sunday mornings, to the service known as 'matins at eleven'.

There were, and are, two Anglican churches at Crowborough: All Saints' was extremely 'low'; St John's, to which my parents went, had been founded in the nineteenth century, like Lancing, to promote the Tractarian cause (the building itself was a replica of Newman's church at Littlemore), but, also to some extent like Lancing, had somehow got stuck at a moderate level — what derisive Anglo-Catholics called 'middle stump'. The proper eucharistic vestments were worn and candles lit (only four of them), but there was never a whiff of incense and — the biggest black mark — this dreary service of matins was the principal event of Sunday. Nor was Holy Communion ever called anything but that, or perhaps the Eucharist; never the Mass.

At Lancing I met a number of genuinely good and 'straight' boys, who no doubt knew about the sexual goings-on of their fellows but did not take part in them. Several of them were the sons of Anglo-Catholic clergymen and were accustomed at home to more elaborate forms of worship than those provided in the college chapel. In this context I recall the names of J. F. Harrison from Guildford (whose sister Joan was to become a well-known collaborator with Alfred Hitchcock in Hollywood) and B. H. Molony. On Sunday mornings, after the early Communion service, we were free to go where we liked, and some of these boys introduced me to the ornate and fragrant ceremonial of the Mass,

sung solemnly with all the trimmings. The aesthetic appeal of such
a service at, say, St Bartholomew's, Brighton – an enormous brick
building, almost comparable with Albi cathedral and now at last
commended by such experts as Pevsner and Ian Nairn – was
immediate. I studied tracts and books about the Movement and
was stirred to read that its devoted priests had been imprisoned
only a few decades earlier for 'illegal practices' (of an ecclesiastical
nature) and were still being harassed by pompous bishops; I got
by heart such manuals as *The Ritual Reason Why*; and learned
most of all from an enormously detailed onslaught, *The Secret
History of the Oxford Movement*, by a Protestant propagandist,
Walter Walsh, which contained such splendid verses as:

God give our wavering clergy back those honest hearts and
true
Which once were theirs ere Popish snares their toils around
them threw;
Nor let them barter wife and child, pure hearth and happy
home
For the drunken bliss of the strumpet kiss of the Jezebel of
Rome.

Although I myself was not much of a Jezebel-fancier, I was all
for our clergy wavering Romewards if this was to involve them in
such entertaining controversies and make church services less
tedious. It was startling, all the same, to find an actual, authentic
Roman missal behind the high altar in Lancing chapel. It had been
left there by Father (later Canon) Dudley Symon, probably the
most 'extreme' of the assistant masters. I remember a sermon in
which he likened the dance of David before the Ark to the movements of celebrant, deacon and sub-deacon as they go to and fro
censing the altar at High Mass: it was frustrating that our own
more austere chapel worship should not be embellished by such
anthropologically instructive performances. We recalled the thrilling report given to an earlier Bishop of London by the chaplain
whom he had sent to see what was happening at the notoriously
'Romanising' church of St Alban, Holborn: 'My lord, I saw three
men in green, and I do not think they will easily be put down.'
But I need not dwell at length on this adolescent liturgical
intoxication: the best account of such matters is in *Sinister Street*

and others of Compton Mackenzie's earlier novels. What is most to the point here is that, by a coincidence, just as I was making these discoveries at school and in Worthing and Brighton – and, soon, in London – a kindred upheaval was disturbing the stuffy tranquillity of St John's, Crowborough. One Christmas holiday, home from Lancing, I was electrified to learn that a new vicar had been appointed and that he was 'making changes' (always a dangerous thing to do in an English parish) of a kind which I now eagerly approved of.

I was told, for instance, that from the moment of his arrival the church's single bell had been rung three times a day, and not rung 'ordinarily' but in a pattern of 3, 3, 3, 9: this, I at once recognised, was the Angelus; my hopes quickened.

My father had lately died, but in a few days' time it would be Christmas and, as in his lifetime, my mother and I would go to early Communion together. For other services she sat in the back-most pew of all (for she had a slight nervous tic which she controlled by resting her chin in her hand, and preferred to do this unobtrusively), but when we were 'going up' to the altar-rail we sat at the front. I could therefore observe closely all the motions of priest and server and was alert for certain shibboleths in their ritual dialogue. I knew that if the service were to begin, as in the *Book of Common Prayer*, with the Lord's Prayer and the 'collect for purity', there would have been no significant change under the new regime. I was not disappointed: a bell pealed, the priest entered, preceded by the server in a freshly laundered cotta. They took up their places before the altar and crossed themselves; and I heard – uttered very fast and *sotto voce* – the crucial words 'In the name of the Father, the Son, and the Holy Ghost. Amen.' Occurring at this point, these were a direct translation from the Roman rite (as it then was). I turned to my mother, kneeling beside me, and said, in an intense whisper: 'Mother, *it is the Mass*!'

So this curious revolution was on. It was, as I say, disturbing, and I was for anything which upset the smugness of Crowborough. There were bitter rows: some of the congregation left; the choir-men walked out because they were expected to bow to the altar and because, as one of them put it, 'he kissed the stole'. (This trivial excuse referred to the fact that a priest, when he goes into the pulpit to preach, puts on a stole, first, usually somewhat

perfunctorily, kissing the cross embroidered in the middle of it.)
Soon the Sacrament was reserved, so that genuflexion rather than
bowing became the required gesture of homage; and matins on
Sunday morning was replaced by the Mass—admittedly not so
well sung or performed as at Brighton but at least a sacrificial
drama, action as well as utterance, not just a static series of psalms,
readings, and prayers; a temple, not a synagogue, function. St
John's now seemed to eye, ear, and nose (with its ornaments, its
'bells and smells') what every Anglican church should be—
uncompromisingly Catholic. Indeed, this little church (in which
there is a memorial to my mother, a Madonna by Sir Ninian
Comper) became, and has remained, the one major exception to
my general detestation of my birthplace.

My mother never bothered with the nuances of the new situation, but stuck loyally to St John's. She liked the new vicar, the
Reverend Basil Gurdon, who came to us from a well-known
London church, St Barnabas, Pimlico. He was a fine man, tall,
slightly deaf, and truly celibate. I hero-worshipped him, sided
with him in the high *v.* low battles, morning after morning walked
nearly a mile from my home to serve his weekday Mass (rewarded
by breakfast in the vicarage), and, doubtless to his embarrassment,
tried to egg him on to further ultramontane practices that might
épater the Evangelicals. Once, in the vestry, I tried on his biretta
and found it becoming. What fun, I thought, to be priest—but
thought also that this would be inconsistent with my sexual habits.
I feel sure that Father Gurdon guessed that I had homosexual
tendencies, if not at the extent of my practice (for at this time,
during holidays from school, I was carrying and using a powder
compact and a little rouge); but we did not discuss the matter and
I never went to Confession to him or any other priest I knew
personally, but only to strangers. At that time I thought, naïvely,
that the practice of homosexuality among the clergy was rare, and
I was even shocked by occasional evidences to the contrary in the
News of the World. Now I know that some of the best priests, like
some of the best teachers, generals, and prison governors, are
homosexuals, practising or not.

The usual shallow sneer at homosexuals in any sort of public life
(or, for that matter, at heterosexuals who indulge their appetites
extra-maritally) is that they are 'hypocrites'. Except in the sense

that the Greek word 'hypocrite' means 'actor', and that, especially
in an intolerant society, all of us have to do a certain amount of
protective or comoedic role-playing, the charge is false. In my
own case, the two interests were parallel and simultaneous, and I
was not a hypocrite: whether functioning as an acolyte in the
sanctuary, or practising *fellatio* in some hotel bedroom or station
W.C., I was doing what I most wanted to do at that moment, and
doing it with complete sincerity.

My only complaint is against the formal teaching, as distinct
from the practice, of the Church, which made me think
that it was 'wrong' to snatch a kiss from a fellow-acolyte behind
the sacristy door and so robbed me of a good many chances of
enjoyment. The difficulty is that, as one advances in years and
status, one becomes identified with the teaching as well as the
practice and may thus be thrust into false positions. In later life, as
an M.P., I was labelled 'Anglican' and required to serve on
various ecclesiastical committees (some of which did indeed interest
me); I had to open church bazaars (role-playing, indeed!) and
preach in school chapels. This last task has been easier since one
has been able to concentrate on attacking, in the name of true
Christian freedom, the puritan and Manichaean backlash against
permissiveness.

'Moderate' as the chapel services at Lancing were, they did at
least introduce me to several kinds of good music, including
Gregorian chant (plainsong), to which we sang the psalms at
evensong, and the *English Hymnal*: this book, whose musical
editor was Vaughan-Williams, was then only ten years old and
represented a big advance, in both words and music, on the
standards of the old familiar *Hymns Ancient and Modern*. Our
charming and whimsical organist Alexander Brent-Smith, himself
a competent composer, used to thunder out Bach toccatas and
fugues, and organ arrangements of some of Beethoven's
symphonies.

There were also a few hymns specially written for use at
Lancing; of these I remember particularly one, in the Sapphic
metre, in honour of St Nicholas (one of our patrons) which must
be unique among all the millions of examples of Christian
hymnody, for it contains one stanza directly, if scornfully, invoking
a heathen deity:

Rouse thee, great goddess of th' Ephesian temple,
For lo! the offspring of a greater Virgin
Armeth his servant to destroy thine oak-tree —
                              Dumb, dead Diana!

The author of this hymn was the Reverend Adam Fox, who on July 15th, 1973, on his ninetieth birthday, preached his last sermon as a Canon of Westminster.

Much intellectual stimulus at Lancing was provided by Evelyn Waugh, whose time there overlapped with mine. Though it has been corrected elsewhere, I had better record here that his account, in *A Little Learning*, of an incident in chapel, when he and I, both sacristans, were getting the high altar ready for a festival, is inaccurate. He says that he indicated to me that he had ceased to believe in God. He did no such thing. When I was fussing about the proper hang of the linen cloth, he merely said: 'Nonsense! If it's good enough for me it's good enough for God.' This may be mildly blasphemous: it is not a proclamation of atheism.

His published diaries show that Waugh, at school, had homosexual inclinations, but that he repressed them. I certainly never heard of him as a practising homosexual until later, at Oxford. Later still (after one false start) he was happily married and became intolerant of homosexuality. It may have been this suppression of his true nature — in his case, bisexuality — that led to the mental breakdown so vividly described in his autobiographical novel, *The Ordeal of Gilbert Pinfold*.

I was surprised by the disparaging references to J. F. Roxburgh in Evelyn's diaries and in his letters to me after he had left Lancing. I found Roxburgh — who left Lancing while I was in the sixth form there, to become the first headmaster of Stowe — a magnetically brilliant teacher: he was a dandy and a sceptic, with a sonorous voice ('*Con*substantial, *co*-eternal ... ' he would quote mockingly, from the doxology of a famous hymn), and he could inspire in us a passion for poetry — English, Latin, Greek, and some French. Evelyn had a theory that the resonant tones of Roxburgh's voice, and his polysyllabically precise delivery, can still be heard in the voices of those who sat under him. This seems true of Lord Molson and one or two others I can think of, and may possibly be true of me.

Partly through the school debating society and play-reading society, but mainly through reading Bernard Shaw — not so much his plays as the prefaces to them — I was now, at the age of fifteen or sixteen, taking an interest in politics and beginning to think of myself as a Socialist. That my leanings should be to the Left was natural: quite apart from the merits of the argument, this was part of the revolt against Crowborough.

Several things happened during my last year at Lancing. Political interest was quickened by the election of the first Labour Government (but without a clear majority) under Ramsay MacDonald. I cannot remember how soon disillusionment set in, but both then and much later the Labour Party (of which I was to be Chairman in 1957–8) seemed to me about as dull as a 'middle-stump' church. During one of the long, boring holidays — when term ended I dreaded going home, when holidays ended I dreaded going back to school — searching for something that seemed more revolutionary, I joined the Brighton branch of the Communist Party of Great Britain, and was assigned the hopeless task of selling the *Daily Worker* (or was it then the *Workers' Weekly?*) at Crowborough.

Now I was leading a triple life indeed. I had to conceal from my new comrades both the fact that I was being educated at a bourgeois public school and, still more, my ecclesiastical and sexual tastes. In its turn, the school must know nothing of the sex or the Party. Only Father Gurdon was mildly amused to find that I was distributing a 'red' sheet, without success, in his parish. Through the Party I was at last able to meet on terms of equality — better still, inferiority, since they had been in the Party longer than I — males of the working class. Unfortunately, those I happened to get to know best were unattractively plain. (Physical beauty is not absolutely necessary to stimulate desire, but it does help. In particular, no doubt because my father had one, I have never been able to abide a beard, and deplore the current fashion for chin-hair among some of the otherwise best-looking young proletarians of my acquaintance.)

But at this final stage in school life my mind, suddenly and alarmingly, had to be concentrated on personal rather than political or ecclesiastical obsessions. I was now head of my house and deputy head of the school, having, to my chagrin, just been passed over for the headship in favour of a straight, square, glowingly healthy and clean-minded boy named Gibbs, a member of an eminent Anglican and banking family. Had I not had this rebuff, would I have controlled my private conduct so that it would be more acceptable to the school authorities or at least more discreet (and therefore more 'hypocritical')? It is possible, but I doubt it. At any rate, two of the boys in my dormitory resisted my nocturnal overtures and complained of them to the housemaster. (One of them was an extremely pretty boy with fair curly hair named Hector Lorenzo Christie. He lived at Jervaulx Abbey in Yorkshire; this he eventually inherited from his centenarian father, who had for some years been 'the oldest living Old Etonian'.) This meant severe punishment, administered in the ways most calculated to make me feel ashamed of myself. I felt no shame; but I felt annoyance at being found out (or, rather, 'betrayed') and acute embarrassment at what was now done to me; indeed, I felt so utterly miserable that I went up one night to a high place — the top of the 'Masters' Tower' — and tried but failed to summon up enough courage to jump from it. I was stripped of all offices — deputy head of the school, head of my house, head sacristan, head librarian and so on — and segregated in a small bed-sitting-room, where I was supposed, without any tuition, to get on with my work in preparation for taking a scholarship exam at Oxford. I was also cut off from the other boys at meal-times; I had to sit at a table on the dais with the housemaster, his wife, and the matron; the conversation was not enlivening. It so happened that the week of my disgrace was a week in which it was my turn as a prefect to read the lesson at morning chapel (then compulsory daily): the most painful part of the whole ordeal was that I was *not* deprived of this duty, but had to leave my place in the choir-stalls, turn and bow to the altar, walk across the enormous chancel, stand up at the lectern — a tarnished cynosure, stared at with pity, wonder or giggling amusement — by several hundred boys and a few shocked or cynical masters — and read, with as little tremor in my voice as possible, some irrelevant passage from the first book of Samuel.

I learned later that these arrangements, depressing as they were, were yet by way of being a concession. My brothers had been sent for and, in earnest conference, it had been agreed to keep the matter from my widowed mother: this could be done only by substituting a closely supervised reprieve until the end of term for the instant expulsion considered appropriate. At the end of that term I must leave; that, too, would be a premature departure, but my mother was told that, as I had failed once to win an Oxford scholarship, I must have some intensive private tuition ('cramming'). The tutor chosen was a good-looking young barrister named Colin Pearson (now Lord Justice Pearson). He helped me to get an open classical scholarship at Christ Church, largely by a process of bluff: I knew no German, but he taught me a few German vogue-words, such as *Weltschmerz* and *Weltanschauung*, and these I scattered at appropriate places in my essays. Nor, being an imaginative boy, already addicted to poetry and the visual arts, did I have any difficulty with such questions as '"Nature is too green and is badly lighted". Discuss.' (I was glad to see, in a recent Christ Church annual report, that philosophy exams are still, as they ought to be, thought-provoking. Question 38 in one such exam was 'Is Question 38 a fair question?')

So I was leaving Lancing, in the traditional phrase, 'under a cloud'. (When I was lecturing there, a year or two ago, the admirable young headmaster, Ian Beer, said: 'I can't think why we haven't asked you back before.' I could have told him.) Despite kind notes of sympathy from Brent-Smith and one or two other masters, and courageous manifestations of affection from a few boys whom I had never thought of in that way, these were the unhappiest weeks of my school life, comparable in bloodiness with the initiatory Sunday night when, as a new boy, I had had to stand on a table in the house-room and sing a song (the one I insanely chose being 'The Bay of Biscay-O', a most unsuitable number for a boy whose voice was just breaking); comparable, too, with the Sunday nights of torment in the dormitory when, since the prefects were taking coffee with the housemaster and were not there to keep order, some really rough bullying went on. In my dread of one such night, I had feebly and ineffectually cut a wrist with a razor-blade. This earned a bandage from the matron, but did not diminish the bullying, since it was recognised as a cowardly kind of malingering.

The most embarrassing part of leaving was the farewell interview with the headmaster, the Reverend H. T. Bowlby, a tall, gaunt, awe-inspiring figure with a pronounced limp. Fortunately, this interview was brief. It consisted merely of a few platitudes: 'It comes to this ... if you have enough faith in Christ, he will see you through' – words which meant nothing to me in my emotionally shattered condition.

Bowlby retired from the headmastership soon afterwards and became a Canon of Chichester. Soon after that, it was riveting for me (and thousands of others) to read in the papers that he had been arrested and charged with molesting little girls in a train. He explained to the police: 'I only treated them as I treat my own grandchildren', and was acquitted (or got off on appeal); but he never fully recovered from the incident. Perhaps I should not have felt a slight twinge of *Schadenfreude*.

5

Oxford

Having left school a term early, but having now, thanks to Pearson, got my scholarship, I had a few months to wait before going up to Oxford. Surprising as it may seem, I had no difficulty in getting a temporary job as a schoolmaster, at another of those awful 'good' prep schools – this one being at Bournemouth. The headmaster's wife was said to be 'a connection' (whatever that is) of Mrs Churchill's. Here I taught English, which for me chiefly meant reading modern poetry with a class. I also had to take the boys bathing in the sea – rather an alarming responsibility, since I am a poor swimmer. For the one term's work I was paid, so far as I can recall, £65 (plus a bonus of £10 for special coaching of a boy who also got a university scholarship; and, of course, 'all found', including the use of a tatty common-room).

Perhaps because of the shock of my departure from Lancing, I seem to have been for a time sexually quiescent. I do not remember any of the casual encounters that there must have been. There was nothing doing in the school: even if I had not had that fright, the boys were too young for me.

Nor can I recall any political activity. There would hardly have been a branch of the C.P. in Bournemouth. I went to one or two of the local churches. St Stephen's, in the centre of the town, seemed prosperous and smug; it is an accomplished piece of Gothic revival, but that was not yet back in fashion and – despite the austere majesty of Lancing chapel, which I had genuinely admired – we tended to look down on the style. I was by now rather keen on Bentley's Westminster Cathedral; but when I mentioned it favourably one day at Lancing, Roxburgh in his sardonic way had growled that its marble-and-mosaic side-chapels were like 'bathrooms by Harrods!' This did not put me off: the 10.30 capitular High Mass sung daily at Westminster was the best piece of liturgy I had ever seen; I took my mother to an organ-recital there by Marcel Dupré from Notre-Dame; and altogether neo-Byzantinism was much to my taste. So, at Bournemouth, I was glad to find a small but rich example of the same sort of thing, at St Osmund's, Parkstone.

By the time I got to Oxford, Evelyn Waugh had gone down and the Hypocrites' Club, to which he had taken me when I had gone up to sit for scholarship exams, had been closed by the proctors. It had been the scene of some lively and drunken revels ('orgies', were they?), mainly homosexual in character: I remember dancing with John F., while Evelyn and another rolled on a sofa with (as one of them said later) their 'tongues licking each other's tonsils'.

I therefore made friends at first mainly within my own college; this was peopled largely by wealthy Etonians who devoted much of their time to hunting, rowing and drinking. During my first interview with one of my tutors, J. G. Barrington-Ward, a young man put his head in at the door and said, with imperious condescension, 'I thought I'd just let you know that I shan't be coming to any tutorials or lectures this term, because I've managed to get four days' hunting a week.' This was my first intimation of the extent of undergraduate freedom, and, after the discipline of school, I found it irresistibly exhilarating. Of course there was really no comparison between that young man's situation and mine: he was wealthy, I was not; he was not a scholar, I was – and was therefore expected to be a credit to the college academically, as well as in other ways. He and his like were the last exemplars I should have chosen. But I was soon behaving in a similar way (though not to indulge in outdoor sports) – cutting lectures and tutorials, drinking too much, and giving or going to lunch-parties: in those days one could order luncheon to be served in one's rooms, and the parties often went on till four or five o'clock.

There were also expeditions for dinner – usually in a fast open car, an Isotta-Fraschini or a Hispano-Suiza, belonging to an American undergraduate – to the Spreadeagle at Thame, kept by the famous innkeeper, John Fothergill. He was famous both for the quality of his food and wines (the latter he would refuse to sell to some tipsy undergraduate incapable of appreciating them) and also for his rudeness, especially to customers whom he happened to dislike or thought unworthy of his (quite expensive) hospitality. The people who made him angriest of all, with some justification, were passing motorists who came in, did not buy even a drink, and wanted only to use the loo. Later Fothergill wrote his reminiscences of these matters in *An Innkeeper's Diary*. Until André Simon, A. J. A. Symons, and the Wine and Food Society came into my life, ten years or more later, I learned as much about wine, if fragmentarily, from this formidable eccentric as from anybody.

To innocent outsiders, Evelyn Waugh's description in *Decline and Fall* of a bump supper and its aftermath have seemed wildly exaggerated. It was, if anything, a mild account of the night of any Bullingdon Club dinner in Christ Church. Such a profusion of broken glass I never saw until, at the height of the blitz on London in the 1940s, a land-mine almost hit Broadcasting House and I found myself in Upper Regent Street ankle-deep in a sort of *porridge* of glass.

One feature of such nights — and of other nights too — was a raid on the rooms of some obvious quarry. As in my earliest days at that prep school, I fitted into this role. In my queerness there was always an element of exhibitionism: I like being 'too far out', I liked shocking — but I feared the consequences of my own behaviour. Thus, this was the period when 'Oxford bags' were worn — trousers very wide and flapping at the ankles, far wider than the Navy's bell-bottoms. In my first year at Oxford I got the widest pair I could find, at Hall Brothers in the High, and in an unusual colour — bright green. This was indeed 'asking for it'. Soon I heard that most terrifying sound, the cry of a pack baying for its victim: a dozen or twenty young men were tumbling up the stairs to my rooms, shouting my name opprobiously. Soon the offending trousers were off me: I heard next day that they had been carried round Tom Quad in triumph, cut up, and hung in strips round the junior common-room. I had probably not paid the tailors' bill: Oxford tradesmen used to encourage undergraduates to run up credit accounts, knowing that in most cases the parents would pay in the end. But I minded about the trousers less than about the Philistine destruction of some wax or glass fruit, bought from

Italia House, a firm specialising in the then fashionable Italian baroque. (The Baroque was beginning to replace the Byzantine as my favourite style, for I had read *Southern Baroque Art* and had met the author, Sacheverell Sitwell, and his brother Osbert.)

Frightening as this raid was for a few minutes, I think, looking back, that it was, in an odd way, fairly good-humoured. They liked to have someone to tease, but there was not much malice in it. I became quite friendly (and wished I could be much friendlier) with the leader of the raiding-party, a blond and handsome rowing man named Tim Shaw. The same was true of the only other raid I ever suffered, a much more civilised affair. This took place in my second or third year, when I had moved into a better set of rooms; I had what was known as a 'drawing-room' in Peckwater Quad — a first-floor suite consisting of a large panelled living-room with two small rooms, a bedroom and a study, off it. (This type of accommodation now has to be shared by two undergraduates.) One night I was giving a party, I think for Francis Turville-Petre, who became a celebrated archaeologist. The room was fairly full, but I suddenly realised that it had become much fuller, with gate-crashing strangers. The motive for this raid, which did not involve any violence or debagging, was semi-political. Perhaps because of a speech at the Union, I had become known as a Communist, and these young fellow-undergraduates, Tories to a man, wanted to see what such a strange beast was like. One of them — the most hostile, but not discourteous — was a hefty Scot named Angus Graham, who later succeeded his father as Duke of Montrose but continued to be known as Lord Graham when he served in Ian Smith's illegal racialist 'government' in Rhodesia. Another, who discussed political issues more seriously and open-mindedly, was Bryan Guinness: he was a budding poet and novelist; later, when his father was assassinated in Egypt, he became Lord Moyne (and in 1954 made an excellent speech in the House of Lords attacking the introduction of commercial television). I once asked him how much income he derived from the family stout: he said that he thought that at that time he got a twelfth of a penny for every bottle of Guiness sold in the world.

But the undergraduate members of the House (as Christ Church, *Aedes Christi*, is familiarly known) were not all of the sort whom my political comrades denounced as the idle rich. The most delightful, and in the long run the most rewarding, friendship that I formed there was with Wystan Auden – destined to become, after T. S. Eliot, the greatest poet of my lifetime. I may possibly have the right to claim a small share in this triumph; for, only a few years ago, he gave me a copy of one of his books inscribed 'To Tom Driberg, who made me read "The Waste Land".' His recollection was correct: we read this truly epoch-making poem for the first time together: read it, standing side by side in my rooms, in a copy of the first issue of Eliot's review, *The Criterion*; read it, at first, with incredulous hilarity (the Mrs Porter bit, for instance); read it, again and again, with growing awe.

Close (though chaste) as our friendship was, I saw Wystan only occasionally during the rest of his life. For many years he lived in New York and in the village of Kirchstetten, in Austria, where he had an unassuming small house (celebrated, room by room, in one of the best of his lighter volumes, *About the House*). In New York I lunched with him and Chester Kallman, the American poet, in the house they shared – a house down-town, in St Mark's Place, which had once been lived in by Henry James. In Austria (having to be in Vienna for a conference) I spent a weekend with him. He cooked the simple meals, played Wagner on the gramophone, and took me for a walk round the village: he spoke German fluently and rather enjoyed being greeted deferentially as 'Herr Professor' by the postmistress and the other locals. They had renamed the road in which his house stood, in his honour, Audenstrasse; there was the official name-plate on a wall.

But he was not altogether happy at this time. Chester, who was away, had sustained a grievous bereavement. Wystan was upset by a bitchy article about him in *Life* magazine (which, I am glad to say, died before he did). He was even angrier with a lesser-known, semi-pornographic, glossy American magazine, *Avant-Garde*, which had printed without permission a long poem of his and had 'had the impertinence' to send him a small cheque. He had returned the cheque and repudiated authorship of the poem.

Wystan's attitude to what is called 'permissiveness' seemed to me ambivalent; we discussed it during that weekend in Austria (when he also, though a high Anglican, proclaimed his adherence to the 'Protestant work ethic' and reaffirmed his devotion to the Teutonic north rather than the torrid south). He set great store by the right to privacy, and regarded sexual affairs as essentially private. He did, however, write some bawdy or 'obscene' poems, whose quality as poetry is such that they ought to be included some day in his published corpus. These, he explained, were intended for private circulation – a dozen copies typed for old friends. Nor did he mind so much that the poem pirated by *Avant-Garde* (which I knew to be genuine, for he had been writing it, and had read me some of it, when I lunched with him in New York years before) had also been published in two duplicated 'underground' papers, *Fuck You* in New York and *Suck* in London. But he shrank from the public exposure of his sexual inclinations that even such limited distribution ultimately – and inevitably – involved.

I have had, or have, three such poems by Wystan. One is a rollicking ballad written by him in Brussels on the eve of New Year's Day, 1939, when Fascism seemed victorious in Spain, Germany and Italy; it contains toasts to his friends, separated but surely also drinking that ominous New Year in. I lost my copy of this for years: Wystan no longer had one himself, so when my copy turned up again, as things, thank Heaven, sometimes do, I wrote out a copy of it for Cyril Connolly, who was much more expert than I at not losing things and was able to identify most of the friends mentioned by Christian name in the poem.

Apart from the poem pirated by *Avant-Garde*, the only other item of this kind which I possess was given to me by Wystan in 1965 when we were both staying in the Deanery at Christ Church with the late Dean, a hospitable and friendly old Canadian named Cuthbert Simpson. This is a beautiful and touching poem, entitled 'Glad', well up to Wystan's highest standard and in his most characteristic manner: it is addressed to his Viennese boyfriend, Hugerl, 'for a decade now' his 'bed-visitor'.

There were two reasons for our presence in Oxford that weekend (and for the presence at the Deanery also of Sir William Walton and his wife). On the Sunday morning I had to fulfil an engagement which, forty years earlier, it would have been unthinkable that I should ever be asked to undertake: I had been invited by the Vice-Chancellor of the University to be that day's Select Preacher, to deliver the University Sermon in the University Church of St Mary the Virgin. Then, in the evening the superb choir of Christ Church Cathedral (which is also the college chapel) were to

give the first performance of an anthem, 'The Twelve', for which
Walton had provided the music and Auden the words.

The preaching of the University Sermon is a formidable for-
mality. The preacher is collected from his lodging, in my case the
Deanery, by a functionary called the Bedel in Divinity, who
precedes him, bearing a wand, through the streets to the church.
The Vice-Chancellor attends, scarlet-robed, in state. There is no
service, in the ordinary sense – simply two hymns and a 'bidding
prayer', delivered from the pulpit by the preacher before his
sermon. In this prayer ('Ye shall pray ... ') the preacher commends
to the attention of his hearers the authorities of the University,
including, by name, the Chancellor (who happened at this time to
be Harold Macmillan), and also the founder and benefactors of his
own college ('our most religious King Henry the Eighth'). I had
a satisfactorily full house for my sermon, which was broadly
Socialist in content; but it went on for about five minutes too long.
For such an occasion one has to prepare a script; one cannot
extemporise. This has the disadvantage that one feels obliged to
hurry towards the end, when one senses that the listeners are
beginning not to listen. As we came out afterwards, Wystan
remarked to me: 'I did not detect any heresy.'

Anthems, even 'O, for the wings of a dove!' used to be merely
interludes during which the congregation could sit inert, with
wandering thoughts. (At school they were opportunities for the
display and nudging admiration of some of the talents of the
prettiest boys in the choir.) For this Auden/Walton anthem we did
indeed sit; but it made us sit up. The sound was dynamic, almost
violent: the words raced and leaped and tumbled, like rivers
joining in a waterfall. 'The Twelve' of the title were the Apostles,
and

> When they heard the Word, some demurred, some were
> shocked, some mocked. But many were stirred, and the
> Word spread.

I last saw Wystan at the 1973 Poetry Festival in the Queen
Elizabeth Hall. The chief performers on this evening were Basil
Bunting (who read some of his splendid Northumbrian poem,
Briggflatts) and Allen Ginsberg. In the interval we drank back-
stage with them and Wystan; Ginsberg recited a mantra, with the

appropriate manual gestures. Wystan asked me to come and stay with him in the cottage in the precincts of Christ Church in which he had lately been installed. I was never able to do so.

A year or two earlier I had heard him give a reading of his own poems. This he had done, as a great kindness, to help two friends of mine, Frances and Graham Long, who had opened a bookshop in Museum Street, Bloomsbury. The reading was to have been in the shop; tickets were offered for sale at a guinea (to include wine and cheese after the reading) in aid of Wystan's chosen charity, Amnesty; so many were sold that the reading had to be transferred to the church next door, Hawksmoor's St George's. The Rector, Father Henry Cooper, readily agreed to its use for this godly purpose. Wystan wore carpet-slippers. The church was packed, and there was a tremendous scrum in the shop afterwards: Wystan consumed several strong whiskies and signed nearly a hundred copies of his latest book. After a time I took him and Stephen, Natasha, and Matthew Spender (with whom he was staying) to dinner in the private room at the Gay Hussar, where, to diversify the company, I had asked Marianne Faithfull and Mick Jagger's younger brother, Christopher, to join us. Wystan's chair was next to Marianne's. As we sat down, he turned to her and said, in his curiously blurred, yet attractive, American accent: 'When you're smuggling drugs, d'you pack them up your arse?'

It was a great grief to learn of Wystan's sudden death in 1973. Yet it was a good death, possibly even in the pious sense of the phrase. He had been lecturing, and reading his poems, to students in Vienna: no doubt there had been a few drinks and some amiable conversation afterwards; and he died in his sleep. No death could be more enviable, if it was painless – save, perhaps, one attended by the presence at one's bedside of one or more of one's dearest friends and lovers, and of a priest to shrive and anoint one (in response to a wink as unfathomable as the one Socrates must have given when he reminded *his* young men that he owed Aesculapius a cock); with, holding the holy oil and standing close by one's feeble, but still just stirring, hand, an adolescent acolyte, even if his fair face were ravaged by acne.

I could not go to Wystan's funeral at Kirchstetten, but Stephen Spender and Charles Osborne of the Arts Council, who did go, reported favourably on it. Wystan's Viennese boy-friend was there, with the understanding wife ('good girl', as he called her in his poem 'Glad'). They gathered first in the house, where Chester Kallman played a record of the Siegfried Idyll, as Wystan had wished, after some preliminary flurry of doubt about which recording was the best. I did go to the memorial service at Christ Church, where Spender gave an admirable address, calling Wystan 'a serious joke', and the cathedral choir sang two of Wystan's poems set to music by Benjamin Britten. One of them was his 'Hymn to Saint Cecilia', and the other had the quaint but, in its effect, moving refrain:

> O lift your little pinkie and touch the winter sky,
> Love's all over the mountains, where the beautiful go to die.

There had been some discussion in advance about the meaning of the word 'pinkie'. It is archaic in England, but still in use in Scotland and also in low slang in New York, where Auden had no doubt learned it. There was no real anxiety: the word simply means 'your little finger'. But the Dean had sought a guarantee of purity from the Chaplain: even after death, Wystan might try to 'slip something past' them. 'Where the beautiful go to die ... ' Auden had profound beauty of mind. In youth he had physical beauty too: he was tow-haired, chubby-cheeked, innocent-looking. In middle and later years his face, quite suddenly, developed that complex network of deep wrinkles and furrows — like a majestic mountain or a river-bed in drought — with which his juniors remember him.

When I first met him, Auden was unknown as a poet outside Oxford. With Cecil Day Lewis he edited the slim annual volume, *Oxford Poetry*, in which a few of my poems were published. But I also made the acquaintance of several established writers. One of the most impressive of these was Robert Graves, who at that time shared a house at Islip, near Oxford, with the American poet Laura Riding. They received me hospitably, and it would seem that the hospitality was returned, for I have a scribbled note from Graves in which he asks for the return of a leather bag left in my rooms and adds: 'I was very pleased with the Mount[1] City Blues and the

---

[1] *Sic*. This was *Mound City Blues*, one of many early blues and jazz records which I was playing at that time.

beer and the company; and if you care to come out here to a meal, we will be glad to see you. Sunday is the best.'

This seemed, and seems, an easy start to what should have been an agreeable friendship. I liked what I had seen of both Graves and Laura Riding. He was already famous for his poetry but had not yet written his first world war memoir, *Good-bye to All That*. (Both Graves and Osbert Sitwell had held commissions in the Army, and when Sitwell, shooting while on leave in Yorkshire, sent a brace of grouse 'To Captain Graves with Captain Sitwell's compliments', Graves replied: 'Captain Graves presents his compliments to Captain Sitwell, and thanks him for Captain Grouse.') Graves was tall and burly, with a heavy, gipsy-like face that looked, in repose, sulky, and a sensual mouth: Riding was slight, pale, and fey, as spare and taut as her verse. As I say, my relations with them should have gone smoothly: I might have been friendly with Graves through all his subsequent marital mazes and even until he reached his present eminence as the patriarch of Majorca. Alas, something went wrong—a misunderstanding mainly attributable to my own social ignorance and *gaucherie*, but also, I think, to unusually thin-skinned touchiness on the part of Graves and/or Riding. Besides the note I have quoted, I also have friendly, informal notes from her inviting me to a meal. Either while they were still at Islip or when they had moved to Hammersmith, in London, I thought that I would like to see them again. I knew or assumed that they were living, as the saying goes, 'as man and wife', but I was genuinely unsure, in my inexperience, how to address an envelope to her. I knew that, in such situations, some women retained their own names, some preferred to be called 'Mrs'. I consulted an undergradute friend, Norman Cameron, but got no useful advice. I therefore thought it safer to write to Graves and ask if I might come and see them. In retrospect, it seems an innocent enough thing to have done, but it produced a shattering reply—an accusation of deliberate rudeness to Laura Riding, since the house was as much hers as his. Why, I wondered, had my stupid, old, unsophisticated parents or my rather more knowledgeable brothers not warned me of the ghastly social quagmires that I might step into when I started mixing with free-living adults? It took me a long time to recover from this—as I felt, undeserved— rebuff. I no longer have this letter, but I have another, almost worse, which shows that some time later I tried – clumsily and, again, ingenuously – to atone for my *bêtise* by praising in print a little book by Graves called *Mrs Fisher, or the Future of Humour*. This was one of a series of 'or the Future of ... ' books, to which Graves also contributed *Lars Porsena, or the Future of Swearing*. No oral oath at his command could have been more wounding than this second letter. It is undated, on paper headed with the Hammersmith address, and runs:

Look here, Tom Driberg,

I am told that the commendation of Mrs Fisher and the attendant comments on my tall, dark and handsome person are by you. I wish to God you'd cut it out. It is some months now since I heard from Norman Cameron about your attitude to Laura Riding but it made me feel pretty sick and the effects are still here. You asked him that entirely unpardonable question as to whether you should address her as Mrs Graves, because etc. – I was so sick that I nearly asserted my Elemental, Virile, Sulky personality and came to beat you up. There were two things bad about it, first that you had accepted L.R.'s hospitality and had been taken into our confidence about things, second that we knew you were homo and therefore we expected none of that conventional tin-arse filth which one finds in the hetero about man and woman relationships; and I should add a third that it seems incredible to me that anyone with any sort of judgement should mistake L.R. for the sort of person you have in mind even on the evidence of a single first glance at her. You probably recall my fury on a previous occasion when you wrote to me entirely disregarding her existence, treating her as a sort of hanger-on of mine. So your hurrahs for Mrs Fisher, though I recognise the ironic undertone, only make me feel bad.

Yours

ROBERT GRAVES

Scrawled along the side of the page is a postscript (the latter lines of it marked '*This is not to be repeated, please*'):

It is the same sort of attitude which ascribes the word-by-word collaboration of *A Survey of Modernist Poetry* to Mr

Robert Graves alone: and does not hesitate to see Mr Graves'
master-hand behind her individual writings, (the boot being
as it happens on the other foot altogether – I contributed
nothing to hers and L.R. did a good deal of the difficult work
in *Mrs Fisher*) and regards this flat as mine not hers.*

It would be useless now to seek to analyse this confusing, and
surely confused, letter, except to say that I was not aware of
having any 'attitude' to Laura Riding except general, uncompli-
cated liking. I thought that Norman Cameron (whom I also liked)
must have made whatever I had said to him seem much worse than
it was. I was surprised by the disrespectful reference to hetero-
sexuality: it did not then occur to me that the violence of Graves's
reaction to my olive-branch might conceal an unconscious homosexual impulse. At any rate, as on the previous occasion, it took
me some time to recover from the shock and depression induced
by this letter; and I do not think I attempted to reply to it. This
was my first and most harrowing experience of what is loosely
called the artistic temperament. I am afraid I still have Laura
Riding's letters filed under Graves, R.

Disgraceful though my academic idleness seemed to my tutors, I
was at least developing, through such contacts as those with Auden
and Graves, the literary and artistic interests that had begun at
Lancing under the influence of Evelyn Waugh and J. F. Roxburgh.
At school there had been an admirable arrangement whereby any
books which the form-master certified as educationally valuable
could be bought and charged against a boy's parents' terminal
account; and by this means, with Roxburgh's connivance, I had
managed to get such books as the Sitwell anthology, *Wheels*, and
Ronald Firbank's *Concerning the Eccentricities of Cardinal Pirelli*,
a title which intrigued me doubly. So now it seemed obvious to me
to explore and champion the *avant-garde* and to reject the boring
old Academy painters, the Georgian poets, and the 'Squirearchy'
or *London Mercury* school (even though J. C. Squire had once
been kind enough to print a bad poem of mine, which he should
not have done).

I obtained a copy of *Ulysses*, noticed with pleasure that a

* See the note on page 256.

previous edition had been seized by the Philistines at Dover, and toiled my way through it with delight.

I was also lucky enough to see several performances in what was to be the last year in London of that most justly renowned of all ballets, the Diaghilev Ballet. Possibly the Bolshoi has an even more disciplined *corps de ballet*; no Diaghilev ballerina danced or acted better than Margot Fonteyn; but it was Diaghilev who risked bringing into ballet all the most advanced composers and designers of the day — Stravinsky, Picasso, Tchelitchev, Sauguet, Bérard. Jean Cocteau caught perfectly in his cartoons the huge, gross figure of this dictator-impresario with, sheltering in his shadow, his waif-like, high-cheekboned, ravishingly pretty favourite, Serge Lifar, or, earlier, the greatest dancer of all, Nijinsky. By the time I went to the ballet, Nijinsky was out of it. But I was glad, in the 1940s, to be able in a small way to help him. He had come to depend entirely on the services of a Swiss valet-companion, and this man, on one of his rare free evenings, had been arrested for importuning in Leicester Square. He had been fined — and the magistrate had recommended his deportation. Nijinsky's wife, Romola, wrote to me in despair, and I took the matter up with the Home Office. The deportation order was cancelled, and Nijinsky's remaining days were as happy as they could be. This was, to me, one indication that Attlee's was a relatively civilised government (as was also the readiness with which, at about the same time, the Foreign Office helped Norman Douglas to get back his flat in Florence — intimating to me that they regarded it as an honour to be of use to that notable writer).

I believe — for I have it on the authority of one who shared a room with him for many years — that Nijinsky was able to perform a feat of which, in certain circles, one often hears at third- or fourth-hand, and therefore unreliably: the feat of (to coin a mongrel word) *auto-fellatio*. (Perhaps it should be called, in current jargon, recycling.) My informant states that this was possible for Nijinsky, without undue difficulty, because of two gifts which he possessed to perfection — the suppleness of a dancer's body, and a penis of extraordinary length. What the dietary effects of this practice can have been, I do not know; but one of my medical advisers has informed me that a daily oral intake of semen furnishes the body with as much potassium as the normal healthy male should need.

My visits to the ballet from Oxford were generously provided by one of the wealthier of the Christ Church undergraduates, Edward James. This young man – slight in build, sanguine of complexion, quick of movement, with a high-pitched laugh – was a son of Mrs Willie James, one of the closest friends of King Edward VII. He used to complain that, while 'everybody' said that he was a son of that robust Teutonic monarch, he himself was by no means sure that it was so. Certainly he bore no resemblance at all, in face or figure, to the dead King. When a boy at Eton, James had attracted the amorous attentions of a celebrated Liberal statesman, Sir William Harcourt. This became known to the authorities and, to avoid public scandal, Sir William shot himself on the splendid marble staircase of his town house in Brook Street, now the Savile Club.

Edward James had the best set of rooms in the House, in Canterbury Quad. They were furnished exotically: the latest French and American music belched from the mouths of the busts of Roman emperors. Later he became a great patron of the arts, especially of Salvador Dali. I liked his company, but there was no special intimacy between us. After the ballet we used to catch the last train – known as 'the flying fornicator' – that would get us back to Oxford before the college gates closed. This was at midnight in all the other colleges, but at 12.20 a.m. at Christ Church, which centuries before had been deemed further from the centre of the city.

It was not necessary to go to London to learn something of the classics of the theatre, for at the Oxford Playhouse J. B. Fagan produced an admirable series of repertory seasons, with a company headed by his wife, Mary Grey. 'Always a poised and handsome woman,' The Times called her when she died in her ninety-seventh year in October, 1974. I remember her as a stately and moving Madame Ranevsky in The Cherry Orchard. Equally remarkable was the performance of Veronica Turleigh, in Strindberg's Spook Sonata, as the woman who, locked in a cupboard, makes parrot noises – in her dark, haunting eeriness the antithesis of Mary Grey. I was lucky indeed to see such plays, for the first time, so excellently presented.

One even more exciting event was the arrival in Oxford of Gertrude Stein and her delivery of a lecture entitled 'Composition as Explanation'. I do not think that we all found the explanation pellucidly clear, but I can still recall the thrill of watching this massive, short-haired woman – rather like a German *Hausfrau* or a good plain cook – declaiming in a completely matter-of-fact American voice statements which, to most of those present, seemed complete nonsense; the thrill, too, of knowing that here among us, in our conservative university, was one of the stars of the Left Bank and *transition*: the revolution of the word in person. When, after the lecture, Lord David Cecil rose, an eel-like figure, and asked in his sibilant voice what was meant to be a devastating question, of *course* I was on her side.

One of my few talents has always been that of the *madame*: I like introducing or recommending suitable people to each other. In an editorial conference I know who the right person is to write such-and-such an article, and can usually telephone at once to him or a friend of his. I felt that the Stein lecture ought to be printed, and wrote to Virginia Woolf suggesting that the Hogarth Press might do so. Mrs Woolf replied thanking me for letting her know about the lecture, and accepting the suggestion; and in due course the thing appeared. (Mrs Woolf's letter contained only a couple of sentences, in her own writing: such now is the prestige of 'Bloomsbury' that I sold the letter at Christie's in 1973 for £85.)

My only essay in visual art was an abstract water-colour which I put into some undergraduate exhibition. It contained no form even remotely resembling the female figure, but I named it *Marion Tweedy Bloom*, after Joyce's heroine. When it had been on view for several days, some joker drew in the middle of it, very neatly, a map of England and Wales. I pretended to be incensed at this act of vandalism, but secretly recognised (though the word had not yet been invented) that it was a surrealist gesture.

The principal artistic performance in which I was involved was rather more pretentious (though equally surrealist or, as we then said, dadaist). A group of us hired the beautiful premises of the Musical Union in Holywell – said to be the oldest hall in Europe designed for chamber music – and presented a concert which we called 'Homage to Beethoven'. No doubt it was this title which

attracted a capacity audience of elderly dons and their wives form
North Oxford; the air was thick with the aroma of moth-balls.
One of those also involved was Eric Walter White, later an
authority on Stravinsky and until recently a senior executive of the
Arts Council. He has provided me with an account of this strange
evening which he wrote soon after the event:

In 1927 I was one of a group of Oxford undergraduates who
wished to honour Beethoven in the year of the centenary of
his death. Tired of the commemorative spurt of performances of his symphonies, string quartets, and sonatas, we
decided on the performance of an original work at the Music
Room in Holywell and chose the concerto as the most appropriate form — but a concerto for what? Not for piano, violin or
flute — that would be too obvious. Not even for saxophone —
Debussy had been there before. We wanted our ground to be
virgin, untrodden. For megaphone then. And Thomas
Driberg was invited to write the words — partly about 'black
and white and cutting in between' — while Arthur G.
Browne (who had been deeply influenced by the four-handed
piano arrangement of Stravinsky's *The Rite of Spring* and had
recently discovered the delights of *Les Noces*) hammered out
the three movements of the score on a piano in his Beaumont
Street rooms, to the undisguised annoyance of his neighbours.

When the evening of the performance came, the concerto
opened with a bang from the band and an entreaty from Tom
Driberg, delivered through his megaphone, that the audience
would 'commit no nuisance'. The scratch orchestra, which
was conducted by Robert H. Hull and consisted of four-
handed piano (played by the composer and myself), strings,
flute, clarinet, and various instruments of percussion, rein-
forced by two typewriters, then sailed into the opening
movement, which led in due course to an extended cadenza
for megaphone solo. The slow movement was notable for the
fact that it was very slow and very long. The typewriters had
been silent during the first movement, and their entry in slow
triplets over a slowly moving ostinato bass in common time,
followed by a unison glissando punctuated by warning bells,
was undeniably moving. Between the second and third

movements there was a diversion. A crescendo roll on the side-drum turned out to be the signal for the whole orchestra to rise to its feet. While the audience was still uncertain whether this manoeuvre was the prelude to 'God Save the King!' or something similar, the roll on the side-drum stopped and from a w.c. just off stage was heard the noise of a flush followed by the slam of a door. This was the cue for the orchestra to sit down and start the last movement. The concerto was brought to a characteristic conclusion by Tom Driberg's final injunction to the audience: 'Please adjust your dress before leaving'.

During the concert (which was crowded) the bust of Beethoven stood on the floor of the Music Room, just in front of the platform under the conductor's *Pult*, crowned with a wreath of laurels.

The text of the 'megaphone solo', which I had laboured at for some days, was eventually published, under the title 'Metropolitan', in the bilingual magazine, *Échanges*, which Allanah Harper produced in Paris. As a sample, I need only quote the final four lines of the piece:

To eat all this is no tangle, cried the deep one in Miranda —
She was so young she didn't know how to pin down little
                                                        spirals.
But little spirals is alabaster, and we were the first that ever
                                                        burst,
And alabaster is alabaster, five six pick up sticks.

The Beethoven concert was in 1927 — my last year at Oxford. But I had not been entirely occupied in social and artistic frivolities. In the previous year, 1926, there had occurred a most unfrivolous, brave, and tragic event — the General Strike. I had maintained my link with the Communists — and the Strike was the first real test of its strength. Most of the undergraduates went off to try to help break the Strike — as we said, to blackleg — but a minority, mainly of Socialists and Communists, put their politics into action by helping the strikers as best they could; in many cases this simply meant driving cars for the T.U.C. (for this was an official strike), carrying messages, or strengthening an occasional picket-line.

Among those who chose this side were Hugh Gaitskell and others of the group of moderate Socialists who used to gather in the rooms of G. D. H. Cole. In a recent letter to me, Dame Margaret Cole gave the names of some of this group: I did not recognise a single one of those she mentioned as having been a friend of mine at Oxford. I found their moderation less exciting than the apparent extremism of the C.P. (now regarded by the youthful Trotskyist ultra-Left as bureaucratic and old hat). Maybe I would have been more interested if I had known that Cole, besides being one of the most brilliant and attractive of the younger dons, had homosexual tendencies; this is disclosed in Dame Margaret's biography of him, published in 1971.

We were, of course, aware that some of the dons were homo-sexual: the enchantingly eccentric Hellenist Professor Dawkins was one such. Another, whom I knew slightly, was reported to have said to a pupil: 'I can't go on teaching you — I'm in love with you.' For some reason, this very unHellenic attitude was thought highly creditable. Perhaps it was only a ploy: let us hope that the boy took it as such. I personally had sex with only one don while I was an undergraduate: probably I should not have done so if I had met him socially: he looked far from donnish when he picked me up in a 'cottage' in Bear Lane. We met two or three times: on one of these occasions, in his rooms, we managed what I have experienced, otherwise, only once in my life — an exercise in *soixante-neuf* culminating in exactly simultaneous ejaculations. He is still alive, still teaching, and I hope still sexually active.

Cole and other dons of the Left naturally encouraged us in our support for the strikers, so there was no trouble with our colleges. (There could hardly have been, since so many others had gone as blacklegs.) But whereas Cole's friends reported to the T.U.C. at Transport House, I went to the C.P. headquarters at 16 King Street, Covent Garden. Here I was seen by a veteran of the party, Bob Stewart, an old stocky Scot with a pugilistic-looking broken nose, who initially showed some scepticism but eventually instructed me to collect a big bundle of workers' bulletins, meet another comrade at one of the northern stations — I think King's Cross — and set off by car to distribute the bulletins in various provincial cities. We kept our rendezvous; the comrade turned up with his car and we were loading the bulletins on it — when the police, whether tipped off or alerted by the sight of so many papers (for no newspapers were being published except Churchill's *British Gazette*), descended on us and took us off for questioning. I don't know where the other chap went; I was taken to Bow Street police station, kept for some hours in a cell, and then, having been identified as an Oxford undergraduate, moved to Scotland Yard. Here I was interrogated by several genteel elderly men, not in uniform, and released. I was, however, followed, and this was slightly embarrassing; for I was staying with my second brother, Jim, then at the height of his prosperity as a consultant surgeon, and his Leicestershire wife at their fairly sumptuous flat in Park Crescent, at the top of Portland Place. As they were both staunch Tories (why are Tories always 'staunch', whereas Socialists are 'rank'?), I had given them only a vague idea of why I was in London; but they had their suspicions of me and were furious when, immediately after my return from the Yard, a copper took up his position on the opposite pavement and proceeded, very obviously and crudely, to watch their flat.

I think that the next issue of the *Cherwell*, then the liveliest undergraduate magazine, must have been rather thin, since most of the contributors were away, either blacklegging or, like me, trying to help the strikers. I used to write various bits and pieces for the *Cherwell*: film-reviews, rude jokes, reports on antiquarian books — I can't imagine how I got the data for these. John Betjeman and Osbert Lancaster were often around the *Cherwell* office. So was Mark Ogilvie-Grant. Many years later I was to go drinking with him in Athens, our favourite late-night bar being the Arethusa. When, later still, I was by chance the last visitor to see him on the evening of his death in Guy's Hospital, I said: 'I'll give your love to the Arethusa.' He just managed faintly to articulate: 'I — don't think — you'll find it much fun now' — for the Colonels were now in power. Nancy Mitford, a great friend of his, wrote a short obituary of him and sent it to *The Times*; it was rejected.

Brian Howard wrote elaborate prose for the *Cherwell* — 'Some days, when I am feeling particularly tired and plain, I see Mr Peter Thursby strolling in the Broad, and at once feel even plainer but much less tired.' A woodcut, the work of Evelyn Waugh some years before, still headed the weekly report of the Union debate.

A caption on it read: 'Europe listens where Oxford sleeps.' Writing for the *Cherwell*, though strictly amateur – amateur indeed, since we were not paid – was probably the nearest I came to doing any sort of regular work while I was at Oxford; and it was in its way a minor exercise in the craft that was to occupy me for most of the rest of my life.

Nor had I abandoned another life-long addiction – my interest in the *minutiae* of church ceremonial. Despite all the other interests that kept me idle and busy, despite the C.P., the Union, the *Cherwell*, and sex, throughout my time at Oxford I went, on most Sunday mornings, to High Mass at Pusey House.

6

Oxford

2: *Vacations*

The vacation periods — especially the long summer vac — are
supposed to be among the benefits of a university education. I
imagine that the year's leisurely schedule was originally arranged
for the convenience and comfort of the dons. Naturally, they
rationalise: the vacations give them time for preparing the new
courses of lectures to which, they hope, the young gentlemen will
flock, ignoring the traditional but heretical advice 'You'll find the
substance of his notes/Much better in the books he quotes.' The
young men, too, are supposed to be studying during vacations.
(Nowadays many of them follow the American example of working
in ordinary jobs to supplement their meagre grants.) Some dons,
even during vacations, take their tutorial duties seriously (or enjoy
the company of the young) and organise those curious excursions —
often to Switzerland or Austria — known as vacation reading-
parties. I never went on one of these. I was not invited to one: I
think they were chiefly attended by the harder-working undergraduates; they would have been a bit too hard-working for me.

During some of the vacations I tried to make up to my Communist friends for that humiliating flop during the General Strike
by doing editorial and reporting work for one of the party papers,
the *Sunday Worker*. This got me into trouble with my college, for,
perhaps foolishly, we published a signed piece by me, as 'of Christ
Church, Oxford', describing satirically the university Boat Race
and the crowds who lined the towpath and, in general, ridiculing
it as a contemptible bourgeois spree. When the next term began,
this led to a severe dressing-down by Dr White, the Dean of

Christ Church, a tiny man with an enormous parrot nose. I doubt if the article converted anyone to Communism, and it may have antagonised some readers. It should probably have been dismissed as a 'Left deviation'. In any case, my main work for the C.P. was to liaise between the city Party and the few members in the University.

During one vacation I tried an experiment which was less futile than the *Sunday Worker* stint—and even slightly profitable. Despite my mother's solitary condition, I could not bear to spend a whole long vacation at Crowborough; I was already fascinated by the sleazier parts of west London; but I had little or no money and could not ask my mother for enough to enable me to get away from home. (She was, after all, making me an allowance which was supposed to supplement my scholarship money adequately, but all this, of course, went in extravagance at Oxford.) From my earliest school-days I had had some small talent for drawing. So I decided to become a temporary pavement artist. I learned that one bought 'four-penn'orth of broken'—i.e., bits of broken chalk of many colours—at an artists' colourman's shop near Drury Lane; that one had to set out very early in the morning to find a good pitch and start drawing on the paving-stones; but that one must on no account try to grab one of the best pitches—for instance, those on each side of Waterloo Place—which 'belonged', and were recognized by the police as belonging, to old men who had been established on them for many years. Others, who merely hired pictures and propped them against railings, were not regarded as genuine pavement artists.

When I had bought the chalk and surveyed some possible pitches, my preparations were almost complete. But, romantically, I thought that I should be more convincing to the public if I wore some really ragged old clothes. So, having borrowed £2 from a man with whom I had been staying for a few nights—my first essay in actual prostitution, and harmless enough—I went down to the Embankment, where also, when out of cash, I had slept on a bench for a night or two. Here hundreds of down-and-outs used to hang about every night, their hopelessness and hunger only momentarily alleviated by free soup from stalls run by charitable ladies. Near one such stall I found a young man—perhaps twenty years old—with a face that was pale and thin and wistfully appealing, and wearing clothes that were indeed more than threadbare, for he was literally out-at-elbows. On his head was a shabby cap. As he was about my height, and I was then pretty slim, I reckoned that his clothes would fit me, more or less, and mine him. I propositioned him: would he come and sleep the night with me at a cheap hotel and then, very early in the morning, change clothes with me? My clothes, though not elegant — probably grey flannel trousers, a 'sports' shirt and jacket — were a good deal better than his. He thought me crazy, but accepted with alacrity.

We walked up Farringdon Street, towards Smithfield, where there was an hotel 'for gentlemen only' at which one could get a double bed for a few shillings. It was a warm night: we agreed to sleep naked, with only a sheet over us. He was reasonably clean (he had been to the public baths that day) and, to my relief, free of 'crabs' — the *Pediculi pubis* which were, and are, so often transmitted in such circumstances. Before getting into bed, we smoked a few cigarettes to drown the smell of his socks. No doubt as a result of prolonged under-feeding, his ribs were too prominent, but his body was well-proportioned, his skin delicate and fair. We spoke little; he smiled — again that wistful look which had first moved me. We turned to each other, and kissed: the alternate thrust and withdrawal of his tongue — soft but firm, warm, and slightly flavoured with peppermint chewing-gum — suggested experience. In view of his general condition, I had not expected a strong sexual response; but now, beating and throbbing against me, was a surprisingly thick, hard organ. Then, still without speaking, he showed what he really wanted, or thought that I did; for, after another kiss, he rolled over with his back towards me, his bottom pressing against my genitals. Sodomy does not happen to be my favourite sexual pastime; but I could hardly refuse so unassuming a charmer. Evidently this move was not made merely to please me — for his member, already rigid, at once became positively adamantine and seemed to be about to swell to a premature bursting-point. The actual entry was, I fear I must say, suspiciously easy: this meant either that the orifice had been coated with Vaseline (or the rather better-class 'K.Y.') to facilitate previous entries, or that my bed-mate was suffering from diarrhoea, a common by-product of dietary impoverishment. The latter, alas, proved to be the case, as a saffron smear on the cheap cotton sheet testified. But before my withdrawal had brought about this regrettable result, he had already, suddenly, uncontrollably 'shot his load' of semen — and a pitiably thin, weak, liquid load it was (poverty, again), not sufficient in quantity to form on the sheet that other stain which chambermaids call a 'map of Ireland'. (Years ago one of these jolly girls must have cried out 'Will ye come and look at this now, Bridget — isn't it just like a map of Ireland!') If a normal emission can form a map of Ireland, my poor lad's puny leakage could hardly have been likened to more than the Isle of Wight.

We were up betimes and I (having given the boy almost all the money I had left) hastened to a pitch that I had thought promising, in Russell Square. First I laid out the cap I had got from my one-night standee, inside up, to receive cash (with a few decoy pennies in it). Then I knelt on the hard pavement — I had not thought of bringing any kind of cushion to kneel on — and started to draw. The only two scenes that I can remember drawing were both illustrative of favourite couplets in English poetry, and capable of dramatically polychromatic treatment. One was Blake's:

> A robin redbreast in a cage
> Sets all heaven in a rage.

The other was Marvell's:

> He hangs in shades the orange bright,
> Like golden lamps in a green night.

The Blake was particularly popular with the customers: bird-loving old ladies would come up to me, press sixpence into my hand, and say meaningfully 'That is for *that* one.' The best results were obtained, I soon found, not by sitting beside one's art-work but by standing, leaning forlornly against the railings, so that one's eyes were on a level with those of the passers-by and it was more difficult for them to avoid one's mute, lost-dog-like appeal. Evangelists (some of them, I guessed, crypto-homo) were a nuisance: they tried to save one, but contributed only mean pennies to the process, and while they were chatting one up other potential clients could hurry past without paying. I found Indians and Africans the most generous: when they spoke to me, I was careful to call them 'sir'.

After two days in Russell Square I got a better pitch, near St Martin's-in-the-Fields. One day a lot of expensively dressed people passed me, on their way to the opening of Canada House. One of them was Margot Oxford.[1] She gave me a shilling. Sixteen years later, when I was an M.P., she came to lunch with me at the House of Commons. I reminded her of the incident but she had, naturally, forgotten it.

I kept up this game for just over a week, having rented a modest room on my first day's takings. I found that, in fine weather, I could average a good £5 a week — not a bad income for those days. Then the weather broke, and it became urgently necessary for me to wear some cleaner and less malodorous clothes. I cannot remember how I effected the change, except that I dumped the dirty rags in a parcel at the house of an old friend and *protegée* of my mother's, named Florence Greenfield. Miss Greenfield kept a superior lodging-house in Beaumont Street, where I had often stayed as a boy, my mother having sent me there for a week or two to be shown the sights of London by Miss Greenfield. Miss G. was a dear: she had a pink, shiny, enthusiastic face and bobbed white hair. She now took charge of my parcel, but some time later opened it and ordered me to remove the rags.

Many years later, when she died, her body was handed over to a hospital, in accordance with her will, to be used for medical purposes. When they had had it for a year or so, and chopped it up, I was surprised to hear that they were now ready to hand over the few bones, or whatever remained, for cremation or burial. I did not want to do anything about this, but thought I had better.

Rather more elevating than the week of my pavement artistry was a Christmas vacation for which my mother, usually so thrifty, took me on my first visit to Italy. (I am being unfair to her: it may have been *because* she was thrifty that she could afford this quite expensive outing.) She had been recommended to go to Rapallo, on the Italian Riviera, and there we stayed for several weeks, at the Hotel Bristol. We went by train, by what was then the very handsome Rome Express: I have forgotten much, but can never forget the first glimpses of the piercing blue Mediterranean, seen in the early morning from one's sleeper or the breakfast-car, as the

[1] The Countess of Oxford and Asquith.

train raced in and out of the many tunnels along that rocky coast. Now almost the whole coast, and in particular Rapallo, has been ruined by tourism and speculative development. Indeed, the Italians themselves, who have allowed this beastliness to occur, seem to realise that it is at its worst in Rapallo, for they have invented the term, *Rapallizzazione*, to describe in general what the speculators have done.

The best description of that coast as it was, and of the peculiar charm that it then had, is in that outrageously sentimental novel, *The Enchanted April*, by the authoress of *Elizabeth and her German Garden*. She understood, as E. M. Forster did in *Where Angels Fear to Tread*, what it is about Italians that makes them at once so infuriating and so irresistible. I can almost forgive my mother for the well-meaning errors of my upbringing when I recall that she was responsible for my first experience of Italy and, unwittingly, for my first taste of Italian sex. I do not refer to the night porter at the hotel, who seduced me late one night: it was not my fault, and he was rather too old (*c.* thirty-five) for me; but he pounced, with what some novelists call a strangled cry, and I felt that it would be ungenerous to rebuff the poor man. No, the best encounter of that holiday (or perhaps the second-best or, as they say in some other sporting records, tied equal) was one which, surprisingly, punctuated and enriched a sedate walk one afternoon in my mother's company.

We walked from Rapallo to Portofino Vetta, the sturdy phallic lighthouse which sticks up from the end of a graceful promontory. On the way, as we walked through a grove of pine-trees, my mother slipped — probably on the pine-needles — and fell. She was not at all seriously hurt, but when we reached the lighthouse she decided to sit and rest outside while I climbed to the top.

There were no other visitors. The lighthouse-keeper was young — perhaps twenty-five — and sensuously attractive: not of the lean dark Roman type of Italian, nor of the invitingly sinister Neapolitan or Sicilian types; almost more Austrian-looking, with a round, tender face, plump but virile figure, fairish hair, and thick, mobile, smiling lips. We climbed the stairs; it was not a very tall lighthouse, but the look-out gallery that surrounded it was protected from snooping eyes by a chest-high barrier. We stood close together: he started to breathe heavily — I caught a whiff of garlic —

and looked straight into my eyes. Contact was instant, consummation almost as quick: he had clearly not had any sex for some days. Within five minutes or so I had rejoined my mother. 'What a long time you were up there, dear.' 'Well, it was a lovely view, mother.' Naturally I was sorry that she had had that fall, but I could hardly not be grateful to whatever tutelary deity (Priapus?) had, perhaps, given her a push and led me up the lighthouse.

The runner-up or tied-equal, already mentioned, was a pick-up in Milan, to which I went from Rapallo for a night or two, to see the Leonardo 'Last Supper' and the ornate silver tomb of St Charles Borromeo in the wedding-cake cathedral. This was a youth of about seventeen, named Aldo; his clothes were far more ragged than those I had worn as a pavement-artist; the aroma of garlic — stronger than the lighthouse-keeper's — was superimposed on a general stench of poverty. But he was well-equipped and randy, and skilfully feigned (I suppose) not only passion but, much rarer, affection. He needed money, of course; I gave him some, and liked him so much that we exchanged addresses. I still have the letter I received from him some months later, on very fancy paper, starting '*Cuore mio!*' (My heart!) and pleading for a little more money. Why not? When there is heavy unemployment and no social security, what else can such boys as Aldo do? At least he seemed to enjoy it, and was probably, like so many men, genuinely bisexual — for when I next saw him, a dozen years later, he was heavily married, living in *petit-bourgeois* comfort, dark-moustached and beginning to run to fat. It had taken me some time to find him: he had moved from his former address in the Via Nicolini. Mussolini was in power, and Aldo had some sort of job as a Fascist bureaucrat. For old times' sake he came back to my hotel — rather grander than the one in which we had first made love, and our mating was now more perfunctory; but, again for old times' sake, I forced a *pourboire* on him. I was now on my way to the Spanish Civil War, and said that I would send him a postcard from Barcelona or wherever the Republican government was still holding out. With sharp alarm in his eyes, he begged me to do no such thing: the postal censors would see the card, and he would be in serious trouble.

Altogether — and not only or mainly because of the sexual opportunities it provided — this visit to Rapallo was an extremely fortunate one for me. Indeed, I can say that, without it, the course of my life might have been entirely different. Certainly I would have missed several most rewarding (and non-sexual) friendships. I had already, at Oxford, met Edith Sitwell. She was not here, but her two brothers, Osbert and Sacheverell, were in the same hotel, and I easily got to know them, and with them William Walton, then only just beginning to practise as a composer. There too was the artist Richard Wyndham, later the host, at Tickerage Mill in Sussex, of some of the best weekend parties I have ever attended. (There would usually be four or five old friends there, some with their latest wives or girl-friends: Peter Quennell, Cyril Connolly, A. J. A. Symons, Constant Lambert, John Rayner and others; and from Dick's marvellous cellar, ranged on the sideboard and decanted well before dinner, would stand six or more magnums of château-bottled claret of the finest years.) Wyndham wrote some good books, one about south-eastern England, one about the Dinka tribe of the Sudan. After the Second World War, he went to Palestine during the troubles there as a correspondent for the *News of the World* (possibly a cover-job for something more secret), stood up out of a trench to take a photograph, and was shot dead by a sniper. At the time of my visit to Rapallo he was driving round that part of Italy in an open grey Rolls-Royce, making drawings of church towers for a projected book.

Another member of this remarkable group of fellow-visitors to the Bristol was Mrs Ada Leverson, herself a novelist of some distinction but more renowned as the hostess who befriended Oscar Wilde both before and, more important, after his imprisonment. She wrote a vivid account in the *Criterion*, called 'The Last First Night', of the *première* of *The Importance of Being Earnest* – a glittering occasion at which Wilde was in her box but was constantly called from it by mysterious or menacing messages. He nicknamed her 'the Sphinx' and she did indeed look sphingine, smiling and nodding her head in pretended comprehension; for she was very deaf. She was elderly, but had a bright-golden coiffure – we assumed, a wig – and was never seen without a massively constructed black hat, which the Sitwell brothers said was actually part of the same edifice as the golden hair. In her girlhood the Sphinx had been to dancing-class with Max Beerbohm, who now lived in Rapallo. She took me to have tea with him; I can remember nothing about what should have been a memorable encounter, except that he worked in a study built on top of his villa and that his manners were, as one would expect from his writings, exquisitely polished and dandyish.

Years later Mrs Leverson invited me to lunch at her London hotel, the Washington. This was kind of her, but I found the meal embarrassing. The two of us sat in a restaurant that was largely empty but with a few other parties within earshot; and the Sphinx, being deaf, spoke very loudly and clearly. When I had told the waiter what I wanted to eat, I realised that she had not ordered food for herself, and asked if she were not going to eat something. 'No,' she said, with what I recognised as a Wildean echo, 'I only eat between meals.'

But it was the Sitwells whom, remembering my schoolboy liking for *Wheels*, I found most fascinating. Though the brothers were very different in character and manner, both were devastatingly witty and each had the keenest artistic sensibility that I had yet known. They were at the height of their campaign to revive appreciation of the Baroque, in painting and architecture. They had founded the Magnasco Society, and such books as *Southern Baroque Art* were either just out or on the way. It was Sacheverell ('Sachie') who told me to go and see the cascade at Caserta, Santa Chiara in Naples and the Villa Palagonia at Bagheria in Sicily, on whose garden wall was a grotesque assembly of statues of dwarfs and monsters.

There is no point in recounting here all the famous Sitwell jokes, especially those about their father Sir George ('Ginger'), which are mostly to be found in Osbert's own writings. I think I like best Osbert's reply to his commanding officer when he had just joined the Grenadier Guards. Seeking to put him at his ease and picking a safe topic, the Colonel said 'D'you like horses?' 'Yes,' said Osbert respectfully, 'but I think giraffes have a better line.'

Sometimes it seemed as if life were offering an endless vista of bizarre or stimulating surprises. I do not know how it came about — perhaps in consequence of 'Homage to Beethoven', which was noticed in the *Sunday Times* as well as in the *Cherwell* — but one day, to my astonishment, I received an invitation to lunch in London at the Eiffel Tower restaurant (now the White Tower)

with Aleister Crowley. I hesitated, but accepted: such an invitation
was too piquant to refuse; but, as the date of the luncheon drew
near, I became more and more nervous about keeping the appointment. Crowley was widely regarded as a sensationally sinister
figure, and the wildest stories about him were circulated: many of
these were exaggerated, some may have been spread by himself to
frighten those in the strange, closed, credulous world of occultism
who had crossed him. The *Sunday Express* had denounced him as
'the worst man in the world'. He claimed to practise magic (which
he spelled 'magick'). He said it was 'white' magic; others said
'black'. Some years before he had organised performances of the
Eleusinian mysteries in the incongruously staid surroundings of
the Caxton Hall. It was alleged that he lured well-known women
to these orgies, drugged them until they participated, and then
had them photographed for blackmailing purposes. The cakes
that he distributed, as a kind of unholy communion, contained
wheat, honey, hashish, and female *menses*. Quite recently an
Oxford undergraduate named Raoul Loveday had died 'in
mysterious circumstances' when staying at Crowley's 'temple of
Thelema' at Cefalu in Sicily. (Crowley said that he had died after
drinking the local water; Loveday's wife Betty May, an artists'
model, in a book called *Tiger Woman*, attributed his death to
physical and mental revulsion at the midnight ceremonies in which
he was required to sacrifice cats.) There were also more creditable
items in Crowley's record: at Cambridge he had been a competent
poet, in the Swinburnian manner; he still played chess masterfully
at the Gambit in the City; in his youth he had also been an
accomplished mountaineer. Indeed, he claimed to have learned
wisdom from the 'secret masters' in Tibet. This wisdom may have
included certain formulae for sexual potency; for, though he was
bisexual, I was to observe over the years that, ugly as he was, he
could exercise a compelling fascination over women, particularly
elderly women with a fair amount of money. He used heroin
freely, saying that he was its master not its victim; his novel,
The Diary of a Drug-fiend, had just been banned.

In short, as I say, nothing would have induced me to cut that
lunch-date – but I was keeping my fingers crossed. Crowley was
already there when I got to the Eiffel Tower. He stood up, stout,
bald and middle-aged, in a well-cut plus-four suit of green hand-

woven tweed, and greeted me. Then, as we sat down, he said, in a rather high, cracked, donnish voice: 'Pardon me while I invoke the Moon.' There may have been some special reason for the brief muttering which followed. It was not his usual grace, which, like the versicle and response which he and his followers used instead of 'Good morning', or at the start of any enterprise, ran: 'Do what thou wilt shall be the whole of the law' – 'Love is the law, love under will'. This exchange, with its echoes of St Augustine and Rabelais, seemed harmless, even admirable. Crowley expressed it in another way when he said that the essence of this teaching was that you should 'discover your own true will and do it'.

We did not on this occasion go into these deeper matters. I asked him whether at this time he was performing any magical ceremonies in London. He took this opportunity to explain that they were very expensive to set up – the pentacle must be just so, et cetera, or it could be dangerous. All the same, a lot of rubbish had been written about his magic. Magic was simply 'the art of causing change to occur in conformity with will'. It operated in quite everyday ways: when you used the telephone it was magic, or would have been thought so a century ago.

After this I saw Crowley from time to time. I suppose that he had hoped that, because I was at Christ Church, I was rich; he may have been a little disappointed that this was not so, for he wanted to get some magical ceremonies going again, and also to go to America to tackle the Rosicrucians who, he alleged, had 'stolen' some property from him in California. One day he wrote to tell me that he had found a reference to myself in the Egyptian Book of the Dead. The actual quote was: 'From no expected house shall this child come' – and 'what house,' asked Crowley, 'could be more unexpected than *Aedes Christi*?' (Christ Church – 'the House'). It was often hard to tell if he were serious or joking, as when, soon after this, he told me that he had decided to nominate me as his successor as World Teacher. He had assumed this role some years earlier, and dated all his letters from the year and day of his epiphany. However, I heard of one other man to whom Crowley had made the same offer, and I hope that he, rather than I, has inherited the burdensome legacy.

I disregarded the more fantastic rumours about Crowley's misdeeds – as that his infant child by one of his mistresses ('an unblemished male') had been found floating down a river with his heart cut out. But I thought disconcerting the fate of one of his followers, a dim, grey little man called Norman Mudd, who used to come up to one at parties and say 'You won't remember me — my name is Mudd.' Because he differed from Crowley on some point of doctrine or ritual, Crowley called him a 'traitor' and cursed him in a way that he must have found alarming — prophesying that he would die 'by water and the rope'. Some years later, in Paris, I read in the Continental *Daily Mail* a small news-item to the effect that an English visitor to Portugal, Mr N. Mudd, had been found drowned in the sea, with a rope round his neck.

One of Crowley's more impressive claims was that he was the Great Beast foretold in the Book of Revelations, whose number was 666. So his followers familiarly called him 'Beast'. He also described himself as 'Sir' Aleister Crowley. When I asked him about this, he explained that he was a Knight of the Holy Ghost, but that I need not put the title on letters to him, as the order was 'not recognised in England'.

Some years after I had left Oxford, when I was working on the *Daily Express*, a man named Cosmo ('The Great Cosmo', a music-hall illusionist) got in touch with me and said that he had acquired from the landlady of his room in North London a trunk once left there by Crowley, either as payment in lieu of rent or in the course of a 'moonlight flit'. In this trunk he had found some letters from me to Crowley: did I want them? I went along to see Cosmo. The letters were not 'compromising', but I relieved him of them. He also let me have something much more interesting — a small square volume, bound in red morocco and encased in baroque silver which must once have held a missal or a breviary: this contained Crowley's manuscript diary, recording his daily magical and sexual doings, for the period covering Loveday's death at Cefalu and Mussolini's subsequent expulsion of Crowley from Italy. (He set up another 'temple' in Tunis.) It also contained a number of pages bearing what may be called oaths of allegiance, signed in Crowley's presence by various devotees. To my surprise, one of the signatures was that of J. W. N. Sullivan, one of the most distinguished mathematicians of the century. In another case, that of Augustine Booth-Clibborn, there was no signature. Instead, Crowley had written at the bottom of the page: 'He was plotting treachery, but he feared terribly.' The first page of the diary, written in Crowley's hand, bore titles he had bestowed on himself, some of them in Greek: ΤΟ ΜΕΓΑ ΘΗΡΙΟΝ (The Great Beast), ΛΟΓΟΣ 'ΑΙΩΝΟΣ (The Eternal Word), and 'The Wanderer of the Waste'.

I was not seeing much of Crowley now, but one evening he invited me to dinner — a curry dinner, cooked by himself at a fine house up the Thames lent to him by a friend and admirer of his, Lady Harris. (She was the wife of Sir Percy Harris, then the Liberal Chief Whip and known in Parliament as 'the housemaid', for, being the most boring speaker in the House, he had an unfailing knack of emptying the chamber. She was also an accomplished artist, painting under the name of Jesus Chutney; under Crowley's instruction, she was working out a new set of designs for the Tarot cards.) The curry was excellent, and was accompanied by a bottle of Moët and Chandon's champagne. Then Crowley did what he had often done before: he drew the little diagram known as the pentacle, used for telling fortunes by the ancient Egyptians, and asked me to stare into the central space between the lines and tell him what I could see. I had never before seen, or pretended to see, anything; but now I recalled the little manuscript diary — which he did not know that I had — and began, in a trance-like voice, to describe it: the shining baroque silver, a monstrance with a Host on one side of it, the red leather, the writing inside which I could not quite read ... I had never seen Crowley so staggered: he leaned forward in desperate eagerness. 'Go on,' he said, '*go on*!' But the vision faded. 'Try again,' he pleaded. 'No,' I said. 'I can't see anything more ... though perhaps if we had another bottle of Moët ... ?' This was, I fear, rather a mean trick to play on the old boy: I excused it to myself by reflecting that it had given him such obvious amazed delight to see one of his own bits of magic actually coming true. I always half-meant to give him the diary back, and I made it available from time to time to people writing books about him. (I no longer have it.) But years passed without my seeing him, and one day I read that he had died at Hastings. He was given a proper occultist's send-off at the municipal crematorium in Brighton; the service included the recital of his *Hymn to Pan*; the town council passed a resolution deploring the whole thing and saying that it must never happen again.

7

Down and out, and in

By the time I was twenty-two years old, Oxford had finished with
me. Unworthy as I had been of the name of scholar, I had made
fairly full use of one of the main advantages of being at a university
– the opportunity of meeting all sorts of people, some 'distinguished', some to be friends for life; not all encountered in the
strictly academic context. And there had been those romantic
walks on the towpath, some with a milk-roundsman who seemed
to smell deliciously of milk.

It had been, on the whole, an exhilarating experience. But then
came the deflating return to Crowborough. My mother, her small
house, and the whole place seemed to have shrunk, almost
physically, into near-insignificance. I knew that I wanted to be a
writer – I had always known this even at Lancing (where I had
contributed some shaming items to the school magazine, including
a poem 'For J.', who was E. J. (Jimmy) Watson, the boy I wor-
shipped most despairingly and could never touch, since he was
younger and in another house). But at home there wasn't even a
medium like the *Cherwell* in which to exercise such talent as one
had. I tried for a time to continue writing poetry, as Edith Sitwell
had urged me to; she even included one of my poems in a lecture
she was giving on texture in verse. I suppose I realised that one
could not make a living out of poetry, and that journalism was
at any rate one way of writing prose. But I had no idea how to set
about being a journalist, and – luckily, as it turned out – I did not
consult any established journalist, or I should have been given the
standard advice that I later gave to others: get a job on a local

paper, and then, after some years, you *may* break into Fleet Street.

My mother was, naturally, at least as ignorant as I was. I am sure that, as usual, she worried, but she knew no journalists. She said, Why not stay at home, write articles here, and send them up to editors in London? This advice was subjective – she wanted me at home – and, though I had never been inside a newspaper office, I sensed its futility: I could imagine the unsuitability of anything I could think of writing, and the stream of rejection-slips that would descend on me. Besides, I was more bored than ever with Crowborough (except, as before, for St John's): I hankered after London, in particular after Soho, and most of all I craved a certain deep and dark doorway in Rupert Street, in which I had stood for hours at a time enjoying the quick embraces and gropings of other young layabouts – an even more dangerous, and therefore more thrilling, alternative to the simple urinals ('cottages') then plentiful in the mews and alleys of West London. Why municipal vandals should have thought it necessary to destroy so many of them I do not know: I suppose it is one expression of anti-homosexual prejudice. Yet no homo, cottage-cruising, ever prevented a hetero from merely urinating; while to do one's rounds of the cottages – the alley by the Astoria, the dog-leg lane opposite the Garrick Club, the one near the Ivy, the one off Wardour Street, the narrow passage by the Coliseum, ending up always in Of Alley,[1] off Villiers Street – provided homos, not all of whom are given to rougher sports, with healthy exercise. It would no longer be possible to write so entertaining and informative a book as one which I reviewed in the *New Statesman* in the 1930s: this was a guide to the West End cottages called *For Your Convenience*, by 'Paul Pry' (a pseudonym of Thomas Burke). I carried this book about with me at night for some weeks: the fact that I was reviewing it professionally (for a typically *N.S.* pittance!) provided a perfect excuse for spending some time in a cottage, making notes on its *décor*, *ambiance*, security, graffiti, and general flavour; and very pretty some of those pierced metal Victorian ones, usually

---

[1] It is typical of the illiteracy of the L.C.C. bureaucrats that, until Kingsley Martin pointed out their folly in the *New Statesman*, they changed the name of this humble lane, not realising that it was called, with the neighbouring thoroughfares, by the name and title of George Villiers, Duke of Buckingham.

painted green, were. Kingsley, with equally characteristic puritanism, cut the best bits out of the review.

Occasionally my Rupert Street vigils led to something more substantial than a casual grope. Once I was picked up by someone rather too ruling-class for my taste, but remarkably handsome: he was a member of the Guards Club, and took me to a deserted upper room there; at the far end of the room was a deep sofa, on which we coupled. I learned later that he was an *habitué* of All Saints', Margaret Street. (The revival of interest in Victorian architecture had not yet made it fashionable to admire this Butterfield masterpiece, and I for one thought it, liturgically, more 'moderate' and less *chic* than the church I was to frequent for many years, St Mary the Virgin's, Graham Street, now Bourne Street, Pimlico, which had an impressively baroque-type reredos.) Another somewhat 'superior' pick-up was, perhaps, a businessman, but he was young and had a North Country accent which appealed to me: he was frantically randy, trousers bulging in impatient anticipation, and we had nowhere to go; we did it in a telephone-kiosk, shielding the manipulation with his raincoat while I lifted the phone and pretended to talk into it. Nothing more than masturbation was possible in the circumstances; and I was surprised when, as we left the kiosk, he slipped into my hand the generous sum of 30s. in notes.

This was welcome, for whatever money my mother had given me to come to London with was exhausted; and I could hardly ask her for more. Nowadays, I notice, the sons and daughters of people in roughly my mother's station in life usually get part-time jobs in pubs. But these are vacancies which employers have difficulty in filling, and in those days there was large and growing working-class unemployment. I was afflicted, too, with a kind of lassitude, as well as a shyness, which deterred me from what I guessed would be useless visits to newspaper offices. No unemployment benefit, or social security of any kind, was available. So I signed on (probably under the name of Hardy, a pseudonym I sometimes used) at the office in Shaftesbury Avenue of an agency named Jay's, which booked actors and extras for film work. This office was at the top of several staircases. There was always a small crowd of out-of-work theatricals hanging about. (This was before the founding of Equity, or I would have joined it.) One was more often turned away with a 'Nothing today' than offered anything, but they did get me a few jobs, at a rate for crowd-work of, I think, a guinea a day. It may have been two guineas if one had to provide evening clothes, which I still could: I had to wear either dinner-jacket or tails as one of the audience at a Queen's Hall concert in a silent movie of *The Constant Nymph*, directed by Basil Dean.

In this way, and with small loans from friends, I managed to keep alive and to pay the rent (7s. 6d. or 12s. 6d. a week, I forget which) of a narrow top-floor room at 66 Frith Street, Soho. The stairs and the bed creaked so loudly, and the walls were so thin, that I hardly ever risked taking anybody in here. Once I went with a red-haired East End boy to Hampstead Heath. It was a moonlit night: there was thick snow on the ground, but we spread a macintosh for our idyll. He wrote me a letter, ill-spelled but full of love: ' ... I think we ad a verry, hapy time.' He marked the back of the envelope 'PIRVIT — XXX' [Private].

The day came when I had no money for the rent, and had long since pawned the silver cigarette-case from Asprey's that my mother had given me for my twenty-first birthday. (I had become enough of a snob to wish that she had gone to Cartier's and got a gold one: I had seen the superb cases or boxes that some people at Christ Church had — friends such as Edward James or John Dumfries or Dick Girouard.) So having parked my suitcase in a cloakroom, I set out in the evening with a few shillings in my pocket and nowhere to go. I wandered round by Soho Square; at that time there was a large cross above St Patrick's church which was illuminated at night. I walked slowly down Greek Street, along Old Compton Street, hesitated outside the café on the corner of Dean Street, which I had often used, but did not go in. Instead, on an impulse or directed by Providence, I made my way round to Church Street (now Romilly Street) and in it found a café, unknown to me, which looked cheap enough. This was to be my home for some months.

There were few customers as yet. This café filled up later: it was open every night from 6 p.m. to 6 a.m. I got talking to the boss, a fairly attractive young man named Tommy. He was single-handed but for the cook, a big, lumpish, nineteen-year-old Irish-man called, inevitably, Paddy. So Tommy needed someone who would work all night as a waiter, and help with the washing-up in the kitchen. After some discussion, I agreed to take the job: he would pay me 5s. a week 'and all found' – meals – and I could sleep upstairs, sharing a big double bed with Paddy. Tommy slept in a single bed in the same room.

Tommy then explained a more interesting side of the job. The house above the café was owned or leased by an old woman known as Mother McCawry (spelling unknown), and the rooms in it, other than Tommy's, Paddy's and my room, were rented by female prostitutes who catered to a special taste or fetish. They were all enormously fat girls, and their beat was the north side of Lisle Street. (Before the Act which followed the Wolfenden Report, prostitutes were allowed to walk the streets.) To Lisle Street, then, went men who had this special taste: they usually seemed to me to be slight, skimpy little men. I got to know some of the girls quite well. All of them were called Fat somebody – Fat Adelaide, Fat Jessie, Fat Mary and so on. One of them, I think Fat Adelaide, was a thoughtful girl and a strong atheist: she lent me the works of Colonel Ingersoll, the nineteenth-century rationalist. Often one of the girls would order a meal from downstairs for herself and her client (for these were mostly not short-timers: the tiny men liked burying themselves for hours in those great earth-mothers' mounds of flesh). I had to take the trays of food up to their rooms. They always made the customers tip me well, and often slipped me packets of cigarettes.

Paddy turned out to be rather a wild one. I tried to seduce him, but he wasn't having it. At that time I had a revolver, a Mauser 32, which I'd bought some time before and hadn't pawned. Paddy got hold of this, loaded it, and waved it around, swearing crazily. He thought he was in love with one of the fat girls, and threatened to shoot her because she preferred to stick to her clients. He cried a good deal about this. However, he didn't mind a non-sexual embrace, and we often slept in each other's arms. But when Tommy tried to get into the double bed with us, I had to push him away, with regret, for I had noticed that he was suffering from gonorrhoea. On the whole, the three of us got along reasonably well: we felt light-headed when the café shut in the morning and Tommy took us down to Lyons Corner House in Coventry Street for breakfast – always porridge and cream.

After I had been there for some weeks I realised that Tommy

was going off more and more in the evenings – to 'the dogs', he said, and this was probably true. I also realised that, since Paddy was in the kitchen at the back and I was the only one at the counter and moving around in the café, this meant that Tommy was relying on me to look after the place and keep some sort of order. This gave me a much greater kick, and a much keener sense of responsibility, than being a prefect at school had ever given me. But, oddly, the public-school ethic and training worked: I did get, psychologically, a kind of control over the regulars who sat around for hours, chatting and arguing in their thieves' slang – and I did it by treating them with respect, clearing away dirty plates and wiping the tables promptly. They were a rough and villainous lot. They called me 'the Baron', could not make me out at all, and teased me a good deal; but I minded this much less than I had minded the teasing and bullying when I was a junior at school. Gradually a mutual regard grew, and I no longer thought I should ever have to use the revolver which I had kept under the counter. The only bad scene I recall was when a one-legged man hopped swiftly across the room and brought his crutch down hard on the head of a man standing with his back to him. Another disabled customer was known as Cripple Ernie from Hoxton. There was also an awkward half-hour when the police raided the house, looking for stolen goods, and disturbed some of the girls upstairs, who had after all paid the local cops regularly not to be disturbed when pursuing their vocation. I had to put on an 'Oxford' manner to keep the police out of the café (for some of *my* clients were getting nervous), assuring them that what might be happening upstairs, and what parcels might be coming into Mother McCawry's premises, were nothing to do with us or with my employer, who was unfortunately away on business. All in all, despite the squalid surroundings, this was one of the most undilutedly happy periods of my life. For the first time I was liberated from the terrible shyness and diffidence that had always haunted me: I began to feel a certain confidence in my ability to cope with situations.

It could not last. On Saturday afternoons, being careful to be back before the café opened at 6 p.m., I had been having a clean-up and going off to Moscow Road, Bayswater, where Edith Sitwell lived, high up in a block of flats without a lift. Every Saturday she had a tea-party—strong Indian tea and penny buns, nothing else, dispensed by Edith and her great friend Helen Rootham: at these gatherings one could meet T. S. Eliot, H. G. Wells, Aldous Huxley and many other of the famous, together with young unknowns like Cecil Beaton and myself; but I found that, though one *could* meet them, one needed more intrusiveness than I had to pin them down, for the famous tended to get together in close little groups and talk, invariably, about money—royalties, and the merits or demerits of their respective agents and publishers.

Sometimes, at Edith's bidding, I would get there a bit early and we would talk quietly. I had merely told her that I was doing 'a rather humdrum job'. One day, when she asked me again, I told her what it was and described it as I have described it here, fat women and all (but not my own sleeping arrangements). She was horrified: I must be got out of there. I at once took, not hope, but fright. I was habituated to my sordid routine: I dreaded the effort involved in breaking with it. What was she threatening? A steady office job—perhaps with a publisher? I begged her not to bother: No no, I would be all right, I could look after myself, I would just stay in Soho a bit longer and look round, meanwhile, for something more 'suitable'. Then other guests arrived. But she did not forget— and she was a woman not only of great compassion, but of great pertinacity. It seemed that the then managing editor of the *Daily Express*, Beverley Baxter, was under some kind of obligation to one or both of Edith's brothers (whom I had seen from time to time since our meeting at Rapallo). Anyway, she got them to get on to him to see if there was any chance of a job there.

Young men are supposed to succeed by their own efforts alone; it is thought wrong, even disgraceful, to 'use influence'. Once I had resigned myself to the break with Tommy and Paddy, and the café customers, I was glad of Edith's intervention; nor have I ever felt ashamed of it since. For in any case there was no automatic open door at the *Express* (nor do I believe that, if I had been no good, I would have got and held a job there). Every editor got, and gets, dozens of solicitations by or for young men just down from a university, most of them with better qualifications than my non-existent degree.

This was less than a year after Evelyn Waugh had arrived at the *Express* as a reporter, also with an introduction to Baxter from

Sacheverell Sitwell. He had a degree, but a poor one. It would have been fun to be there with him, but he lasted only a month or two. Had he stuck, and hardened into a full-time *Express* news-hawk, we might not have had those novels (except, perhaps, *Scoop*). Had I not stuck, and hardened into a full-time columnist, I might have become a good poet — which Edith Sitwell thought I was and wanted me to be but effectively prevented me from being by getting me this job.

Perhaps because of his recent disappointing experience with Evelyn, I had to telephone Baxter's secretary several times before an interview was fixed, and then it was not with him but with the Features Editor, Reginald Pound, a genial, stocky, curly-headed man who now lives at Tenterden, Kent, still, in his eighties, writing major biographies. I was, of course, in a state of terrified self-consciousness. Possibly seeing this, Pound, without any severe quizzing, told me to go away and write an article on a subject on some aspects of which I was by now expert: it was either 'London by night' or 'London after midnight'. I cannot remember at all what the article was like; I am pretty sure it was never published. But a few days later, in January, 1928, I was told that I could have a job as a reporter, on trial for six weeks, at £3 a week. This was exciting, but also alarming. I knew nothing of the technique of news-reporting. My boss, the news editor, was an unflappable, episcopal-looking man, J. B. Wilson, who had a comfortably plump, middle-aged secretary, Miss Secker. The night news editor was a 'character' — an exaggeratedly Welsh little Welshman named Alan Jones. When a reporter returned from some disaster, Jones, parodying the hard-faced newshawk of legend, would shout in his Welsh accent: 'Any babies dead, man? What! No babies dead! ... *Damn!*' All these were extremely kind to me. So was Hannen Swaffer, then the dramatic critic, who took me one evening to his regular haunt, the Savoy Grill. I soon picked up the technique of the standard news-story: facts — who, when, where, etc. — in the first paragraph. I was sent out on all the usual jobs: tram accident (there were trams in London then), fires, sudden deaths. (I learned that what is condemned as 'intrusion into private grief' is not always unwelcome. Sometimes the door would be flung open: 'Are you from the press? ... Come in ... [then, dramatising] He was a wonderful man ... ') Once, but only once (it would have been unprofessional to do it too often) I telephoned my story from a kiosk and returned to spend some hours with a bereaved husband, providing consolation that he was unlikely to get from any other source that night.

As though fate were paying me out for this bit of fun on the side, an extraordinary coincidence tested my equanimity – the mask I wore – when I had been at the *Express* for only a few days. A job came up that would go to a junior reporter: there had been an airplane crash at the Royal Air Force College, Cranwell, and I was told to ring the Air Ministry and get any details and the names of those killed. Fortunately, only a few had been killed (fortunately for me, too, since I did not do shorthand). The names were read out to me, and the last name was Watson, E. J. – the boy I had been most in love with, at a distance, at Lancing.

On reflection, I don't think poor Jimmy Watson would have made the Ideal Mate whom so many of us are vainly looking for all our lives. As Dorothy Parker said, the promiscuous are 'pursuing monogamy from bed to bed'. I used to correspond with him in the holidays and when I had gone up to Oxford: trying to impress him, I sent him the most expensive Turkish cigarettes from S. P. Ora, which he probably loathed, and tried to fix a date for tea at the Ritz. (What could have happened there, and then!) My only souvenirs of him are a blurred snap of him in cricket gear and a letter from him which is an almost unbelievably awful specimen of its type and period (and also, perhaps, a pathetically fictitious attempt to warn off a menace):

Hopedene,
Willingdon,
Eastbourne

Dear Tom,

Lots of exciting things have happened since I wrote last ...

Last hols I took a wench to Brighton for the day. Perfectly priceless wench so much so that I missed the last train home and had to taxi with her for thirty odd miles. I nearly committed a grievous sin but I just managed to control myself.

The other day I had a letter from an infatuated female whom I had never seen in my life she told me that she loved

me and all that sort of cock, and begged me to meet her. I
have just done so she's not a bad girl quite pretty in fact.
Yesterday I had five girls on hand but I've just 'divorced'
one, four's quite enough ...

On Tuesday I'm going to take my exam. There's a little
hope, but a *damned* little. Still, I've got another chance, and
my tutor thinks that I ought not to find any difficulty in
passing finally.

Yours sincerely,

JIMMY WATSON

His exam was for entrance to Cranwell. He passed.

I turned his and the other names in. I can't remember if the
story got into the paper. It wasn't worth more than a few lines.

My six weeks' trial was up, but Miss Secker went on making out
my chit for £3 a week and paying my expenses. As nobody noticed
I was still there, I stayed on; and in due course somebody did
notice and gave me a sort of contract, at slightly higher pay. The
real turning-point came, not when I joined the *Express* on trial, but
when, some months later, I was transferred to a column called 'The
Talk of London', by The Dragoman, to assist the man who was
writing it single-handed, Colonel Percy Sewell.

It is almost like re-reading a school magazine of one's boyhood
to skim through the yellow files of the *Daily Express* for my first
months there. The circulation then was about 1,152,000. It was to
rise much higher. The lay-out and typography of the paper look
quaintly old-fashioned now; and the advertisements, even more
than the editorial matter, convey a sense of period. Whisky was
offered at 12s. 6d. a bottle. Women were encouraged to buy
dresses with 'the dripping hem-line'. Consumers of Sanatogen
were alleged to be 'feeling like ten men and a boy – especially the
boy!' Selfridge's store took full-page ads. In the early days of
Beaverbrook's ownership of the *Express*, Selfridge had been a
'good friend' to the struggling paper, booking and paying in
advance for substantial series of advertisements. There was therefore an absolute rule that (as in the case of other big advertisers)
nothing was to be printed editorially that could offend Selfridge or
his shop. Some years later, when a hideous clock was erected
above the main entrance of the store – it is still there – I wrote a

paragraph regretting the clock, on aesthetic grounds. The paragraph was killed. This is a trivial instance of the influence exercised by advertisers on the editorial content of newspapers – a phenomenon familiar to all journalists, though press lords and their senior executives obstinately deny that it exists.

There was also a curious little directive, which had originated with Beaverbrook himself, on the style by which Selfridge was to be referred to in print. He was never to be called by his full name, Gordon Selfridge, but always simply 'Mr Selfridge'. Sometimes, I think, press lords issue these directives on the spur of the moment and forget about them: their sycophantic hacks obey unquestioningly and treat the directive, however pointless it may be, as immutable. Thus, too, the Aga Khan, but no other oriental potentate, was to be 'H.H. the Aga Khan'; while Bonar Law was always just 'Bonar Law', *tout court*, without 'Mr' or 'Rt Hon.'. So were fossilised the master's passing whims.

Another speciality about which I soon learned was the dreaded 'white list', so called because 'black list' sounds too menacing – the list of people whose names were never to be mentioned in the *Express*, or not to be mentioned without consultation with the editor. This ban might be defensible if the names on the list were only those of people who were what lawyers call litigious – people who had brought or threatened to bring actions for libel against the paper. It has sometimes been suggested that this was so in the case of the *Express*. This is not entirely true: besides the names of the litigious, many of the names on the list were there at the caprice of Beaverbrook; they were the names of people who had offended him personally or crossed him politically, and the punishment inflicted on them was to pretend that they no longer existed – in the grim Soviet phrase, that they were 'former persons'. The victims may not have minded very much: to be mentioned in the *Express* is not everyone's idea of bliss; but in so far as these were names of people in the public eye, their relegation to this limbo may have deprived the readers of information which they were entitled to have. In my evidence to the first Royal Commission on the Press I mentioned this, as I thought, bad practice, citing in particular the inclusion in the white list of two distinguished Roman Catholic writers, Hilaire Belloc and G. K. Chesterton, who had incurred Beaverbrook's anger. The *Express* put forward supplementary evidence to try to prove me a liar. This was some years after I had left the paper, and unfortunately I had not kept a specimen of the white list (which varied from time to time as names were added to it or taken off it) and so could not show it to the Commission. Later a friend who was on the staff gave me a copy of the list: Belloc's name was still on it, but Chesterton had been released by death; other names included were those of Noël Coward, Douglas Fairbanks, jnr, Charlie Chaplin and Paul Robeson.

My full knowledge of the white list came much later, when I was running a column on my own; but it did not take me long to realise the truth of the adage that freedom of the press in Britain means freedom to print such of the proprietor's prejudices as the advertisers don't object to.

I had been at the *Express* for little more than a month when I provided the news editor with my first 'scoop' — an account, I think the first in a mass-circulation paper, of the revivalist cult led by Dr Frank Buchman from Pennsylvania. This movement, which was beginning to be called, misleadingly, the Oxford Group, was to become world-famous, from 1939 onwards, under the name of Moral Re-Armament. I had heard about it from friends still at Oxford, which Buchman was then visiting. I went there, attended one of the group's sessions in the lounge of the Randolph Hotel, interviewed the Vice-Chancellor, Dr Streeter, Dr A. E. J. Rawlinson, Father Ronald Knox and other senior members of the University, and printed what I saw and what they said. The *Express* thought the story worth running for several days, starting on the front page on February 28th, 1928.

Some time later, in the summer vacation, I went to Oxford again and talked to Dr Buchman personally. I still think that the best description of him is that given by an early disciple, Harold Begbie: 'tall, upright, stoutish, clean-shaven, spectacled, with that mien of scrupulous, shampooed, and almost medical cleanness or freshness which is so characteristic of the hygienic American'. I remember him walking bouncily towards me across the lawn of the women's college at which the Buchmanites were having a house-party, greeting his followers as they gathered round him. One of them was Austin Reed, of the men's-wear chain of shops. Buchman was good at remembering names. 'Hullo there, Mr Austin Reed!', he cried. 'How's that lift-boy of yours coming along?' I thought it clever of him to remember, in England, to say 'lift' instead of 'elevator'.

From then on I took a desultory but increasing interest in the Buchman movement. I kept newspaper cuttings about it and discussed it with people who had direct experience of it; some of them had got out of it, disillusioned. In the 1950s, to my surprise, I was invited to lecture on it at two Scandinavian universities, Oslo and Göteborg. The lecture was printed as a pamphlet, and this in turn prompted my friend David Farrer, of Secker & Warburg, to commission from me a full-length book on the subject. I went to Pennsylvania to find out about Buchman's origins there, and acquired some interesting facts. The book – *The Mystery of Moral Re-Armament* – was published in 1964. Both in that book and in everything else I have said and written about M.R.A., I have tried to be fair and objective. I am afraid I have not succeeded; at least, the Buchmanites don't seem to think I have.

One of the characteristics of this movement is its hypersensitive vindictiveness against anybody who has uttered a word of criticism of it, however mild, or has mentioned such inconvenient facts as the interview in the *New York World-Telegram* on August 26th, 1936, in which Buchman, who had just been visiting Nazi Germany, said: 'I thank heaven for a man like Adolf Hitler, who built a front line of defence against the anti-Christ of Communism.'

Since I have been regarded for many years as an enemy, M.R.A. has a copious dossier on me – some of which is wildly inaccurate, though some, I must admit, will find confirmation in parts of this book. In 1960 I was one of three speakers invited by the World Council of Churches to address their European Youth Conference, at Lausanne. This assembly was organised by a French Protestant pastor, Michel Wagner, and some time before it met he was put under heavy pressure by M.R.A. spokesmen, who demanded that they should be allowed to send delegates to take part in the proceedings. The pastor, a shrewd and experienced Christian, was determined to prevent this intrusion: he explained that delegates were not being invited on the basis suggested by M.R.A., and continued to resist their pressure. In consequence, just before the assembly opened at Lausanne, a press conference

was held at the M.R.A. centre at Caux, also in Switzerland, at
which a fierce attack was made on the Lausanne assembly. The
chairman of it, who is now the Dean of Liverpool, was falsely said
to be a card-carrying Communist. Others connected with the
assembly were branded as homosexuals: so far as I know, this was
also untrue, except of myself, and it will be realised that I would
not regard the allegation as particularly shocking or my presence
at Lausanne as tending to corrupt the youth of Europe. (It was in
fact, so far as I was concerned, a completely chaste occasion.) The
correspondents who came on from Caux to Lausanne reported to
us all these slanders. They were felt to be disgraceful, and the
General Secretary of the W.C.C., Dr Visser 't Hooft, a Dutch
veteran of the ecumenical movement so venerable and so univers-
ally respected that even M.R.A. would not dare to try to smear
him, issued a solemn rebuke to the slanderers.

   The most fantastic of all the Buchmanite inventions about
myself concerned my brother Jim, of whom I have written. At
some time during the latter, unfortunate part of Jim's life, when
he was drinking heavily, he encountered Dr Buchman, who
apparently recognised his talents and his potential, took him in
hand, and actually cured him of drinking. If this is true, it is
greatly to Buchman's credit. But then, alas, Jim reverted to his
old ways — and, according to the M.R.A. myth, it was I who, in
sheer wickedness, lured him back to the demon drink. Nothing
could be more remote from the truth: as I have explained, Jim's
drinking became both boring and, to me, expensive; I should have
been delighted had he been able to give it up. But Buchmanites,
like other believers, can construct the most grotesque fables to
embellish their propaganda and to discredit those whom they have
labelled enemies.

I have only vague memories of the *Express* in my first months
there. This was before the erection of the big black-glass building
in Fleet Street, and we came and went by an unimpressive door in
Shoe Lane, where there was a 'sausage-shop' that we frequented
for cheap meals. Both J. B. Wilson and Miss Secker treated me
with great kindness. So did Baxter, who was managing editor, and
an eminent veteran journalist, R. D. Blumenfeld, who was by
now described as editor-in-chief; when I came into the office one

afternoon rather the worse for all the champagne I had drunk at the wedding of an old friend, 'R.D.B.' administered the gentlest of reprimands.

Besides all the reporters and sub-editors, I gradually — very gradually, for I was still shy — got to know the 'characters' who lurked in various corners of the shabby old building. There was an old man with a lean grey face who spent the entire day going through back numbers of American newspapers, cutting out items of news or comment and passing them to anyone on the staff who might use them. His name was Gask; I learned that he was, in the world outside the *Express* office, an internationally recognised authority on antique silver spoons. In the library — chiefly devoted to reference-books and long buff envelopes full of millions of cuttings about every conceivable subject and person — worked a tall, ruddy-faced, fast-moving youth, obviously homosexual, with whom I soon struck up a furtive friendship. In the library also worked a plump little birdlike elderly woman called Mrs Van Someren, whom I greatly regret not having got to know better. I had never heard the name before: this was long before A. J. A. Symon's brilliant biography, *The Quest for Corvo* — from which I was to learn of the hospitality provided for Corvo in Venice by this same Mrs Van Someren and her husband. How, I wonder, did she and old Gask find their ways into these modest jobs in Fleet Street?

On the whole, I enjoyed being a reporter, but after a few months came the intimation that I was to be transferred — to the vocal disgust of Alan Jones, who had begun to find me reliable — to Percy Sewell's 'Talk of London'. This was a column of social gossip, which Beaverbrook was later to kill: it was not so malicious as some present-day gossip-columns, but was equally futile, in that it largely chronicled the doings of what were called the idle rich. The main difference between then and now is that the people whom Sewell wrote about — the people he knew — were of aristo-cratic, or at least gentle, birth. Now the names which fill the gossip-columns are those of *parvenus* — Greek shipowners, oil millionaires or film stars — who are thought important because they have a lot of money. Looking through 'The Talk of London' of those days, I can distinguish between paragraphs written by Sewell and my contributions. His would contain the names, for instance, of Lady Maureen Stanley, Sir Horace Rumbold, Lady Sybil Grant, and Lord Crewe: mine contained mostly the names of my school and Oxford friends, people of a younger generation than Sewell's, many of them not rich or aristocratic, some of them writers or artists. I recognise as mine some paragraphs about a party attended by the composer Constant Lambert, the artist Oliver Messel, and the writers Peter Quennell and Harold Acton, and by Stephen Tennant, who 'wore a football jersey and earrings' and 'arrived in an electric brougham' ('like riding in a bow window,' he said). I also recorded the literary progress of Nancy Mitford, John Betjeman and Evelyn Waugh – and wrote of Christopher Sykes, Waugh's biographer of nearly half-a-century later, that he had 'a taste for massive splendour and two ambitions: (1) to be elected Pope, and (2) to conduct a great orchestra in Wagner.'

All this was pretty frivolous stuff, though not, I venture to think quite so vulgar and trivial as some of today's gossip, since it was often about people, such as Mitford and Waugh, who were intrinsically interesting. And I did manage more and more – particularly when writing for Monday's paper on a Sunday, if Sewell was off and I was left in charge – to introduce references to more serious subjects, such as capital punishment, Soviet films (praised, and the monstrous Home Secretary, Joynson-Hicks, attacked for banning them), modern architecture, and *avant-garde* movements in the arts; this greatly to Baxter's distaste, since he said that nobody was interested in ballet, that nobody had ever heard of Stravinsky or *Façade*, and that Epstein and D. H. Lawrence were 'ugly'. (The Philistine police had raided a gallery showing Lawrence's paintings. When *The Well of Loneliness* was suppressed in 1928, I backed it but the *Express* editorially said that such a 'flagrant and infamous' book meant that England was 'in deadly peril'.)

I always wrote with respect of artists whose work I admired, and never ridiculed my Oxford friends; but the tone of the column, so far as I could influence it, became more and more satirical. I described in detail the absurdities and extravagances of the ruling class, in a way calculated to enrage any working-class or unemployed people who might chance to read the column; at a time of mass-unemployment I felt that I was doing something not without value to the Communist Party, to which I was still attached. (A few years later, when Beaverbrook supported Neville Chamberlain and Halifax in their policy of appeasing Hitler, and *Express* writers were forbidden, e.g., to print anything that might upset Hitler's clownish ambassador, Ribbentrop, I told John Strachey how awful it was to work on the *Express* under these restraints, and said that I felt I must resign: he urged me to stay on, since I could still get in a few jabs at our rulers, while if I left my place might be filled by someone explicitly pro-Fascist.)

It took me over three years to get my own by-line – 'By T. Driberg, *Daily Express* Special Correspondent' – on a story. This was an extremely bitchy, column-long piece about a ghastly song recital by Ganna Walska, the divorced Polish wife of an American millionaire.

After I had been Sewell's assistant for some time, he retired. He was a sad and secret man with stooping shoulders and a droopy moustache, conventionally dressed, and with a quiet wit; 'crossed in love', they said. It was rumoured that he had fallen deeply for a woman who had turned out to be an inflexible Lesbian. I liked him very much, and learned a lot from him – though some of his wisdom was of the nature of old wives' fantasy, for instance his belief that each human male has a foreordained and fixed number of seminal emissions allowed him, and that when you've come this number of times you're finished sexually. He must have been aware of my sexual habits, but we never discussed the subject. Fairly soon after his retirement (though not very old) he died – possibly by his own hand: it was not certain. I took over the running of the column, and was able to introduce more of what I wanted to print.

Then, in May, 1933, came the big change, which was to determine my future as a journalist. For one reason or another – perhaps he sensed my hidden motive – Beaverbrook decided to abolish 'The Talk of London', and 'social gossip', altogether. As I wrote in the introduction to my book *Colonnade*:[1]

His onslaught was characteristically ruthless and total. He knew (or rather, he felt, for Beaverbrook was essentially an intuitive impresario) that no half-measures or 'tapering-off' would do. They had been tried before. 'Goddammit,' he had

[1] Pilot Press, London, 1949.

snarled at his gossip-writers, 'write about people who *do* things — who do real work — not about these worthless social parasites and butterflies ... ' The response was a piece of praise of two ravishing débutantes who had embarked on real work — in a Mayfair flower-shop. So the time came to make a clear break with the past. 'William Hickey' was born. It was not a painless birth. Those who have worked for Beaverbrook will know that, when he is in labour with an idea, it is hard labour for all concerned. I need not here go into all the details; but one of the main inspirations of Beaverbrook's new-style column was the American magazine *Time* — and the harrowing discipline imposed on the new-style columnist was to emulate and even to surpass *Time*'s sharply flavoured and jagged prose style. A staccato telegraphese emerged which was certainly not English: it had few verbs and no definite or indefinite articles; it consisted almost entirely of adjectives — often elaborately quaint and neologistic — and such gruesome portmanteaux as 'cinemagnate'. It was shock treatment, but it worked: there was no more social gossip in the *Daily Express* — no more 'Lady X, who is, of course, Lord X's third wife, was charming in blue'; no more, 'The Aga Khan, looking bronzed and fit'. *Time* had a feature, called 'People', whose standing text was 'Names make news: last week these names made this news'. So the new *Express* feature was called 'These Names Make News'. After several weeks of uncertainty, Beaverbrook decided that it should be signed, pseudonymously, William Hickey, thus reviving the memory of a great diarist of the late eighteenth century who had, says the *Oxford Companion to English Literature*, 'a weakness for women and claret' (which I should have thought were two separate weaknesses, if indeed weakness is the word).

I do not know where Beaverbrook got the idea of reviving the name of Hickey; the suggestion may have come from his crony Lord Castlerosse, himself a gossip-writer on the *Sunday Express*.

One of Beaverbrook's more engaging qualities was that he was a *tease*. He enjoyed pulling our legs — an alarming process until you were used to it. One of the best examples was his brush with an executive who had failed to carry out Beaverbrook's instructions exactly as he wanted. One morning his Lordship's voice came rasping down the telephone: 'You've *thwarted* me once, you've *thwarted* me twice' — and what a good word 'thwarted' is for roaring in a rough Canadian voice — 'and if you *thwart* me again I shall ... go back to Canada! Come to dinner this evening. Good-bye to you' — the last phrase being the invariable termination of a Beaverbrook phone-call.

Another example, which illustrates both Beaverbrook's habit of teasing and his preference for people who were not mere stooges but would answer him back when teased, is contained in the following paragraphs from 'The Londoner's Diary' in the *Evening Standard* of May 19th, 1938. Here (for the first part was dictated by him) he was inciting one of his own columnists to tease another of his own columnists, without however mentioning that the latter was the pseudonymous Hickey; but in the latter's 'reply' — which would have been read to him before it was printed — he was allowing the victim of the tease to snap back:

THE CAFÉ COMMUNIST

The Café Communists are one of the more recent products of our modern social life.

They are the gentlemen, often middle-aged, who gather in fashionable restaurants, and, while they are eating the very fine food that is served in those restaurants and drinking the fine wines of France and Spain, they are declaring themselves to be of Left Wing faith.

One of them is Mr Victor Gollancz, not actually a member of the Communist Party, but a staunch Left Wing supporter, who lunches each day off the best fare that London can provide. Another is Mr John Strachey, a prominent member of the Communist Party, who may from time to time be seen supping in a certain grillroom.

REPLY

Another is Mr Tom Driberg, the columnist. When taxed with this incongruity between his views and his surroundings, Mr Driberg retorts that he does not see why he also should be a victim of the malnutrition which is an endemic disease of capitalism; that clear-thinking need not imply poor feeding;

that since the most painful part of his job is to associate
occasionally with the rich and powerful, he naturally, on such
occasions, needs an anaesthetic; and that he has yet to discover
a really 'fine' Spanish wine anyway.

One of the night-clubs that I used to frequent was called
Frisco's. Frisco was the name of the jovial black man who ran it
and sang with great gusto some of our favourite songs; one was
'Lullaby of Broadway', which seemed exactly suited to the feel of
Soho at dawn: 'When Broadway babies say Good-night, it's early
in the morning ... Sleep tight, baby, the milkman's on his way.'
During the Abdication crisis, I was in Frisco's one night with
Frank Owen and one or two others, when news came through of a
public statement by Mrs Simpson starting with the words: 'The
situation is unhappy and untenable ... ' We pounced on these
words, which seemed to fit a West Indian rhythm then favoured by
us, and composed a whole calypso around them. So little did we
care about the sufferings of that unfortunate woman. In this we
were following the example of my employer, who said many years
later that he wouldn't have missed that crisis on any account
'because of the fun I got out of it'.

She has had her revenge for the callousness or hostility of the
royal family and others in Britain—if it is true, as she has told
many friends, that she is leaving to the French government the
valuable royal heirlooms which she obtained from Edward VIII.

8

Hickey at large

The jerky, *Time* style influence was still verblessly present when I covered the Coronation of King George VI in May, 1937. A few days before this ceremony I went to the final rehearsal in Westminster Abbey. The piece I wrote opened: 'Overture. The Archbishop on the air ... Crowd waiting in the rain.'

'The Archbishop' was Dr Lang, of Canterbury, who had earned much obloquy in the previous year by his comments on the abdication of Edward VIII. He was white-haired, exquisitely groomed, like a delicate old lady. I can still recall this graceful old thing wandering about the Abbey, during the chaos of the rehearsal, wringing his hands and crying: '*Where* is the Lord of the Manor of Worksop? Where *is* the Lord of the Manor of Worksop?' This improbable title was that of one of the feudal functionaries – persons of the utmost unimportance – who had a traditional right to appear for a few seconds at a coronation, to hand the new monarch a rose or a peppercorn or whatever; in this case an embroidered glove.

For the *Express* readers I explained about the 300 Gold Staff Officers – the ushers for the ceremony – and the class they belonged to: they had been 'selected for several reasons – some because they are peers' sons, some via Admiralty, Foreign Office, etc., some simply because the Duke of Norfolk knew them personally as presentable chaps'. I was always careful to stress the predominance in our society of unearned privilege, and to write without reverence of those who enjoyed it – referring, for instance, to these Gold Staffs as typical of 'the "young men about town" who act as ushers at snob weddings'.

I also, again as always, loftily analysed for the instruction of the bemused public the ritual and ceremonial of the service – 'ritual' being the thing said, 'ceremonial' the thing done: 'Few people seem to realise that the Anointing of the King is not merely a formalized gesture. Oil really is poured on his chest, head and hands. He is unbuttoned for this purpose. Lord Ancaster does the unbuttoning.' Unbuttoning was my forte, too: Ancaster, I noted, 'had some difficulty at one rehearsal in getting at the buttons of [the] gigantic guardee who was standing in for the King ... Oil is poured on the King from a pearl-studded, silver-gilt spoon; into spoon from beak of eagle-shaped ampulla, whose head unscrews for filling.'

What the editor made of the ampulla I don't know; but nobody dared to cut such fragments of superior knowledge. Then I vouchsafed: 'It is the Anointing rather than – as people, misled by the name of the service, ignorantly write – the Crowning which is the "supreme moment" of the service. The Crowning is merely the symbolical demonstration of what has already been done.' Such observations cannot have endeared me to other commentators. I was indeed getting above myself. And in describing at length the Coronation itself and those attending it – from a seat in the triforium measuring, I complained, 1ft 7in. by 2ft 1in. – I was, again, 'objective'; that is, I wrote deliberately not to convey that sense of hushed awe considered appropriate in most of the press: 'St Augustine and St Gregory, in Victorian stained glass, looked rather yellow; but Mrs Tate [a Conservative M.P.] looked extremely well ... resting her chin on her white-gloved arm. Wilfrid Roberts [a Liberal M.P.] rubbed his eyes sleepily.' I rarely allowed honorific titles: 'Italy's Grandi and U.S.S.R.'s Litvinov were next to each other in the procession; Abyssinia was all in black, had curly black hair ... Juliana [of Holland] chewed the end of her lorgnette ... Lloyd George folded his arms, looked bored. Ribbentrop appeared to go to sleep ... From above Sir John Simon's head is like a pink egg.' I missed seeing Queen Mary's arrival 'because at that moment an official, enjoying his moment of power, barred me brusquely from a corner in which Gold Staff in charge of us had said I could stand.' Then: 'Zero hour, 11 a.m. Bells pealing outside. Women preened themselves, patted their hair; as though anyone was going to look at them ... ' Both archbishops were here this time: 'York plump, Canterbury very old and grave, acidly beautiful.'

More titbits of liturgical knowledge: 'It is not an "unvarying" rite, as people say. There have been at least six revisions. There are three changes this time. But its essentials take you back ... to dark primeval times.' The English coronation service was copied so closely in Europe that 'centuries ago a Milanese coronation service contained a prayer that the local king might continue to rule over the Saxons, Mercians, and Northumbrians.'

I also emphasised that the service did not support the theory of the divine right of kings. Its structure was 'based on the idea of a contract'. If anyone had shouted 'No' when the Archbishop 'presented' the King to the people, the service couldn't have gone on.

For the anointing the King stripped off his robe 'like a tennis-player taking off a sweater'. The oil was left over from the coronation of Edward VII; it had been consecrated in 1902. 'King's chemist recently tested it, found it "perfectly pure".'

Then 'they dressed him up'. The Archbishop's hands trembled as he popped on the Crown; 'his pince-nez, secured by broad black tape, were well down his nose'. Then Enthronement (with a reminder that, if crops failed, kings had often been sacrificial victims), Homage, and Communion: 'Caesar and Caesar's wife (certainly above reproach, this one) went up to the altar side by side.' And so on. I quoted a dock-worker from East Ham, on duty in the Abbey as an ambulance man, as saying: 'Candidly, I'd sooner be me than him. Brought up different, of course, but I couldn't stand it.'

This account of a big occasion contained no explicit republicanism, no libel on the King or anyone else; but it excited a storm of shocked rage among the middle-class readers of the *Daily Express*: dozens of letters of protest came in. It was the *tone* of the report that they disliked. One detail that particularly upset them was the description of the villainous Simon's head as 'like a pink egg'. My offence seemed to be that, by watching the coronation in the way in which a dramatic critic might watch a stage show, and by treating those taking part as moving, breathing human beings and as performers, I had in some way robbed the ceremony of its glamour and the monarchy of its mystique.

Two years later, in March 1939, the *Express* sent me to a coronation on an even grander scale—that of Pope Pius XII. A month earlier I had also gone to Rome, for the funeral of his predecessor, Pius XI. (I went to this a week after returning from my second visit to the Spanish Civil War.) His corpse lay, 'stiff, still, waxen-faced', in a chapel on the right of St Peter's basilica; the body was propped up at an angle, so that one could see purplish patches on the face, indicating rapid decomposition. It was clad in Mass vestments, with a mitre on the head. On the day of the funeral Swiss Guards hung around chatting; the upright bars of the gate of the chapel 'made a good test of the immobility of the Noble Guards who have stood about the body watching it four days and nights. I fixed my eye on one bar. It exactly bisected a guard's face, hiding his nose. It still bisected the face each time I looked back at it.'

The service was in the late afternoon. The Pope's body was carried from the chapel to the area near the high altar in which it was sealed in the coffin and lowered into the crypt. There was a long delay: we were told afterwards that they had 'run out of the lead needed for sealing the coffin and had had to send out for more'.

This funeral expedition provided several opportunities for my tiresome knowingness or, as we have learned to call it, one-upmanship. *The Times*, I remarked, had said that the lying-in-state had been in a chapel on the 'south' side of St Peter's: 'It was on the north; though in a less learned journal the mistake might have been overlooked, for St Peter's "faces" west instead of east.' Then there was the common error, perpetrated by the B.B.C., of supposing that St Peter's is a 'cathedral'. (St John Lateran is the cathedral of Rome.) I also debunked the myth, revived by several papers as historical fact, that 'the Cardinal Camerlengo calls the dead Pope by his baptismal name and taps his forehead thrice with a small mallet. No such ceremony took place'.

However, I charitably added that I was 'resolved never again to make fun of brother journalists guilty of using clichés. When one is writing in a hurry ... one always tends to use four words where one would do.' After telephoning my description of the funeral from my hotel to London, I had been 'horrified to find that I had written "sank to their knees" when I only meant "knelt".' In Rome at the same time was the novelist Hugh Walpole, covering the papal ceremonies for the Hearst news-syndicate. He said: 'All one can hope for is a few fine phrases floating in a sea of clichés.'

Whereas I had to return to London and my daily column for the weeks between the two events, Walpole was lucky enough to stay in Rome for both the funeral and the coronation. I found him a congenial companion and, since he was a quick worker, suggested that he should fill in the time by putting his impressions of Rome into a book. This he did; the book was called *Roman Fountain*. I do not think he had been in Rome before: the book, though probably not his best, sparkles with fresh observation. He lunched with me at Alfredo's, in a mood of gratified exaltation: that morning, he claimed, a handsome attendant at the Borghese gallery had insisted on pinning him against a wall and buggering him.

When describing the papal coronation, I again found myself disposing of some popular ideas. I stressed, for instance, not the elaboration so much as the austerity of the Roman rite: 'For the King's coronation Westminster Abbey was profusely adorned with flowers: flowers are not permitted on or above a Roman altar, and there was not a flower in St Peter's today except a few formal bunches carried in one of the processions. At quite ordinary church functions in England or France you see blazing clusters of hundreds of candles: today, apart from a few extra carried in procession, there were only seventeen candles alight in the whole of St Peter's — seven on the high altars, eight about the crypt, two before St Peter's statue.'

None the less, this was one of the most magnificent ceremonies I have ever attended; nor was there any need either to embroider the facts or to demythologise. As the Pope was carried in and the 40,000 people packed into St Peter's cheered and clapped, we really did witness that astonishing encounter of which I had read: 'Three times the procession halted, the Pope rested from his gestures of blessing. Three times the Master of Ceremonies turned to face the Pope, set fire to tow in a tall portable silver burner. The flame blazed up splendidly for a moment; died swiftly to ashes. Three times, as it died, the Master of Ceremonies cried, in a low voice, '*Pater Sancte, sic transit gloria mundi.*'

Early in the Mass which followed, chasubled dignitaries went up to the Pope's throne to do him homage. This I described with my customary precision: 'Cardinals kissed the Pope's foot and hand; archbishops and bishops kissed his foot and knee; mitred abbots his foot only.'

A newspaper description of such a function had to be one long purple passage. The piece that I telephoned to London, sitting on my hotel bed, was one of the longest I ever wrote for the *Express* and I think one of the best. (It was praised for its accuracy in some of the English Roman Catholic reviews.) Communications are so fallible that I was glad to find that only one word had been mis-heard: 'rode' (of the Pope in the *sedia gestatoria*) was printed 'rolled'. This hardly mattered.

The frantic scene on the steps outside afterwards was described thus by Hugh Walpole in *Roman Fountain*:[1]

> Policemen had been driving back the front rows, and the back rows were pressing forward. The women began to scream. The pressure grew more active. The great mass became rhythmical as though following music. A townsfellow behind us began to shout as though demented: 'Basta! Basta!'
>
> I had been in many many crowds and I knew well that moment when one sets one's shoulders and presses back with one's calves, laughing good-humouredly, calling out to people to keep calm. But, quite suddenly now, there was no good-humour at all. People began to strike with their hands. The huge monk with the beard turned furiously to the man who was shouting 'Basta!' A woman began to cry that she was falling.
>
> And then I felt myself lifted and knew that I was carried off my feet. I was helpless and the sense of that was so ominous to me that it was as though I were about to be crushed to death.
>
> 'So this is the end of my Roman adventure!' I thought.
>
> I fancied that I had a last vision of Hilaire Belloc, lifted up, transcended, in air, waving a sandwich. I heard people call out 'The steps! The steps!' I saw Tom Driberg in his elegant evening dress and white gloves, still smiling and courteous

[1] Macmillan, London, 1940.

although he seemed to be bent sideways. 'The steps! The steps!'

They were to the left of us, a whole flight of them, and if at the top of them people fell there would be a dreadful disaster to record in the evening papers of the world. I was being carried as though a wind drove me, nearer and nearer to the steps, and I remember that I thought, 'It's an omen. If we get safely over this there'll be no war.'

I saw a woman disappear. A great wave hit us in the back. I saw Driberg's white gloves. I slid. I slipped. I slid. I was almost down. I was up again. I rushed, as though I were eagerly greeting a friend, to the outer wall. I stayed, breathless; my waistcoat was torn, my shoes trampled to pieces.

I looked to the balcony, but the ceremony was over.

I never saw Pope Pius XII crowned.

Walpole, who did care a good deal for the English language, once told me that I used too many adverbs. I still do, but I cut out a lot of them from everything I write for publication.

These visits to Rome were among several memorable trips abroad that I reported on in the Hickey column in 1938 and 1939. In February, 1938, I went to the Middle East: that was the time of the Arab revolt in Palestine. I wrote serious interviews with Dr Weizmann, the Zionist leader, with the Emir Abdullah of Transjordan, and with Peake Pasha and Glubb of the Desert Patrol; visited Petra, the 'rose-red city half as old as time'; learned about the brutal tortures inflicted by the (British) Palestine Police when interrogating suspects or witnesses (details of which were deleted editorially); and spent the most curious evening of the tour – an evening on which two British soldiers had been shot dead by Arab guerrillas ('terrorists') – at a Hunt Ball at Government House, Jerusalem, residence of the British High Commissioner, Sir Arthur Wauchope. Here were 'no Jews or Arabs (except for the servants and the Jewish police band). It was immensely county ... the women wore long white gloves and carried little pink programmes with little white pencils. There was a good deal of Scottishness: Black Watch pipers performed ... Guests were carefully sorted out [by an anxious young ADC, I recall] for a reel

("*nothing* annoys H.E. more than an eightsome danced badly") ...
Hounds were paraded in the ballroom. The Hunt is called the
Ramleh Vale. They kill mostly jackal.'

This was a farewell party given by Wauchope, who was just
retiring. 'Criticism of his policy,' I wrote, 'is qualified by affection
for him personally ... He is small, slight, soldierly, with a large
moustache, a bald head encircled by grey fleece ... He doesn't
suffer bores gladly. At dinner it is a danger-signal if he says
"Speak up. I can't hear you." It means he hasn't been listening. It
is followed at once by "Don't shout. I'm not deaf."'

In grim contrast to this ball was a day in a military court. These
courts had been passing heavy sentences: a nineteen-year-old
Arab had got ten years' jail for being in possession of a revolver
and one round of ammunition. On this day, 'prisoner was a slim,
22-year-old Jew with an open-necked shirt, a self-conscious,
centre-of-interest smile ... He was said to have fired at a bus.' The
evidence was confused, but the man was sentenced to death. (The
sentence was later commuted.)

This visit taught me lessons about the Middle East which I have
never forgotten — the first being that all the long-drawn-out
trouble in Palestine began because, as District Commissioner
E. Keith Roach ('dear old K.R.') put it, successive British governments had 'sold the same pup twice'.

One evening I was in the lobby of my hotel, the King David,
when a young soldier of the Black Watch came in, bringing a
message. He was a sandy-haired Scot of remarkable beauty, with a
fair, freckled skin. I asked him how soon he would be off duty and
if he would like to come back for a drink. He was very ready to
do so. I adopted a device which I have often used in hotels whose
receptionists or porters begrudge one the company of one's
friends. I addressed an envelope to myself, wrote on it 'To be
delivered personally', gave it to John — (for that was his name), and
went to my room. Half-an-hour later he was with me, stripping
impatiently: he had had no sex for some time, and offered just the
right combination of lust and affection. He was also unusually
articulate: when our passions were partially assuaged, he leaned
back on the pillow and said in his Scottish accent, gnomically:
'Only sissies like women ... Real men prefairr male flesh.'

I have mentioned my two visits to Spain during the civil war. The first of these was early in the war, when Madrid was still holding out against the Fascist siege. The other correspondents whom I saw most of included Tom Delmer, also from the *Express*, and Ernest Hemingway; with him was the brilliant American writer, Martha Gellhorn. I enjoyed Hemingway's company, and we drank a good deal: it is galling to have to record, of a writer much of whose work I admired, that I cannot remember a single thing he said. I think that Geoffrey Cox was there for the *News Chronicle*: in 1955, when commercial television started in Britain, he became head of Independent Television News, and later Chairman of Tyne Tees Television. The great tragedy of Spain at that time — one reason why the rebel Franco won the war — was the mistrust and divisions between the two main forces supporting the Republican government, the Communists and the Anarchists. Propaganda and press facilities were looked after by the Communists: of them I remember best an able and handsome woman of aristocratic ancestry, Constancia de la Mora. She wrote a book entitled *In Place of Splendour*,[1] and after the Fascist victory went to Moscow. There was a dark-eyed youth, Francisco Ramos, with whom I formed a romantic liaison. Our meetings had to be at night, in dark streets and doorways. He wrote to me afterwards once or twice, but I do not know what happened to him.

Equally unofficial during this visit was the purchase, for about £1, of a finely embroidered baroque chasuble, possibly looted (or rescued) from a church. That formidable scholar Sir Stephen Gaselee, who edited anthologies of medieval Latin verse, corresponded regularly in Latin with three priests, in Portugal, Transylvania and Italy, and was Librarian of the Foreign Office (and used to lunch at the Athenaeum wearing a top hat), had asked me to look out for some such trophy for him.

The circumstances of my second Spanish visit, in January, 1939, were very different. I had been travelling elsewhere in Europe; by pre-arrangement, at Perpignan I met two comrades from Fleet Street — one, Harry Harrison, was killed in the Second World War, one, Lou Kenton, is still around. They were driving a food lorry into Spain on behalf of the Printers' Anti-Fascist

[1] Michael Joseph, London, 1940.

Movement, a purpose for which we had for some time been raising funds.

As we drove into Spain we should have realised that the war was almost over and the government defeated; for, trudging up the road towards us and towards the French frontier, alone and carrying a pack, was a stout middle-aged figure whom I suddenly recognised: he was Alvarez del Vayo, Foreign Minister of Spain. (He was not, in fact, running away from Spain — only taking some government documents to safety in France.)

Our lorry was laden with food: 'Women with faces of agony stretched out their hands to us crying "Bread, bread!" It was horrible to have to say: "We are here to help you but we can't give you bread," and to explain that we had to go on to the central depot ... They clawed at the side of the lorry. Carabineers moved them on.'

We also carried a supply of insulin for diabetics — among them the chief censor, José-María Quiroga, formerly Professor of Spanish literature at Salamanca.

During this visit I became accustomed, for the first time, to being in air-raids, an experience which the British people were to suffer in the following year. Of one such raid I wrote:

We were in the street when the alarm went again. This time we were near a refuge, though only for splinters — a stout wall built in an aisle of an ex-church; we could see the sky, the distant planes. Where we stood there had evidently been an altar. On the wall above there was still a text: 'VENITE AD ME OMNES'.

It was far better here, huddled with a few dozen peasants, than alone in one's room. Three German girls joined hands and started to sing: old German songs, marching songs, International Brigade songs, a song of the German who yearns for the fatherland he cannot go back to. The peasants closed in round them; their brown anxious faces began to smile ... The raid passed quickly.

When we came out into the sunlight, I felt exhilarated. A raid is like that most drastic of hangover remedies, vodka with red pepper in it; it's kill-or-cure — at least if not cure, it does free you from pettier worries, desires, dislikes, grievances.

Again and again, in the blitz on London, I was to have the same sensation. It is part of a columnist's function to describe in advance what his readers are going to experience.

By this time Barcelona had fallen. The temporary capital of Spain was Figueras. Here, late one night, in the cellars of the old castle, I attended what must have been one of the last meetings of Spain's democratic Cortes:

The moon was up, but veiled, luckily, by low clouds; we came out of dark passages into courtyards over which the sky looked a pale bluish-grey; then, past armed sentries, down a staircase; they had not forgotten to put a strip of carpet down.

We came into a vast, echoing, round-vaulted crypt, with roughly whitewashed walls and pillars. Part of it was set apart for Parliament's meeting. There was some semblance of pomp — carpets, gilt chairs, a table hung with red brocade, the Republican colours above it. Naked electric bulbs, hastily rigged up, shone overhead; Parliament was only an oasis in this long, cathedral-like cavern, in whose dim aisles soldiers sat about smoking.

At the red brocade table sat the 'Speaker' and four vice-presidents (who stood while he spoke, sitting). At a table below them sat official note-takers; one, a woman, had propped her handbag against the red brocade. Opposite us, on one long bench, at the Speaker's right, sat twelve Ministers — Negrin at one end, almost crowded off the seat, del Vayo next him, stout Minister of Justice Peña.

Few Parliaments have ever met in more dramatic circumstances. Negrin read the first part of his speech quietly. He seemed less exuberant than when I had talked to him a few days before.

Del Vayo looked, for him, worried. Peña yawned, doodled, rubbed his eyes, chewed his pencil.

Negrin, still reading, passed his hand over his eyes and back over his hair, as if tired. Then he paused, got away from his script, began strolling as he spoke. Fire came into his voice. He thumped the table only once — when he said that such was the arms shortage that soldiers were waiting in the trenches for the men next them to be killed, to grab their rifles. When he sat down they clapped loudly.

There were other speeches, mostly long. It was well after midnight before we got away. At the end there was a vote. Each Minister, each M.P., stood up in turn, announced his name, added '*Sí*' (Yes).

They were of one mind. The war was to go on. Then they shouted '*Viva España!*'

I have never been back to Spain since then, and have watched with disgust the rush by British tourists, including many working-class Labour voters, to help Franco's economy by crowding his repulsive beaches. (Okay, the package-tours are cheap, but so they are to Yugoslavia and Malta and other non-Fascist countries.) I may or may not be on some Spanish official black list; I could probably go there as a tourist – but then I might be watched, followed, and framed. So, having learned something of the courageous underground resistance to Franco at the Spanish Socialist Workers' Party conferences in Toulouse, I will wait until the Spanish workers have had their revolution. But I should like to find Francisco again; or his grandson.

There were at least four other foreign visits during these two crowded years of 1938 and 1939. In August, 1938, almost on the eve of Munich, I went to Prague and Sudetenland and watched the failure of the Runciman mission. Lord Runciman, a dim little man who looked 'like Stan Laurel just after he's been sacked', entertained the Czech Prime Minister, Hodza, to a long and boring dinner at the Alcron Hotel. The air was thick with espionage: the hotel head-waiter turned out to be a Nazi.

In April, 1939, Easter was a welcome break, at Boulogne and Le Touquet. I went with friends. On the Sunday we drove out for a country lunch:

> At Inxent there is an inn, with big, fragrant log fires. The widow Lechevin serves you a 3s. lunch which includes her own *pâté*, fresh trout, chicken, a light crisp pancake. While it is cooking you can walk down the lane opposite (by a villa called 'May Fly') to the quick, clear stream that the trout come from. Waxen yellow celandine grows beside it for your button-hole.

A crimson-faced goose flaps his iridescent inky-green wings. Across the plough, among the straight birch saplings, are magpies. A sheep's jaw lies by the path. The bridge over the stream is not 'rustic' but, sensibly, of concrete.

In the warm sun some fruit blossom is smelling strongly; there is already a summery buzz of insects.

Then, as we finished our coffee after lunch at an outdoor table, a great jangling began from the two bells of the small, white-walled church. The church is so narrow that the ringers were stooping and swaying in its very doorway, their muscles bursting through their Sunday black. As we looked in, the old priest lifted his biretta politely to us. Apart from them and the little red-cassocked boys lighting up the candles, the church was empty.

Ten minutes later it suddenly filled — as suddenly and 'from nowhere' as a town street-crowd gathers after an accident.

They sang Vespers, despite the competition of a stertorous harmonium.

In the casino at Le Touquet a piquant fragment of dialogue occurred:

A man whose red carnation buttonhole was outshone by his face tackled me. 'Wrote about me once,' he snorted. 'Didn't like what you said. Nothing against me, what? Didn't like what you wrote in your — hah — rag.'

'What did I say?' I asked, having no recollection of having wasted space on him before.

'Can't remember,' he said. 'Know I didn't like it. Don't ask me what it was.'

A few weeks later I went (for the second time) to the United States. Here I was too busy with specific enquiries and interviews to make any of the generalisations about the American culture that I made on other occasions. Having studied Fascists in London, I thought it would be interesting to see Fritz Kuhn, leader of the German-American *Bund*. He assured me that they had got no ideas and no money from Germany:

Kuhn, a bull-necked, heavy-faced but mild-mannered,

sprucely dressed ex-serviceman, has been in USA since 1924. His German accent is still thick. He is a chemical engineer by profession; leading his hundred thousand local Nazis is now his full-time job.

I use the term Nazis because their views, methods, salute, swastika emblem — despite Kuhn's 'no ideas' claim — are indistinguishable from official German ones. Above Kuhn's desk hangs a portrait of Hitler. A portrait of Abraham Lincoln eyes it quizzically from another wall.

'Anyway,' I said to Kuhn, 'you admire Hitler, you approve of what he has done? 'Of course,' he said. 'He has saved Christianity.'

After a moment's pause, to take breath, I tentatively raised the subject of religious persecution in Germany.

'That is just publicity,' said Kuhn. 'It is not so. Why, when I was in Germany last year I heard nothing of it. In my opinion Hitler has nothing to do with it. There always was a row between the religious people, even before the war. That's all it is.'

'Then why is it necessary to detain people like Pastor Niemoeller?' I asked.

'He has done something wrong,' said Kuhn, in the tone of one explaining a simple sum to a child. 'He has broken the law. He must have, or he wouldn't be in jail.'

So impeccable was this logic that I reverted to another topic — Kuhn's visit to Germany. I asked him if he had met any of the leaders while there. He shot me a sharp glance before replying: 'No, not one. It was purely a holiday.'

I reverted to his statement that his organisation did not get its ideas from Nazism. 'Do you accept the racial theories of National Socialism?' I asked. 'If one of your members, for instance, married a Jewish woman, would he be expelled?'

'Most certainly. I should hope so!' he said, explosively — then quickly added, 'I didn't like the way you put that question. We are not against the Jews. We do not want to deprive them of their rights. We simply ask that we shall keep our own company. For, after all,' he went on — and the lightning tangents of his arguments left me following far behind, dazed — 'after all, you, coming from England, should know even better than I do that the Jews are the root of all evil.'

'Why specially England?' I asked.

'The British Secret Israel Service,' he said, 'is the most powerful in the world.'

'The what?' I asked.

'The British Secret Israel Service,' he repeated, with melodramatically guttural emphasis.

'We never hear about that,' I said. 'I suppose we are not allowed to?'

'Hah! That is so,' he said, glad that I was getting the hang of it.

He also seemed surprised that I had not heard of a petition signed, he said, by two million Englishmen who were against war against Germany.

He believes strongly that America should not get mixed up in a European war. But he added that, should America unfortunately go to war on the opposite side to Germany, his organisation would, 'as loyal American citizens', take part. In any case, he added, only about half his members are of German origin. He has Scots, English, many Irish.

The subject of Roosevelt excited him so much that he almost forgot his syntax. I asked him whom he would prefer as President. 'Anybody is better,' he cried. 'Regardless who comes. Everything better than Roosevelt.'

Much more agreeable were outings to the New York World's Fair and Coney Island. These I took with the family of a friend I had met in Spain, where he had been serving with the Lincoln Battalion of the International Brigade. They were a Jewish family, living in Queen's, and they hospitably allowed me to stay with them when I found the Waldorf-Astoria Hotel intolerably uncomfortable. They told me that Maxim Gorki had once visited Coney Island and said that the Americans must be a very unhappy people if they had to have such a place to keep them happy. I disagreed with this uncharacteristically priggish remark. I also liked all the scientific gadgets at the World's Fair — for instance, the exhibit displaying the processes of birth. A bewildered-looking woman next to me asked: 'At what point does the soul come in?' 'I don't have that information, lady,' said the attendant. 'You'll have to ask the supervisor.'

Best of all was an exhibit in the American Telegraph & Telephone Company's building:

From long queues always waiting in there, a few are chosen by lot for the privilege of making free long-distance calls – the only condition being that the several hundred others can listen in by earphone.

This is really a beautiful stunt. It gratifies on the one hand the eavesdropper, on the other the exhibitionist, as well as giving careful out-of-towners, who feel they've been spending too much, something for nothing. Also, many of the chosen free-callers are excellent comic turns.

When I was there a stout priest from the Middle West had won a call. I think he regretted it as he stepped up into the glass-sided booth and the crowd, all earphoned, waited to hear him talking to his distant family.

His brother answered. 'Is that Martin?' said the priest. 'This is brother John. I'm speaking from the World's Fair. They give us a free telephone call, you know.'

'Why, that's swell,' said Martin. 'How're you making out up there? We're all fine, but——'

'Listen, Martin,' said the priest, with an anxious glance at us, 'be careful what you say. [Laughter] There's a whole lot of people listening.'

'What's that?'

'I said don't say anything special, there's about four hundred people listening in.'

'What makes you think so?' said Martin – and went ahead to talk about family worries.

Mother, it seemed ('You know how bad her legs are'), had 'fallen all the way downstairs and bruised herself up.' Roars of laughter from the unfeeling crowd. Then that business about auntie——

'Hey, Martin,' cried the priest, in agony, 'I told you there's a lot of people can hear us. Can't you hear them laughing?'

'No,' said Martin, obviously not believing a word of it.

Brother John was gladder than the crowd when his five minutes were up.

I can't remember whether it was during this visit or an earlier one, in 1937 (I think 1937), that an elegant New York gourmet, Lucius Beebe, took me to a male brothel kept by a Mr Fox. In my inexperience of such places I did what one should never do — liked one of the boys there, a tall blond Lithuanian with a superb figure, so much that I arranged to meet him outside and took him to my hotel for the night. I am usually a light sleeper; he must have got up very quietly, and early: in the morning he was gone and with him went an expensive pair of shoes, newly bought in London.

The only other brothel I have used in America was at San Francisco in 1942. It was a modest but clean resort, kept by a Mr Robertson, and incredibly cheap (for a 'short time'): one dollar for the room, two dollars for the boy. It was also reputed to be safe from intrusion by the police: this was because it was in the same house as a 'numbers' game which paid the local cops for protection. Some well-equipped trade was provided for the clients — Marines, truck-drivers and other delights of the 'butch' sort. (In such company I always think of St Mary Magdalen's motto: '*Deliciae meae sunt apud filios hominum.*') Mr Robertson was apt, like many madams, to be superstitious. One evening, I remember, several clients were waiting in the small square anteroom — but none of the boys. When we had been there for some time, Mr Robertson remembered a charm that he had heard of from a female of his profession: you peed on the stairs and burned a piece of string. I cannot imagine the origin of this homely magic, but it seemed to work: within minutes we heard the clump of several pairs of heavy boots on the stairs.

After the war, back in San Francisco, I went to call on Mr Robertson. Alas, the place was shut. I made inquiries. There had been a raid and — though a senator, a former client, had flown from Washington to try to fix things — there had been prosecutions; and Mr Robertson had died 'of a heart attack' under interrogation.

Despite these fairly frequent journeys overseas, most of Hickey's time was spent at home: it was primarily a London-based column.

Looking back over it, I find that it had a stronger political flavour, explicit or implicit, than, perhaps, I realised at the time. In March, 1939, soon after returning from Rome, I described the home life of a miner at Porth, in South Wales, who had been unemployed for seven years and was dying slowly of silicosis. I was taken to see him and his family by one of my local contacts, a Communist councillor:

It was as well that I didn't arrive in time for dinner. Neither Dai nor Gwyneth Davies had anything at all to eat for dinner today. 'You've come on the hardest day,' she said. 'Tomorrow he will draw his weekly 45s. from the Public Assistance Committee.'

But there was dinner for their seven children. 'What did they have?' we asked. Mrs Davies hesitated; then said, with a slight look of pride, 'Faggots and peas.'

Now faggots and peas is a great Welsh dish. Faggots are little cakes of liver or lights minced up with onion and bread-crumbs. My companion was a little surprised that this family could run to them.

'How much did the dinner cost?' he asked. She hesitated again. 'Go on, Gwyneth,' said her husband. 'Tell them all. It is for our help that they wish to know.'

'Sixpence,' she said.

She had been able to buy two faggots, one pound of peas. Later I weighed a faggot at the butcher's. It weighed $2\frac{3}{4}$ oz.; $5\frac{1}{2}$ oz. of diluted mincemeat, some peas, some bread, had made seven children's dinners.

'They're very hearty on bread and butter,' said Mrs Davies, anxiously. 'Sugar again—they're heavy on that. I don't take any myself, of course.'

Of the 45s. they get each week, 10s. 3d. goes in rent. 'This is a big house,' said Mrs Davies, again with a touch of pride. (It has four bedrooms.)

She is, indeed, evidently house-proud. The larder's empty shelves are white and clean. The brass kettle by the empty grate in the living-room is brightly polished. So is the brass ash-tray on the table. In a little vase are two vivid purple artificial carnations.

Then there is 2s. 6d. a week for coal. 'You must have a little coal,' she explained.

Which leaves perhaps 25s. or 26s. for the food for the nine of them – clothes being also a considerable problem.

The eldest child, a 14-year-old boy, goes to school a mile-and-a-half away. 'He's many times got to go without any breakfast,' said his father.

They are also proud of this boy. He is a scholar at the County School, which means the best hereabouts. Just now he is not going. 'It's his clothes,' said his father. 'His mother's trying to patch him together.'

'They dress so nice up there,' said the mother. 'It do break your heart when you can't buy them those expensive clothes ... '

I travelled back to London with another Communist – Arthur Horner, the cheerful and indomitable president of the South Wales miners:

Horner's hatred of Fascism is intense. The Communists held a big dance the other night at Cardiff's grandiose City Hall: it was the first time that dusky lovelies from Tiger Bay – Cardiff's Limehouse and Harlem – and boys from the pits, who had to be up at five next morning, had stepped out in such surroundings. (A marble St David smiled thoughtfully down on them.) Horner – still as staunch a Communist as before he had to mix with coal-owners – went to the dance. He flew into a rage, nearly walked out, when he saw a comrade who, with perhaps ill-timed humour, had come dressed as a Nazi storm-trooper.

In the same month I attended a Fascist meeting in London at which Sir Oswald Mosley spoke. I sat, of course, at the press table: this is traditionally neutral ground, but I was recognised and denounced by people in the audience. There were 'bestially savage cries and yells. It was difficult to distinguish the words, but I heard "Jew!" and "He's a Jew" and, from a witty woman, "Hickeystein".' Then, to avoid worse trouble, the stewards insisted on showing me out by a back door. I described this scene, and Mosley's flashy oratory, in detail, and ended by saying that, though not a Jew, I would rather be a Jew than a Fascist.

Two weeks later I was at an equally uncongenial meeting, attended by a rather more upper-class audience (for Mosley's Fascists were mostly *petit-bourgeois* or *lumpen-proletariat*). This was a gathering—a 'victory celebration'—of Franco's British supporters, who called themselves the Friends of Spain. I cannot remember which, but I know that it was one of these people who first described Franco as a 'gallant Christian gentleman'. Possibly it was Major-General Sir Alfred Knox, a Tory of the far Right; he spoke at this meeting and I noted that he claimed: 'All generals are not absolute fools'. Another speaker was Lord Phillimore, of a weighty ecclesiastical/legal family. I quoted him as saying: 'The God of battles, ladies and gentlemen, is best wooed with clean hands.' Franco was also described as 'Our generalissimo' and the 'heaven-sent chieftain'.

Apparently some woolly British liberals had been organising appeals to Franco for clemency towards the defeated Republicans. This was condemned as subtle Red propaganda—and a Spanish ex-diplomat who spoke at the meeting, the Marquis Merry del Val, 'his pointed white moustaches quivering with aristocratic rage', asked if the Republicans were to go 'scot-free' and to have 'an unjust immunity'. The ladies and gentlemen shouted 'No!'

There were a good many interruptions. When the writer Douglas Jerrold gave 'an unfamiliar line-up of European powers—"the four great western nations, England, France, Italy, Spain",' there were a number of shouts of 'What about Germany?' and 'Not France—Jewish-controlled.' The jolliest interruption was 'one which broke the pause after Merry del Val's flamboyant peroration. A meek little man (or so he sounded) got up and said (so far as we could hear) "Might a member of the public denounce you as traitors?"' He was thrown out.

In restful contrast to such ugly metropolitan manifestations were occasional weekends at Oxford or Cambridge. Once, at Gaselee's invitation, I went to the Peckard Feast at Magdalene College, Cambridge. 'It was a grand feast: seven courses, of which I liked best the snipe pie; five wines, of which I liked best the Cockburn 1900.' (The oldest port I ever drank was as an undergraduate in the 1920s, staying with Mr Sparrow of Albrighton in Shropshire for a hunt ball: on his table after dinner were two decanters of port—vintages 1849 and, I think, 1854.) The

Peckard Feast was held by candle-light: 'we are proud,' said my host, 'of never having allowed gas or electricity in hall.' Next day I was taken to Evensong in the Perpendicular-Gothic chapel of King's College:

> As we arrived the choir scurried in, panting, from the snow. A small boy with big spectacles, big top-hat, gown slipping off his shoulder, dropped a big book, said 'Dash', picked it up, hurried in to put on his red cassock.
>
> The chapel seemed vaster than ever in the darkness. Modern floodlighting might show its fan-vaulting more clearly; but there was no light except from the scores of glass-shielded candles flickering at our stalls. The choir sighed their incredibly expert pianissimi; the Gothic soared numinously into infinite blackness.

A bit earlier than this, I wrote a column which, for some reason, stuck in the minds of many readers: even quite recently, in 1975, somebody reminded me of it. It was headed 'My Double Quits', and it described how I went with a friend (who was actually a policeman off duty) to a South London music-hall where a young man had been passing himself off as William Hickey. (This couldn't have happened ten or twenty years later, in the age of television.) We met in the bar of the theatre, with the pretty show-girl whom he had been courting. First we led the impostor up the garden:

> It gave me keen pleasure to say to him all the silly things that are always said to me: 'What an interesting life you must have ... What a lot of interesting people you must meet.'
>
> He was admirably ready with the correctly *blasé* answers; said what a bore it was, for instance, to have to go to lunch today with Sir C—— C——, eminent arms magnate, instead of playing shove-ha'penny in the pubs at Putney (where he lives).
>
> Friend, recalling my visits this year to USA and Spain, asked about them. On USA, 'Hickey' side-tracked the talk to Walter Winchell. On Spain he said, 'Oh, I never went anywhere near the front ... '
>
> 'Oh, but,' said friend, 'I thought you wrote ... ?'

'You mustn't believe all you see in my column,' said 'Hickey'. 'Why, I might write that I'd had four light ales in this bar when I'd really had ten!' ...

The time for the Grand Dramatic Exposure drew near. I didn't feel a bit heroic; nor think him a bit villainous. His puny evasions made me sorry for him. I looked at his shabby coat, floppy felt hat, weak chin, rather pleasant face, nicotine-stained fingers. He was obviously just a fool. He had plenty of money; there was no question of any offence, of obtaining cash or credit by false pretences. But why pick on me? ...

I said: 'I think this has gone on long enough. Will you tell me why you are passing yourself off as Hickey?'

He did not look at me or the girl, looked straight ahead, said in a low voice, 'I don't know what you mean.' He didn't want her to hear, took me aside; made no attempt to bluff it out.

Within a few minutes we knew a good deal about him. I won't print all the details. He says he makes his money backing dogs.

'But why did you do it?' I insisted.

It was because of the girl. 'I wanted to *be* somebody,' he said.

'Be yourself,' I said.

After some further sententious advice, my friend and I took him to the West End for a few drinks. The friend said goodnight. The impostor came home to my mews-flat in Kensington, where a more intimate identification occurred.

9

Against the law

By the autumn of 1935 I had been on the *Express* for more than
seven years, for several of which I had been running my own
column. My name was, therefore, becoming known in Fleet Street,
though the *Express* device of pseudonymity ensured that it would
be known to few outside. Over the years it gradually became known
more widely that I 'was' William Hickey (should the quotation-
marks go round the 'was' or the pseudonym?), but this process had
not gone far by 1935 – for me, as I was to learn, unfortunately.

One night, well after midnight, I was walking through Cran-
bourn Street, about to take a taxi home to Queen's Gate Place
Mews. On the corner of that street I was stopped by two men, the
older of them – dark and ruddy-faced – about thirty years old, the
other a good deal younger, also dark but less dour and with more
charm than his mate. The older one, in a strong Scottish accent,
asked me if I could tell them of any place where they could get a
night's lodging. I mentioned one or two of the obvious places –
Rowton House, the Salvation Army – but these were ruled out,
either because it was too late for them to get in, or because these
places were full, or because the men were, understandably, choosy:
they knew how, literally, lousy such places could be. They were
decent men, anxious to work but caught in the disaster of mass-
unemployment, Scots who had been driven south, like thousands of
others, in search of a living. I questioned them, and learned that
they were unemployed miners.

By a coincidence, I had at that time been involved in fierce
political arguments in the *Express* office: as a Communist, I

condemned the Tory government for the miseries of the unemployed; I had seen something of these miseries in South Wales; and I had argued that the situation in the Scottish coalfields deserved a full-length eye-witness article, either by myself or, perhaps preferably, by the industrial correspondent (whom I believed to be at least sympathetic with Labour). Here, in these two men met by chance, were witnesses who might carry more conviction than I had if I were to present them to my colleagues, the news editor or the features editor. It was also genuinely difficult, at this time of night, to advise them where to go; and it was not a warm night. After some minutes of conversation, I told them that there was room at my place and invited them home. It was an invitation that I was to regret.

Most people's motives are mixed, a lot of the time. It is impossible to analyse one's own motives for an action taken spontaneously forty years ago. I know that the professional and political consideration — possible favourable publicity for the miners' cause — was present in my mind. If I were required to say with absolute certainty today whether I would have taken these men home if they had been elderly and unattractive men — with, maybe, just as moving a story to tell — I suspect that I should have to answer No. But that may be because I know my own character and motivation better now than I did then. Both motives may have been there: I am sure that the more 'respectable' one was. (It must also be remembered that I was then much more diffident and self-conscious, and less reckless, than I have become.)

We took a taxi home, and talked for an hour or two. Then arose a question to which I had not given enough forethought: where were they to sleep? I had said that I had 'room', but I had not *rooms*, in the sense of spare bedrooms. My mews dwelling had a living-room on the ground floor, with a large sofa and easy chairs: upstairs, in my bedroom, was the only available bed, slightly wider than an ordinary single bed. Despite my earlier experiences in Soho — which had given me a fairly low view of human nature — I did not trust my own judgment of the character of two strangers who had been under stress and might yield to temptation. I had a few things just worth stealing; rightly or wrongly — almost certainly, with hindsight, wrongly — I thought it better not to leave the two of them to spend the rest of the night together downstairs.

I will call my guests by their initials, A.L. and J.K.R. (No risk of libel arises, but I see no reason why these elderly men, if they are still alive, need be reminded of an incident which they probably came to regret almost as much as I did.) I need not go into all the details – even if I could remember them – of the tedious discussion which followed, or of the dormitory permutations which were proposed. It is sufficient to say that we ended up, ludicrously enough, with all three of us in my bed, myself in the middle; that that was not, after all, the end of it, for presently J.K.R. (whose penis, I had become drowsily aware, was erect) leaped out of bed, and A.L. accused me of attempting to seduce one or both of them; that the argument was then resumed downstairs, but in a decidedly more ugly tone; and that when eventually they left, having agreed to let the matter drop, instead they went straight to the police and insisted on pressing a charge of indecent assault.

I slept for an hour or two, went to the office, and tried to compose a readable column. I did not yet know that L. and R. had broken their word and reported their suspicions to the police; I am sure that, of the two, the dour, no doubt Calvinistic, L. was the prime mover. But then Westlake, who worked for me at the time, living in, rang me at the *Express* and said that the police had 'been round' making enquiries and would like to see me at the mews at seven o'clock that evening. Such a message fills anybody – certainly any homosexual, at that time or even now – with foreboding; but I was not seriously disturbed. I assumed that there would be a few slightly awkward questions, to which I could give satisfactory answers; and that would be that.

There were no questions (other than one to establish my identity). When Westlake showed the two policemen in, the senior of them, having asked this identifying question, immediately arrested me, correctly citing the often (in fiction) incorrectly quoted formula: anything I said 'will be taken down and may be used in evidence'. All that I said (and it was duly taken down) was 'Fantastic!' It did indeed seem fantastic that the night's happening, which had begun, at least in part, as a genuinely professional and friendly exercise, should have led me into this alarming personal crisis. (Indeed, from then on for some weeks I seemed to be living in a world of fantasy, in a dazed nightmare; it was probably as well that I had to go on writing my column daily, and certainly as well that I had some good friends – notably Frank Owen – to help sustain me.

Then the two policemen escorted me to Kensington police station. I knew of no suitable solicitor whom I could telephone to at this hour; so I could not be bailed out, and spent the night in a cell; and in the morning was taken with others in a 'Black Maria' to West London Magistrates' Court. (I had not previously known that these vehicles, which I had often seen from outside, were divided by metal partitions into narrow spaces in each of which there was room for one person to stand.) I had by now contacted a solicitor; on his advice I pleaded 'Not guilty' and was remanded on bail to the Central Criminal Court.

I at once went to the editor of the *Daily Express*, who was then Arthur Christiansen, and told him what had happened. I also went to see Lord Beaverbrook, who helped me in two ways: with enough money to cover the cost of my defence (since I had a leading counsel, J. D. Cassels, K.C., this came to something like £600); and by ensuring, so far as he could, that nothing about the case should appear in the press (which was, fortunately, full of the General Election at which Baldwin was returned to power). In theory and in principle, I deplore such suppression of news, if what is kept out is newsworthy (which my trial perhaps, just marginally, was); but I am bound to admit that when it is something which concerns one personally, the suppression is jolly welcome. Beaverbrook was able to get the message to most of the newspaper proprietors, though I had to go to see the editor of the *News of the World* myself. (It was a reciprocal courtesy: Lady Astor, for one, had successfully appealed to Beaverbrook to prevent his papers from publicising the imprisonment on a homosexual charge of her son, Bobbie Shaw.) In my case, my special anxiety was that my mother, now a widow of nearly seventy, should not hear about the case. If only I had known her better, and she had been younger, I could have discussed it with her objectively; but this was impossible. So far as I am aware – and she could hardly have hidden the knowledge – she never did learn about it. The only mention of my name in print was in the official 'calendar' of cases in *The Times*. But that was in very small print and merely read 'A.L. and J.K.R. *versus* T. E. N. Driberg'. and if anybody had pointed this out to her, I was going to say that it was merely some

Tom Driberg as a young man

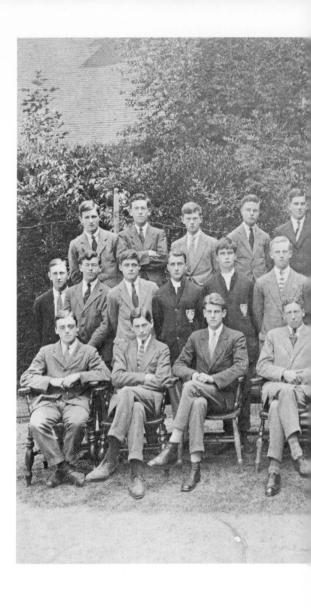

J. F. Roxburgh (centre of the front row) with his Sixth Form, Lancing, summer 1921.
In the back row Tom Driberg is second from the left, with Evelyn Waugh third from
the left and A. H. Molson, later Lord Molson, fourth.

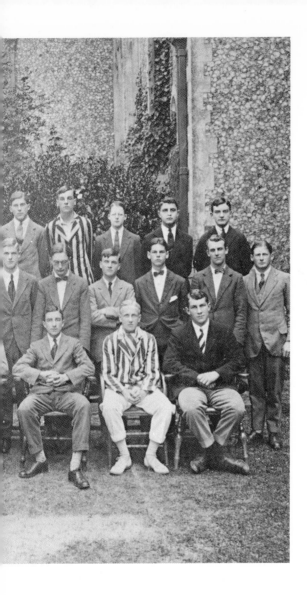

John Trevelyan, later Secretary of the British Board of Film Censors, is in the blazer, fourth from the right, and M. E. L. Mallowan, later Sir Max Mallowan, the archaeologist and husband of Agatha Christie, is at the end of the row on the right

(*Right*) **Alan Jones, 'the exaggeratedly Welsh' night news editor of the** *Daily Express*

(*Below*) **At a Mayfair fashion show, April 1933. Tom Driberg sits next to Lady Pamela Smith, later Lady Hartwell. Also in the photograph Mrs Archie Campbell, Mrs Somerset Maugham, Miss Olga Lynn and Mr Philip Kindersley**

(*Above*) **Guy Burgess and Tolya in Moscow**

(*Right*) **On television with Dame Edith Sitwell, November 1962** (*BBC*)

(*Below*) **'William Hickey fights a by-election.' Campaigning as an Independent in Maldon, 1943**
(*Radio Times Hulton Picture Library*)

(Above) With Harold Wilson at the 1955 Labour Party Conference in Margate

(Radio Times Hulton Picture Library)

(Below) Leaving for the 1963 Scarborough Conference with Jennie Lee and Anthony Wedgwood Benn

(Keystone Press Agency)

(*Above*) **With Pandit Nehru**

(*Right*) **With King Hussein of Jordan**
   (*Keystone Press Agency*)

(*Below*) **With Pope Paul VI**

(*Above*) **Talking to Barbara Castle at the Labour Party Conference, 1971**

(*Below*) **Tom Driberg's home for many years, Bradwell Lodge, Essex.**

debt that I had overlooked (though that would have shocked her enough: she had what such people call 'a horror of debt'). I do not know how much she surmised about my character. By her later years she had given up the nonsense about finding a nice girl and settling down. Once, not at the time of this court case, she left at my flat, by hand, an envelope containing only one leaf from a daily tear-off calendar, bearing the text:

> Avoid society which is likely to mislead you; flee from the shadow of sin.
>
> NEWMAN

So she may have rumbled something (or merely been distressed by some worldly crack in my column).

The period which I have called one of dazed nightmare between the lower and the higher court hearings, numb though I felt, was not painless: conferences with lawyers, curious glances in the office, invitations that I thought I'd better refuse, apprehensions of the worst ... The detective-sergeant who had arrested me kept in touch with me, and we became friendly. (He was later promoted to a senior position at the Yard.) One day he asked me to take him to the *Express* office and introduce me to a senior executive: I suppose he wanted to check on my position there. I took him to the room of E. J. Robertson, the general manager, and left him there. When he came out, his face registered amazement, and he said, in a low voice of great intensity: '*Why didn't you tell us who you were?*' Apparently Robertson, besides saying that I was a 'most valuable' member of the staff, had also told him that I did the Hickey column. The implication of what he said was clear: had the police known what he now knew, I would not have been arrested. The detective-sergeant had already told me that when the two Scots had first put in their complaint, they had been advised to go away and think it over. But they had returned in an obstinately determined frame of mind. Had the police then known that the charge would be against a leading columnist on a national newspaper, the Scots would have been given the same advice, much more rudely. Some time later Beaverbrook told me that he had discussed the case with the Lord Chief Justice, Lord Hewart, himself: Hewart had told him that he understood that 'it had all been a mistake'. Some of the implications of this, and of the detective-sergeant's remark, are disturbing; but – as with the suppression of the news, I cannot pretend that I wouldn't rather have escaped this ordeal.

At any rate, by somebody's mistake or not, in the session beginning November 12th, 1935, I found myself in the dock in No. 1 court at the Old Bailey, charged with indecent assault. It was disconcerting to see that, in the time that had elapsed, my two accusers had joined the Army and presented a brave appearance in uniform as they stamped into court. I was still in a state of confused shock, from which I began to recover only when I was giving evidence and was prodded into sharpness by the feeble, almost senile, performance of prosecuting counsel. On the whole, the judge's interventions seemed to me sensible, and 'on my side'. As always happens to people not accustomed to being tried on criminal charges, I was amazed – and alarmed – by the casual way in which my expensive counsel came in late, glanced at some papers that he seemed never to have seen before, had a whispered colloquy with his junior and my solicitors, and proceeded to deliver what was probably an effective speech, for it may have been one of the factors that got me off. I cannot recall any of the rhetoric on either side, but I have kept, all these years, the following transcript of part of the proceedings, starting when I am in the witness-box being examined:

I am sorry my lord. It was L. I said that I hd nothing to own up to. This argument seemed like being endless. I was very cold and bored and irritated. L. sd very solemnly 'If you will own up we will do nothing more about it and not fetch the police.' I sd 'I'll own up to anything – to murder if you like if only you will get out and let me go back to bed.' They sd 'Well own up to this' and I replied 'I am sorry if anything happened unintentionally. It ws a mistake.'

COUNSEL: Had you any thought in your mind of acting indecently? — No sir.

Did you do anything which wd justify this charge?——No.

You were interested in the men?——I ws interested in the men primarily because I happened just at that time to be writing abt miners and there ws a considerable dispute in my office abt it. I thought I wd certainly be able to get first-hand information and I might have taken them to my office the following morning to get additional information and then have written an article on the subject.

Mr Cassels produced a newspaper cutting which Driberg identified as the article he hd written the day he met the plaintiffs. This ws passed to the jury. It ws not read in court.

COUNSEL: In your office you wd have completed your inquiries with these men and hd their pictures taken?——Yes.

You have collected stories in this way from all sorts and conditions of men?——Yes sir.

MR BEAUFOI MOORE (cross-examining): You are a journalist and know a great deal abt London?——Yes.

When L. spoke to you abt finding a night's lodgings why did you not recommend him to one of the places such as a Rowton House which you know so well?——I did. I recommended him to the Salvation Army or to a Rowton place where he cd get a bed for shilling.

Why not to Bruce House in Drury Lane which was only a few yds from where you were standing?——They sd they did not want a cheap place as they were afraid they wd catch something verminous.

You knew Bruce House didn't you?——Yes.

I put it to you that you never mentioned the place?—— I have sd sir that I suggested the Salvation Army and a Rowton House.

There were two reasons why you took these men to your home and one was philanthropy?——I was in a genuine dilemma as to where they cd go.

And the other was that you thought you could get some useful copy from them for a story?——Yes.

Two or three in the morning is not the suitable time to get copy?——It was actually I think 1.30. I had as a matter of fact accumulated a certain amount of information from them. I intended to accumulate more detail next day.

Would it not have bn better to make an appointment with them for the next day?——I might have done if I cd have thought of any suitable place for them to go.

You knew they knew no one in London?——I gathered that.

I put it to you Driberg that if you had an ulterior motive you cd not have found two more suitable and convenient victims?——Supposing I had had an ulterior motive.

These two young men stranded in the wilderness, friendless, and without a roof to cover their heads?——But I did not in fact have an ulterior motive.

They wd have bn very convenient victims?——I had no ulterior motive so the question does not arise.

One of them charged you with having that in your mind?——I don't remember that charge.

You agree generally with the evidence they gave?——Yes but not in many of the details.

I quite understand that you deny the indecency. Was it because you wanted to get rid of them that you owned up? You admit that you did own up?——Yes but in the tone of voice that I have described.

Why when you realised the accusation they were making against you did you not order them from your house?——I was constantly doing so.

JUDGE: Do you tell the jury that?——I told them repeatedly to hurry up and get out, my lord.

Is that ordering them out?——I did not use the word order but I said constantly Hurry up and get out of the house.

MR BEAUFOI MOORE: You did not say that in your examination-in-chief.——I think I did sir.

When you went into your sitting room after they had talked alone you realized what the charge was against you?——It was very indefinite.

JUDGE: You were charged with indecency?——Yes my lord or the preliminaries to it.

COUNSEL: When you returned to the room you knew what L. was charging you with?——Yes but you will remember he sd to me that he ws not suggesting I had done anything wrong. He sd 'I have just got an idea'.

Why did you not extend your Good Samaritanism further and let them sleep in your bed while you slept on the sofa?——I did not want to leave them alone upstairs just as I did not want to leave them alone downstairs. As a matter of fact it never crossed my mind to let them share my bed with myself on the sofa.

It would have bn kinder to let them sleep together with you downstairs?——I have already said that it did not cross my mind.

You knew they had only the clothes they stood up in?——I gathered that.

They had no luggage with them?——No but they might have left it in the place where they had something to eat.

It did not occur to you to lend them any pyjamas?——No. As a matter of fact I don't think I had any spare pyjamas that night.

Did you own up to the offences?

JUDGE: I have not heard that he has been accused of any offences by these men.

COUNSEL: You understood what these men were saying against you?——I understand what they were hinting at.

Did not L. say he had hd experience of this sort in Canada? ——Yes.

Did he not say the man's actions in Canada were similar to yours?——He said it began the same way. I told him not to be ridiculous.

Did he say he wd give you – a perfectly innocent man – the biggest thrashing of your life?——Yes.

Did you not agree to be thrashed rather than that he shd go to the police?——Certainly not.

It is not true?——No.

Did you ever say I am sorry for what I have done?—— When I owned up under compulsion at the end I sd that I ws sorry if I hd done something by mistake.

JUDGE: What do you mean by compulsion? You cd have opened the door and ordered them out at any moment?—— No my lord. They were threatening me with physical violence and with the police.

COUNSEL: Is that the compulsion?——Yes that is what I mean by compulsion. When they sd if you will own up we will say no more about it I sd I will own up to anything if only you will go away.

When you came back into the room where these two men

had spoken together the question again arose about sleeping. Did L. say he wd not sleep with you alone for £10?—Yes.

Why shd he say that?——I can't imagine. I asked him at the time what he was suggesting.

You can't imagine?——No because nothing hd taken place at all.

Did you go to sleep or did you pretend to go to sleep?—— I went to sleep.

What R. sd took place must have bn done then in your sleep?——I do not think it was done at all.

Then why did R. jump up?——I don't know why he jumped up.

They jumped up and went downstairs—a perfectly innocent man?——Yes a perfectly innocent man.

Did you plead with them not to go to the police?——I did not plead with them. I sd I don't see what good that wd do either to you or to me.

You were in your pyjamas?——Yes.

You actually went to the door to plead with them did you not?——I saw them to the door when they left.

Did you not say 'Is there any way I can fix it?'——L. sd that. He put the words into my mouth.

True or untrue it was a serious matter?——Yes I quite realised that.

No money was mentioned?——No, unless that was the suggestion when he spoke of fixing it.

That was your suggestion?——I have already said it was not my suggestion but L's.

What did you think they were referring to when they spoke of fixing it?——I am trying to explain it to you. L. sd what are you going to do abt it. It immediately crossed my mind that this was some kind of a blackmailing conspiracy.

That is the first time that word has been mentioned in this case?——And that was the only time that money was mentioned.

Driberg you are a man with a great deal of experience of London life ... Don't you know that the man who attempts blackmail clears off afterwards as quickly as possible?——Yes.

He does not go straight away to the police?——No.

I put it to you that it was because these men were disgusted with your conduct that they went straight to the police——? I do not agree.

It is not true?——No it is not.

Can you suggest why two perfect strangers should launch such a charge against you——*Mr John Moore (counsel for Driberg) submitted, quoting King* v. *Baldwin, that this was an improper question to ask.*

The Judge held against him.

DRIBERG: I am at a loss to answer your question. They are very simple people and I think they must have become vindictive after some misunderstanding.

JUDGE: What was the misunderstanding?——I say that nothing happened and one of them thought something did, because of the size of the bed.

COUNSEL: What was the motive?——That is all I can attribute it to as I have already sd.

When you were arrested you said 'fantastic'. When formally charged you said nothing?——No.

You knew what a serious charge it was?——Certainly yes.

Why when formally charged did you say nothing. Is that the act of an innocent man?

JUDGE: He had already sd 'fantastic'. What more cd an innocent man say? Is there any obligation for a man to make a statement.

COUNSEL: He made no reply, my lord.

JUDGE: That is what a wise man does – he keeps his mouth shut – when he is in the presence of the police on a serious charge.

COUNSEL: Very well my lord. [*To Driberg*]: You must have bn very hard asleep not to wake up when R. was tapping you on the chest?——But I did wake up.

Driberg then returned to the dock.

Albert Westlake of 5 Queen's Gate Place Mews sd he had been manservant to Driberg for the past three years.

COUNSEL: Is your master one who works very late at night and comes home in the early morning?——Yes.

JUDGE: Do you live there?——Yes.

COUNSEL: On the morning of October 23 were you in your

bedroom and did you hear voices downstairs?——Yes sir. It was about 7.30 but I cd not be sure of the exact time.

What did you hear Mr Driberg say?——I heard something to the effect 'Will you get out now. I want to go back to bed.'

Have you measured the bed on which Mr Driberg sleeps?——The frame of the bed is 3 ft 6 in and the mattress slightly smaller.

Next morning you cd tell that someone hd bn in the sitting room?——Yes sir.

MR BEAUFOI MOORE (cross-examining): You heard nothing till about seven o'clock?——After seven o'clock sir.

About the time you got up?——Yes.

Did you go down and listen to the discussion?——As I came out on the landing I heard Mr Driberg pass that comment. As I came downstairs I heard the front door slam and Mr Driberg came up the stairs.

Is it a converted mews turned into a flat?——Yes.

JUDGE: It was a coachman's place?——Yes.

COUNSEL: You were sleeping upstairs so if Driberg called out you wd have heard him?——I doubt it. I am a very heavy sleeper.

You did not hear the conversation?——I heard some of it when I woke up at my usual time.

The head of Driberg's bed is against the wall so that you can walk up and down on either side?——Yes.

JUDGE: In a mews flat you have a front door and then go up some stairs before you get into the flat?——No my lord. You go along a passage and then come into a hall on the ground floor about six foot square and then to the sitting room and kitchen. The bedrooms are on one floor—Mr Driberg's, a spare one not furnished which we use as a boxroom, and mine.

JUDGE: They are quite small?——No I wd not say that my lord. Mine is two yds by three yds, the boxroom slightly larger, and my master's slightly larger again.

What time do you go to bed?——I can never tell. Sometimes I am late when I am driving.

You are the chauffeur as well as looking after the flat?——Yes.

Colonel the Hon. Wilfred Egerton of 38 Albemarle Street was the next witness.

COUNSEL: How long have you known Mr Driberg?——About seven years.

Have you and your wife met frequently and visited him and dined together?——Yes.

Have you had many opportunities of studying his character?——Plenty.

How have you found him?——Perfectly honourable.

Would you say——

JUDGE: This is not proper evidence. It is not a question of how he has found him.

COUNSEL: I submit it is. [*To witness*]: What is his character among his friends?——Excellent.

MR BEAUFOI MOORE: Beyond the times you have occasionally met him, you know nothing of his habits?——No.

JUDGE: By asking that question learned counsel for the prosecution now lets him give the evidence that I had to exclude from the defence.

WITNESS: I have always found him most honourable and a perfect gentleman.

Lord Sysonby of St James's Palace said he had known Driberg for ten years.

COUNSEL: You meet him frequently?——Yes.

What is his reputation?——Exemplary.

There was no cross examination.

I attribute my acquittal to the evidence of these two character witnesses as much as to any other factor. Colonel Egerton was a wonderful figure from Edwardian times – a brother of Lord Ellesmere, a dandy who always wore a high stiff collar whose points were not bent back; tall, ramrod-straight, eminently 'distinguished-looking', with a carefully brushed silver-grey moustache. He and his wife had been hospitable to me: on many Sundays I used to lunch with them at their house. Lord Sysonby had been Gaspard Ponsonby, son of Sir Frederick Ponsonby, private secretary to successive monarchs: hence the address in St James's Palace – on the recital of which one could sense a delicious *frisson* running through the collective consciousness of the jury. These admirable men reached their indubitably just verdict fairly quickly, though it seemed to me to take them a long time. This is the worst bit: they take you down to a cell below the court while the jury are out. The best bit is to hear the golden words 'Not guilty', and suddenly to be out of the dock and surrounded by a crowd of colleagues congratulating you; for of course they all knew about it. The only comment in print was in the trade paper, the *World's Press News*, and it didn't mention my name. The Hickey column at that time was headed 'These Names Make News', and this comment ran:

> That was a curious case that Fleet Street was talking about last week. Not all names make news.

I didn't mind that joke at all. What I did rather mind — since the case lasted more than one day — was having to go back to the office, on bail, each afternoon when the Court rose and write a light-hearted Hickey column.

I have often reflected on the series of chances which enabled me, less than seven years after standing in the dock at the Old Bailey, to become a Member of Parliament. I have yet to describe how this came about. Here I mention it simply to try to dispose of the notion that, because I was in this respect exceptionally lucky, there is no discrimination against homosexuals in public life. During my years in the Commons, large numbers of M.P.s, including Ministers, were involved in divorce actions, often as 'guilty' parties: the experience may have been personally painful, but it did them no harm at all in the eyes of the world or their constituents. One — Anthony Eden — even became Prime Minister after going through the divorce court and remarrying (and thus, ironically, became responsible for the appointment of the bishops of a Church which does not recognise the right of the divorced to remarry in a former partner's lifetime). But no homosexual M.P. — and there have been a few, again including Ministers — has survived the shadow of public scandal.

One back-bench M.P., who had visited two public lavatories on his way to a Council meeting, merely smiled at a youth in the second lavatory: he was prosecuted, convicted, and forced to resign from Parliament. A junior Minister, who had committed no offence, was regarded as guilty of an indiscretion: he had to resign office, though remaining an M.P. It is clear that, with rare exceptions, any extra-marital sexual activity is 'scandalous' *only* when it is homosexual.

In the often ridiculous document called an election address, which every candidate issues, such details as 'Married, with two children' are usually included, and there is a corner for a cosy contribution by the candidate's wife. In a civilised society, tolerant of minorities, it ought to be possible – if these private details were thought by a candidate to be publicly relevant – for a male or female homosexual candidate to print in an election address such words as 'Homosexual, enjoying stable relationship with structural engineer', or 'with sub-postmistress', or whatever. If I had thought the electors entitled to such intelligence when I first stood for Parliament, I should have had to put 'Homosexual, promiscuous', and I don't think there would have been many votes in that.

I must also add that, if the news of my trial had not been kept out of the papers, it would have come up when I stood for Parliament and, even though I had been acquitted, my chances would have been damaged. As it was, political enemies tried to start what is called a 'whispering campaign' against me. One of these, a well-known lawyer who lived a few miles from me, presumably knew about the Old Bailey trial. He broke the news of my, to him, unnatural tendencies to three families, of varying degrees of sophistication, in my own parish. One family did not understand what he meant; the second did not believe him; the third didn't mind. Such campaigns of personal vilification often misfire. None the less, a would-be M.P. who had been exposed to one of them is less likely to be selected as a candidate by one of the major parties. (I was not so selected until I had been an Independent M.P. for three years.)

As had happened after my sacking from school, the fright I had had cooled me down – 'steadied' me – for a time; but fear of the consequences, penal or even medical, does not for long deter the incorrigible practising homosexual, any more than fear of the rope deterred the average murderer. If anything, I became more promiscuous after my election to Parliament, relying on my new status to get me out of tight corners. The narrowest shave of my

life — apart from the Old Bailey affair — occurred in Edinburgh,
where I had gone, as a newly elected M.P., to speak at a by-election
for the Northern Midlothian constituency in support of another
Independent, Tom Wintringham. The meeting was a crowded one,
in the Usher Hall; no doubt we had the customary few drinks
afterwards. Later I was walking along Princes Street towards my
hotel. The war was still on, and the whole city was blacked out.
In such dim lighting as there was, one could just make out the
forms of passers-by — and I bumped into a tall figure in a foreign
naval uniform. One of us struck a match to light cigarettes. He
was a Norwegian sailor, typically Scandinavian in appearance,
flaxen-haired and smilingly attractive. He may have had a few
drinks, too: he was eager for anything, and perhaps lonely.
(Loneliness is as strong an incentive, often, as lust.) I recalled that
there was an air-raid shelter under the gardens a few yards from
where we were standing. Neither of us could speak the other's
language, but he readily came down to the shelter with me. Down
there it was completely dark, but another match showed a bench
running along one side of the shelter. There was no air-raid, nor
alarm, on at the time, so we were alone. In a matter of seconds he
had slipped his trousers half-way down, and was sitting on the
bench, leaning well back. We embraced and kissed, warmly
enough, but my interest was concentrated lower down, on a long,
uncircumcised, and tapering, but rock-hard erection; and I was
soon on my knees. Too concentrated, and too soon perhaps; for
in a few moments the stillness of the shelter was broken by a
terrifying sound — the crunching, very near at hand, of boots on
the gravelled floor. Instantly the blinding light of a torch shone full
on us, and a deep Scottish voice was baying, in a tone of angry
disgust: 'Och, ye bastards — ye dirty pair o' whoors ... ' No
concealment was possible: we were caught almost wet-handed;
the sailor pulled his trousers up over a prick that was rapidly losing
its pride, and sat forward, his face buried in his hands; and I stood
up, to confront a young Scottish policeman, of about the same
height as myself, with an older special constable lurking behind
him.

He wanted to take us straight to his station ('Ye can do your
explaining there'); but I (with, I am sure, a subconscious recollection of the detective-sergeant's remark at the *Express* office) said,

with such firmness as I could muster, 'First, you'd better just see who I am.' I was still on the *Express*, and had been equipped with visiting-cards bearing my name, the words 'Member of Parliament' — and, in the lower left-hand corner, the columnist's pseudonym. The policeman scrutinised the card gravely. Then he exploded. '*William Hickey!*' he said. 'Good God, man, *I've read ye all of my life!* Every morning ... '

After a few more exchanges, he turned to his colleague, the special, and told him to go, saying that he would handle the matter himself. My hopes rose a little, but it was not until he shooed away the Norwegian sailor ('Get awa' oot of it, ye bugger' — and get awa' the poor lad did, scampering out of the shelter like a rabbit: I still regret having had to leave that bit of business unfinished; but I don't suppose he picked anyone else up that night) — and it was not until this moment that I began to feel fairly safe, and suggested that we should continue our talk upstairs in the gardens.

So we did. He was seven years my junior, but talked to me 'like a father'. I lied to him as convincingly as I could, swearing that if he would let me off I would never do such a thing again; it worked. In twenty minutes of so, we were good friends, on a writer-and-reader basis. ('Ye must meet a lot o' interesting people ... ') His name was George Crowford. He had a ruddy face, and a markedly cleft, strong chin. I liked him and thought him attractive (but judged that it would be going too far, in the circumstances, to make a pass). When we said goodnight, we shook hands, and he even gave a — not too formal — salute. I was sure that it would be unwise, as well as wrong, to give him any money; but, having ascertained his address, I sent him from London, a few days later, book-tokens to the value of six guineas. I thought it thoroughly decent — and Scottish — of him not to pretend that this was a surreptitious gift, or bribe, in any way connected with the shelter incident, and to write me a literate, though prim, letter of thanks, telling me that he was spending the tokens on books that he had 'long coveted', I think some special edition, or a life, of Robert Burns. I have mislaid this letter, but have another from him, in the same fine calligraphy, dated April 7th, 1951. I had written to tell him that I was coming to Edinburgh again, and he replied:

Dear Tom,

It was with the greatest possible pleasure I received your letter and kind remembrances ... I have many times thought of you ... I will be delighted to meet you again ...

My interest in Robert Burns has in no way diminished ... I have on several occasions been given the opportunity of expressing myself and my views of the man, at a number of functions, an opportunity I have seized with alacrity ... I look forward to seeing you, D.V., when time and circumstances permit ...

                                        Yours very sincerely ...

We met and had a few drinks in a pub. The friendship neither receded nor progressed, but remained agreeably equable. Then, in 1955, I was shocked and grieved to get a letter from his wife telling me that he had died, aged forty-three. She spoke of his 'high regard' for me, and enclosed a cutting from a local paper with a tribute to him and a photograph of the face I remembered so well in its differing moods.

Because I had made this good new friend, the adventure of the Norwegian sailor — despite the sad frustration of the *coitus interruptus* — was much less traumatic than the encounter with the Scots miners had been. When I got back to London next day, I was able to describe the incident, almost as a joke, to at least two friends, Harold Nicolson and Bob Boothby. One of them, I think Bob, subsequently recounted it to Compton Mackenzie. Either Mackenzie had started on, or this anecdote gave him the idea for, a novel called *Thin Ice*, about the precarious life of a homosexual politician — and in particular including a passage that was clearly to me, based on my Edinburgh experience. 'Monty' Mackenzie was a man I liked, and a novelist whose books I have enjoyed, and I had no objection to his using this story, but there was one detail in his version which I did take strong exception to: at the end of his politician's conversation with the policeman, the policeman refused to shake hands with him. This was inaccurate, and I found it deeply offensive.

I was also sorry that Tom Wintringham did not win the by-election (the Tory defeated him by 11,620 votes to 10,751). He would have been an enlivening colleague in the House. He was a

Marxist who had been a leading member of the Communist Party; he had been an officer in the International Brigade in the Spanish Civil War and had written a good book about this called *English Captain*; he had been wounded in Spain and had married the woman who nursed him in hospital; and for this, because she was said to have the 'wrong' political affiliations (i.e., Anarchist rather than Communist), he had been 'excluded' from the C.P. I had sometimes stayed with him and his first wife during vacations from Oxford, and regarded him (as I did J. D. Bernal, J. B. S. Haldane, and, later, Canon Stanley Evans of Southwark) as a kind of *guru*. When the Second World War started, the War Office recognised his abilities and put him in charge of a school at Osterley Park, Middlesex, for training soldiers in unarmed combat and other unconventional techniques of war. Early in the war there was a great popular argument in the *Daily Mirror* and elsewhere (including my column) about 'spit-and-polish' and was all such bullshit necessary in wartime. I asked Wintringham why did he think the Guards regiments, which were the most spit-and-polished of the lot, were also among the toughest in battle. He gave an answer calculated to cause maximum offence to all concerned. 'Because', he said, 'broadly speaking, if you can't get proper officers, gentlemen make the best substitute.' At the time of his death in 1949, he was planning a major history of weapons of war throughout the ages, from a Marxist point of view.

I recall only one other brush with the police. It was a sordid little affair of a few minutes in the charmingly called Jockey's Fields, off Theobalds Road — another handy cottage (though risky because it had two entrances) which the bureaucrats have closed. This incident was mainly sordid because the younger of the two policemen involved acted as an *agent provocateur* — choosing, out of half-a-dozen empty stalls, to stand in the one next to me, and lying about what he was doing out at that time of night (on his way home from work in an hotel, he said). Initially there was vulgar abuse by the older policeman, but he calmed down and the matter was closed when I again used the formula that had been successful in Edinburgh — reinforcing it with an assurance that any charge would be hotly resisted, with benefit of learned counsel and the evidence of a genito-urinary specialist, if necessary in court after court, and

pointing out that magistrates do not always look kindly on un-
corroborated police evidence. The police like quick convictions, of
accused persons who have been foolish enough to accept their
advice to plead guilty. They do not relish having to spend day after
day in court on some piddling little case in which there is no
prestige for them and the risk of an acquittal.

So this line of argument is to be recommended to everyone,
M.P. or not, who finds himself in this predicament. The likelihood
that the night-wanderer will get into this sort of difficulty varies
according to the prejudices of chief constables; Manchester was
unpropitious a few years ago. When visiting a strange town, one
should look at the advertisements in *Gay News* and seek advice
from the local branch of the Campaign for Homosexual Equality.
The passing of the Sexual Offences Act, welcome as it was, really
made no difference to the problem of the lonely and promiscuous,
those who have not the gift, or the chance, of fidelity to one
partner. For them, the best solution would seem to be the licensing
of male brothels on a modest scale, run by respectable persons,
with charges strictly controlled – they could yet be 'free at the
time of use', as the N.H.S. was meant to be – such as I have
occasionally patronised in New York and San Francisco.

10

Phoney war and real bombs

In August, 1939, there were practice blackouts in London.
Describing one of these, I said that it reminded me of the closing
lines of Pope's *Dunciad*:

> Nor public flame, nor private, dares to shine;
> Nor human spark is left, nor glimpse divine!
> Lo! thy dread empire, Chaos! is restored;
> Light dies before thy uncreating word;
> Thy hand, great Anarch! lets the curtain fall
> And universal darkness buries all.

These exercises were just in time. On Sunday, September 3rd,
at 11 a.m., we heard on the radio the voice of that dull, grey man,
Neville Chamberlain, telling us that we were at war with Hitler.
I heard the broadcast at the door of St Mary's, Bourne Street; the
Vicar, Father Humphrey Whitby, had brought down his radio set
and delayed the start of Mass. His very English and matter-of-fact
reaction to the news made a good headline for the column I wrote
for next morning's paper: ' "That's that," said the Vicar.' During
the Mass, an air-raid siren shrilled. The Vicar said quietly: 'People
must do what they like – what they think best.' No one went out.
Remembering Spain, I moved with some others to a windowless
aisle. The Mass went on. We learned afterwards that the air-raid
warning had been a false alarm.

That column ended with the words 'We're all in it.' This was
not in line with the policy of the Communist Party, which did not
regard this war as a genuinely anti-Fascist war until Hitler was
crazy enough to invade Russia in 1941 (though in these first days

the Party's general secretary, Harry Pollitt, deviated as I did: despite all the horrors and suffering that we knew lay ahead, there was an enormous sense of relief that the contemptible period of appeasement was at last over). I have often wondered whether this deviation was one of the reasons why, a year or two later, I was expelled from the Party. This shattering news was conveyed to me in a curiously hole-and-corner manner. I was on my way to a branch meeting with the comrade whom I liked best in Fleet Street, a print-worker named Harry Kennedy. He had called for me at the *Express* office. We stopped at a pub for a drink; he was rather silent and seemed ill-at-ease. Then he said, in an unnaturally formal way: 'I have been instructed to inform you that you are no longer a member of the Party ... You have been expelled.' I protested furiously and asked why. Harry didn't know: he was merely a messenger. I went to see the most influential Party members I knew, Robin and Olive Page Arnot and Dave Springhall (who was later jailed for espionage). *Why*, I asked: was it because of sex? Or religion? Or something I had written in my column? They were acutely embarrassed but seemed genuinely as much at a loss as I. And there was no appeal.

As it turned out, there was one good consequence of my expulsion. When in 1942 I stood for Parliament as an Independent — obviously an Independent of the Left — I was able truthfully to tell the electors that I belonged to no Party (nobody asked if I had ever belonged to one) and would not join any Party without consulting them at another election (which was why I did not join Common Wealth when Richard Acland founded it after I had got into the House).

Until that traumatic message was conveyed to me, I was able in the first years of the war to conform pretty well with Party policies and to take part in Party activities. In particular, I played a leading part in an unusual form of industrial action in the *Express* office which was warmly approved of by the Party in so far as, besides safeguarding the interests of the workers, it tended to obstruct the newspaper's contribution to the war effort. More than a dozen different trade unions were represented in the *Express* building, each with its branch or 'chapel', and the more militant union members were always hoping and trying to create what was called a Federated House Chapel, in which all the unions could join for concerted action on matters of common interest. This prospect was regarded as a threat by the management of the paper, who obstinately refused to recognise or negotiate with such a body.

So, as a step towards our end, we formed an *ad hoc* body which we called The Federated Committee of Chapel Officials — i.e., it consisted of the chairmen ('Fathers') and secretaries ('Clerks') of all the union chapels in the building. I was the Father of the National Union of Journalists chapel, and I was elected chairman of the new body, the C.P. members in the building having done some intensive lobbying on my behalf.

We met and discussed the various problems — many of them arising out of the war and the blitz — with which we were all (genuinely) concerned. We wanted to see the management to discuss these problems. But the management — foolishly, as most industrialists would now agree — refused to meet us. How could we force them to? Then a brilliant idea occurred to us ...

At that time — the winter of 1940–1 — the blitz on London was at full blast. Quite early every evening the sirens would go off, and many people, especially the old and the children, would start making their way to the shelters, in accordance with government instructions; that, after all, was what the sirens were for. On most nights, however, it was some hours before the bombs started to fall; often they didn't fall at all near London. Obviously night workers, such as most of the *Express* employees, couldn't go down to the shelters as soon as they heard the sirens and wait there for hours. If they had done so, the paper couldn't have come out. Usually they took shelter only when they heard the bombs falling unpleasantly near at hand.

So, as the Federated Committee instructed me to, I wrote to the General Manager of the *Express*, J. E. Robertson. The tone of my letter was coolly polite, but it contained what must have seemed to him a dangerous threat indeed. The central part of it ran something like this:

I am therefore instructed to inform you that, unless you agree to meet representatives of our committee, we expect to have difficulty in persuading the members of our respective unions to disregard government regulations and remain at work in the course of air-raid warnings ...

That did the trick, as I knew that it must. Robertson at once agreed to see us; I took with me some of the toughest of the print workers' chapel officials. It was a stormy meeting: Robertson, usually the mildest of men, fumed and banged his desk. 'This is workers' control', he shouted, 'and we're not having it at the *Express.*' The assistant who seconded him was, oddly enough, Leslie ('Dick') Plummer, who later become a leftish Labour M.P., a knight, and a friend of mine. Between the wars he had been well to the Left; but in August, 1939, when the Nazi-Soviet pact hit us staggeringly, he burst into my room and exclaimed: 'You can include me out as a Friend of the Soviet Union.'

I don't know if any real good came of the meeting with Robertson; but it was an interesting exercise in a pressure technique.

Meanwhile, the Hickey column, adapting itself to the war, remained mainly home-based, as in peacetime. But when I went overseas, it was mostly as a war correspondent. The work of the best of the war correspondents — Alan Moorehead of the *Express* and Alex Clifford of the *Mail* were outstanding — was of immense value. They informed the reading public and helped to sustain the morale of the fighting troops. They were a kind of *corps d'élite* of their own, moving freely, in considerable style, from battle-front to battle-front and talking on equal terms to generals and to private soldiers, whose dangers they shared. (Later wars took their toll of some of the best of the correspondents: Ian Morrison of *The Times* and Christopher Buckley of the *Telegraph*, who once said to me, 'I dine with the Left and vote with the Right,' were killed in Korea; Nicholas Tomalin of the *Sunday Times* in the Arab-Israeli war of 1973.)

For the first winter of the Second World War there were few dangers to share. There was an unnatural calm: it was called the 'phoney war'. No doubt appeasement was continuing underground: strenuous secret efforts were being made by pro-Fascists in the West to do a deal, if not with Hitler, then with Goering. 'We're fighting the wrong man,' they used to say. When I went to France at this time, accredited to the forces on the Western Front, I was interested and somewhat shocked to find that a senior R.A.F. officer was billeted on the Prince de Polignac and his wife, and that they were still living in their château and entertaining this officer

and others to dinner in the evenings. The Polignacs owned the
Pommery champagne business. They were among the most
notorious of the pro-Nazi faction among the rich families of
France; the Marquis (his Christian name was Melchior) had been
president of the Comité France-Allemagne, which corresponded to
the Anglo-German Fellowship. Before Ribbentrop became a Nazi
ambassador, the Polignacs had employed him as a champagne
salesman. (He had performed the same office for a German
'champagne' family into which he had married.) Several years
before the war I had attended a festivity at the Pommery château.
The celebrations had included a ball for the vineyard workers and
their families. Princesse de Polignac, who was American, told me
that the head *vigneron*, who was a Communist, had actually asked
her to dance with him. 'What do you think I should have done?'
she asked me, clutching her diamond necklace with prehensile
blood-red talons. So now, in 1940, this fanatical pair – of whom I
thought the woman the more ferocious – were still going on about
the evils of Communism and lecturing young R.A.F. officers about
the 'wrong war' that they were engaged in. Because of the libel
risks, I was not able to print a full account of this strange treachery,
but I mentioned it to people at the Air Ministry, and I hope that the
R.A.F. officers who were the Polignacs' guests were advised not to
become too friendly with them. After the war the Polignacs were
tried for collaboration with the enemy, but with what result I
never found out.

One other incident of this wartime visit to France remains in
my memory, though again I could not write about it in the
puritanical *Express*. I had become friendly with a 'Redcap' – a
Military Policeman – and one night he took me to visit a brothel at
Arras which was reserved for the British troops. It was like any
other heterosexual brothel. The girls sat around downstairs; the
chaps came in, chatted them up, had a drink, and then went
upstairs with any girls they fancied. (Quite a few didn't.) Other
ranks could use this brothel up to 10 p.m.; officers after that. It
amused the other ranks to think that the officers were 'playing on a
wet deck'. I corresponded with the Redcap for a few years after
this, but eventually lost touch.

Some time after I returned from France, I was invited by Lady

Astor, M.P., to lunch at Cliveden — probably because I had used in print or in a speech the famous phrase, the 'Cliveden Set', and she was anxious to prove to me that no such set existed. In one sense she was right: as a hostess she was brilliantly catholic; her friends and guests included Bernard Shaw and T. E. Lawrence as well as Tories. But it was also true that at such crucial moments as Munich an inner circle of appeasers would gather at Cliveden and would plan some such infamous gesture as *The Times* leader which first mooted the carve-up of Czechoslovakia.

At any rate, I was glad to spend a few hours with Lady Astor, whose company I found stimulating, if painful (for she had a habit of emphasising her points with blows on one's arm with her hard little fist). Her prejudices were confused, her chief hates being Communism and Roman Catholicism: I could never make out whether she thought the Pope ran the Kremlin, or vice versa. She was an ardent Christian Scientist: whether or not she persuaded Chamberlain to visit a Christian Science practitioner, it always seemed to me that his policy of appeasement fitted in well with the Christian Scientists' refusal to recognise the reality of evil. I remember also her passionate antipathy to alcohol: once during the war when Churchill was Prime Minister and he had turned down an M.P.'s suggestion that there should be a milk-bar in the House of Commons, she got up, an avenging fury, and asked her right honourable friend if he was aware 'that *no* government had *ever* cared *less* for *temperance* than *this* government' (which was no doubt true, if by 'temperance' was meant, as it usually is, an intemperate loathing of fermented drink).

Though no wine was served with it, luncheon at Cliveden was good by wartime standards. Afterwards I talked with Lady Astor for a while: her slender figure and elegant bone-structure confirmed all that one had heard of her great beauty as a young American débutante. She showed me the manuscript of Lawrence's tale of life in the R.A.F., *The Mint*, which she kept in an unlocked drawer. I told her about my visit to the troops' brothel at Arras; at which she wept. Then — perhaps because I had told her this — came an ordeal which I had not foreseen. In the grounds of Cliveden had been set up, in a number of Nissen huts, a Canadian military hospital. She took me out to look at this, and without any warning led me into — the V.D. ward. Waving her arm punitively at the patients, she cried: 'You're a lot of naughty boys ... and here's Mr Driberg goin' to tell you so!' I told them no such thing: I merely thought what a handsome bunch they were, what a pity they had fallen (as most of them probably had) into heterosexual vice, and how clever it had been of Nancy Astor to trap me into this predicament.

During a fine weekend in September, 1940, I was at my home at Bradwell; several neighbours and I were picking a rich crop of mulberries. Suddenly we heard among the leaves above us a pattering, as of raindrops from the clear blue sky. They were bullets: the Battle of Britain had begun. From then on I wrote many descriptions of the heavy bombing of London and other cities. One of the first was of a night spent going the rounds of his parish with an East End parson, Father H. A. Wilson, Vicar of St Augustine's, Haggerston – a tall, nonchalant man in a black cassock, who 'permitted himself only one expletive, when a bomb fell too near: the appropriate "Blast!" ':

First he took me into his church hall, where a hundred or two people now regularly spend every night. Though of concrete, it is not technically a 'safe' building, he warns them; but they prefer its cosiness to the bleak, cold, unlit little brick surface shelters, some of which, in this parish, are still roofless. They smoke, play cards, play the piano.

In a corner of the floor a youth and girl were playing draughts. We picked our way among huddled groups; many were already asleep, wrapped in rugs. The vicar stopped to talk to a jocose old lady. 'This is the worst woman in east London,' he said, with an affectionate pat on her shoulder. 'She cheers me up a lot.'

'Bin 'ere forty years,' she said to me, 'and don't owe nobody a penny – through no fault of me own.'

At the side, on duty, sat one of the vicar's assistant curates, reading the letters of Mme de Sévigné, seventeenth-century French wit and beauty ...

Meanwhile, we called at an almshouse; the aged inmates were sitting up in a downstairs room happily saying 'he's givin' us a quiet night, touch wood' ... At a public shelter in

the cellar of a disused brewery — the safest place in the parish
— I thought I saw the vicar slip some sweets to an old
woman ... At a convent ... also a recognised public shelter.
Along its narrow corridors the people slept sitting upright,
crowded on narrow benches; one had to edge past them, now
and then gently lifting and lowering a tousled cockney head,
its owner too tired to wake.

The air was hot and acrid. In each room sat a white-coifed
nun; when raids get bad they lead the people in singing hymns,
to try to drown the bombs. Rollicking hymns go best. 'We
Fought the Good Fight about fifty times last night between
midnight and 5 o'clock,' said a nun.

Back at the clergy-house, I dozed. At 4 o'clock I was woken
by a truly terrifying explosion; confused cries and wails followed it. I fumbled in the dark for my shoes, got them on
somehow, went out. The vicar had been out and about all the
time; blast from this bomb (or 'aerial torpedo') had rushed
past him as he stood just inside his open front door. He
thought it had hit the crowded hall; it hadn't; he hurried in
there to comfort the people. An old woman ran past him
wailing, 'Oh dear, I think it's our 'ouse, oh dear ... '

In fact, the bomb had fallen some seventy-five yards away,
wrecking a few small houses. When we got there they were
carrying out a dead child. 'They're getting a young girl out;
she's still alive,' said an ARP man. Over the shambles and
misery an infernal glow in the sky shamed the first streaks of
dawn.

There were many such nights to stay awake through, not all
tragic. I formed a close friendship with two Canadian soldiers, S.
and M., and we used to roam the streets for hours, taking shelter
for a while only when the bombing got too near; sometimes calling
in at nightclubs for a few drinks; or going down to the shelters
under the Dorchester or the Savoy and scrutinising the rich and
famous sleeping in relative comfort; on several occasions, at dawn,
ending up near the Tower of London and persuading the man in
charge of a wine-vault to sell us a bottle, which we opened and
drank then and there, in the quiet sunshine of the morning street.

I wrote of the blitz in city after city — Liverpool and Wallasey,

Bristol, then the so-called 'Baedeker raids' on such cathedral cities as Coventry and Exeter. Strange how insignificant fragments of dialogue remain in the memory ... In the hotel-lounge at Bristol a dignified middle-class lady sat nursing two pekingese dogs and her knitting. When an exceptionally fierce blast rocked the walls, she said, 'Was that a *bomb*? ... It *sounded* rather like one ... ' 'M-m-m-m-m-m,' grunted her husband indifferently, from behind the *Tatler*. But the best blitz-time example of English sang-froid was a card which I pinched from my room at this hotel, and still have. On it is printed the words: 'If you wish to be called during an air raid, kindly hang this card on the handle outside your bedroom door.'

Then, at Exeter, as I walked up from the station at dawn after their worst bombing, river-haze mingled with the smoke from the devastated city: over the hedge of a garden bright with blossom, against bird-song, I heard a trembling, elderly, feminine voice say: 'We are glad that she saw the lilac.' Then I caught the sour, smoky smell characteristic of air-raids.

Censorship prevented me from mentioning the damage to Exeter cathedral and one unexpected reaction which I got from several townspeople – resentment *against* the cathedral: since this was a Baedeker raid, it was the cathedral that had attracted the bombers to their city. I think that this was a passing mood, natural enough in one whose home had just been destroyed.

Again and again throughout history these English cities have suffered through misplaced or perverted zeal: many of the ancient images of the saints have never recovered from the iconoclasm of the Reformation; the *Luftwaffe* was the worst of all; but almost as bad, since the war, have been the depredations of speculative property developers. To those who have not been in England for some time, London in particular has become almost unrecognisable – the worst vandalism being the crowding-in of St Paul's and the other Wren churches by high-rise office-blocks, and the building of similar monsters – hotels and barracks – on the very edge of Hyde Park, so that the park seems to shrink in size and lose its quasi-rural character.

The worst of all the blitz nights I remember was the one in April, 1941, that came to be known as 'the bad Wednesday night'. In the *Express* office they heard that Broadcasting House had been hit; the news-editor asked me to hurry along there. In fact, it had been a near-miss; but two firewatchers on the roof of Broadcasting House had been killed. Certainly it was a big 'incident' (as the effects of a bomb were called in official jargon):

A hundred or more yards from it the air smelt charred; drifts of dark smoke began to obscure the tiaras of flame that hovered above us, as in some hellish pantomime or firework pageant.

As usual, all the burglar alarms had been set ringing; nothing would stop them for the rest of the night. Scores of shops were wrecked; as I got near the incident I had to step over doors and window frames that had been hurled bodily into the road.

Wading at last through an ankle-deep porridge of glass and water, I looked at the slagheap that had, an hour earlier, been a block of – fortunately – empty offices. Less fortunately, one corner of it had been a pub; 'there was usually 20 or 30 of 'em in there about that time,' said a copper.

I was glad of living human company – glad when the ARP people stopped me, took me to see their Incident Officer. Half-sheltering in a ruined shop that was his office-for-the-moment (two blue lamps and a wooden flag mark it), he was a shadowy, lean, quickly-moving figure under a white tin hat. Henry, they called him. He used to make Savile Row suits.

Decision and a clear head are needed. Henry had them. In this half-light of flame and smoke there were even forms to be filled up and signed. A man came up with a form. 'CD driver,' he announced himself. 'Mortuary. Got any particulars about this body over there? Approximate time of death? Time when found? Sex?'

'Female, what's left of her,' said Henry.

Then the driver said, in his routine voice, 'Got any idea of the cause of death?'

'Well ... ' said Henry, 'I could have a guess at it ... '

'Enemy action,' I supplied, appeasingly.

Stretcher-parties were waiting. It would be many hours, perhaps daylight, before they could be used. The men waiting made the usual simple cracks – 'Just like old times' ... 'He ain't half cross with us tonight.' They coughed a good deal in the acrid smoke. One had been gassed in the last war. 'You all right, chum?, they asked him. 'All right,' he would gasp. 'It's only me old complaint.' They speculated constantly—with variations as wild as any untrained civilian's—on the nature of the bomb that had caused this incident; reckoned it was of the size and type nicknamed Satan.

All this time, intermittently, more bombs were swishing down. As they fell, or as a plane sounded like diving, we stepped back a pace or two into the gaping shop, crouching instinctively in unison, hardly needing to say, 'Here's another.' Again instinctively, with a protectiveness that might have been pathetically futile, the men would shield each others' bent shoulders with their arms. Twice, as we crouched, the blast—a foul, hot giant's breath—swept sighing through the shop, tore its way through glass at the far end.

A rosy judgment-day glow shone down on us. Some of the men moved over the road to a darker place. 'It's funny,' said Henry. 'When it's bright moonlight and they're overhead, you instinctively walk in the shadow … '

It was time for the Incident Officer to go and look at some other incidents; wardens, sometimes girls, had turned up, panting, but collected, to say, 'Incident in —— Street, between —— and —— Streets,' or 'They want help badly round at —— Buildings.'

His blue lamps, his flag, were moved to another street. We set off swiftly but circumspectly, skirting the buildings to dodge the tinkling shrapnel, pausing in doorways when we heard the death-whistle. There were some odd little freak effects of blast. It had somehow switched on a torch in a battered shop-window; we switched it off. All this time, too, the traffic lights went on winking meticulously, though no ordinary traffic was passing this debris-strewn way.

We looked in at several public shelters. None of these had been hit, nobody in them was worse than shaken. They all seemed to know Henry; the sight of him reassured them. 'What's it like outside?' they would ask. 'Oh, not so bad,' he would lie.

For the raid's ferocity had been suddenly intensified. Fires that had seemed quenched flared up again. New fires began, in every quarter of the sky; they even lit up pinkly the balloons floating high above.

We turned a corner. Henry ran on quickly. Ahead was a tall house, nearly every window alight with a cosy, crackling, Christmassy flame.

His face was drawn, agonised, in the leaping light. 'God!' he said. 'That makes me feel bad. There's a lot of old ladies live in these chambers—retired nurses and such.'

As good wardens do, the wardens of this district knew pretty accurately how many people are sleeping in a building each night. Henry reckoned there would have been 36 here.

'About 30', we learned, had been brought out alive, taken to hospital, some able to walk. Two, still in there, had been certified dead by a doctor. 'Which doctor?' said Henry. 'How d'you know he was a doctor? Where was he from?'

'Well, he was in a dressing gown,' said a girl. 'He came over from the hospital—said he'd be there if wanted again.'

Arguing fiercely that it must be possible to reach that room or that, where the fire didn't yet show, Henry dived straight into the house. The sparks danced about him; he vanished behind fallen, flickering timbers. 'Henry, come back, it's no use,' cried the girl who had spoken before.

It was five anxious minutes before we saw him again, on the stairs, helping two firemen undo a knot in the hose they were playing up the liftshaft. Their figures stood up darkly against the evil red light—three men walking unharmed in the midst of the burning fiery furnace.

Before we had begun to think that this night could be nearly done—so timeless seemed its incidents, so endless the tread-mill of its grim routine—we looked up ... and the light in the sky was not all from the fires.

The chill dawn wind fluttered burned paper into our faces. Already men were sweeping up the crunching glass. A big lorry switched off its lights as it stole past us: 'That's the street-barriers arriving,' said Henry. As thousands have said after a bad raid night, he added, 'It doesn't seem so bad by daylight, does it?'

There was time to visit his snug post, where a kitten played perilously with the iodine that was being dabbed on a warden's cut hands; time to relax in a canteen over a cup of tea.

Then Henry told me what his ambition had been: to leave ARP, to get into the RAF 'Oh, no,' his chief had said, you'll only leave the ARP when you go out in a coffin.'

I hope, and think, that the war will be done before coffins are carved for the men whom I saw, on the morning of April 17th, walking in the midst of the burning fiery furnace, and the fire had no power on their bodies.

Henry survived the war. I saw him, by chance, quite recently: he is working again in a humdrum job. I don't think he will forget that night and hundreds of others like it. The bombs of the Second World War were puny compared with the atomic bombs of 1945 or the bombs that may destroy us all; but the London blitz had its place in the history of that war.

One controversy in which I became involved at this time concerned the extent to which our bombing of Germany should or should not be indiscriminate. As a test of readers' opinion I printed a paragraph quoting a letter to his wife from a Briton in a German prison hospital. He wrote of a 'sweet little' six-year-old girl named Hilda who had been visiting him: 'she is never tired of perching by my bed and looking at the photographs of you and the baby.'

Ever since Chamberlain's first broadcast of September 3rd, 1939, official British policy had been 'We have no quarrel with the German people'. But Sir Robert Vansittart had been advocating, very ably, a tougher line, and to saloon-bar strategists all Germans were 'Huns'. Raids such as those I have described had intensified anti-German feeling. This biting quatrain has been attributed to A. P. Herbert:

> We have no quarrel with the German nation—
> One would not quarrel with a herd of sheep—
> But, generation after generation,
> They throw up rulers who disturb our sleep.

I therefore dramatised the argument by asking bluntly: should we bomb Hilda? (I think she should have been spelled Hilde.) The editor asked me to let him know what sort of response I got. As I

expected, it was strongly in favour of bombing Hilda. The score
was at first 21 to 1. After a bit more argument in the column, it
ended up 37 to 20 (rather fewer letters than I would have got if I
had attacked dogs or the Royal Family). Most of the letters in
favour of bombing Hilda were hysterically shrill and vindictive:
one actually said, 'We want revenge.' Others said: 'She will grow
up to be a Nazi.' They thought that I was being sloppily emotional,
whereas I thought that they were being sloppily emotional in
wanting to divert our bombs from essential military and industrial
targets in order to gratify their blood-lust. Their only rational
argument was that civilian morale *was* a military objective. Much
later in the war, they won: the obliteration bombing of Dresden
was an appalling atrocity and did nothing to shorten the war. The
best letter on Hilda — i.e., the one that most eloquently put my
view — was from an O.C.T.U. cadet:

> Indiscriminate blood-lust is depressingly common among
> middle-aged and elderly people ... Before I was called up, I
> taught in a secondary school. Nearly all the staff were in the
> fifties and sixties. They used to sit round the staff-room fire
> and work themselves up into a frenzy of hatred against the
> whole German people ... They found in the war a magnificent
> outlet for their ... bile, a compensation for the *ennui* and
> disappointment of their private lives.
>
> When I entered the Army I was delighted at the change of
> atmosphere. These young men ... for the most part bear
> hearts free from malice. You will often hear them express a
> desire for vengeance on the sergeant-major, but upon German
> women and children — hardly ever. Thank God the future is
> with them ...

Yes, but those young men are now in their fifties. Many of them
must have suffered disillusionment, '*ennui* and disappointment'.
Some of them may be among the magistrates who say: 'I wish I
had the power to have you soundly thrashed.'

Early in 1941 the *Express* sent me on a tour of Britain: no specific
engagements, just 'taking the temperature', so to speak, of the
nation and its workers, not staying only in 'posh' hotels (which
weren't so good then, anyway), but stopping, for instance, for tea

in a miner's cottage at Staveley. It was, I am almost sure, during this tour that I had an unexpected meeting with one of my closest friends, the composer Constant Lambert. I had come from Glasgow to Newcastle, and was delighted to find that the Vic-Wells Ballet, of which Constant had since 1938 been the conductor, was appearing in a theatre there that very night – with Constant himself playing the piano. (Owing to wartime dislocation, the Ballet was on tour without an orchestra: the accompaniment was provided by two grand pianos, one played by Constant, one by Hilda Gaunt.)

I can't remember what ballets they danced that night. I remember only that the evening saw the start of a notable literary enterprise – Constant's series of limericks about the bishops of the Anglican Communion, especially those with more than one place-name in the titles of their sees; the disestablished Church of Ireland is particularly rich in these, because so many dioceses were merged. Limericks were a hobby of ours: one of the best inventors of them was Philip Heseltine (the composer Peter Warlock), who had been a great friend of Constant's and had committed suicide. (Constant was deeply depressed by this loss; he composed his abrasive Piano Concerto in Warlock's memory.) As I say, I had just been in Glasgow and had noticed that the local bishop fitted neatly into limerick form.

So, without letting Constant know that I was there, I bought a ticket for the front row of the stalls, ascertained which piano he he was playing, went in early, and, above the music on his music-stand, placed a card on which I had written:

> The Bishop of Glasgow and Galloway
> Preferred Artie Shaw to Cab Calloway ...

He entered impressively, leaning on his stick, bowed to the audience, sat down, shot his cuffs, looked at his music and – it was a moment worth waiting for ... He knew at once who the culprit was, and we met for supper afterwards. By then he had completed the limerick, relevantly to the two distinguished jazz musicians whom I had named in the second line. I have the two cheap blue exercise-books (one, the rough copy, bought at Christie's, the other, the fair copy, given me on my seventieth birthday by his widow Isabel) in which Constant wrote out the whole of his 'bishops' series. I should like to have them printed: they are no more 'obscene' than the contents of Norman Douglas's famous limerick-book; and libel risks would hardly arise, since nobody could take seriously the attribution to these holy men of the bizarre vices with which Constant endowed them — for instance, in one of his neatest efforts:

> The Bishop of Central Japan
> Used to bugger himself with a fan;
>   When taxed with his acts
>   He explained: 'It contracts
> And expands so much more than a man.'

Constant Lambert was one of three or four friends in the course of my life — others were Dick Wyndham and A. J. A. Symons — whose deaths have left gaps impossible to fill: often it is simply something unintentionally comic in a newspaper, an ambiguous headline or a misprint, and one thinks how uproariously Constant would have laughed at it. He had a gift for becoming involved in extraordinary situations. In a contribution to a radio programme about Constant, his friend Michael Ayrton, the artist, gave a rather extreme example of this gift:

He had what he believed to be an occult ability to raise these happenings. I personally can vouch for an occasion in Albany Street, Camden Town, when Constant challenged those present to put on a show. Well no one could. 'Watch this!' he said, and round the corner of the turning out of Regent's Park came a compact group of Negroes of both sexes dressed from head to foot in tartan and all riding tricycles. 'The Mac-Gregor tartan,' said Constant with great satisfaction.

Sometimes this almost psychic gift took the form merely of conversational cross-purposes (and this may have been partly due to his slight deafness). Once he arrived to stay at a friend's house after a long and tiring journey. He was shown into a room in which music was being played. His host said: 'Ah, there you are. How are you?' Constant: 'A little *piano*.' Host: 'No, it's a new radio set.' Host's wife: 'If you mean that stuff like cough-mixture they give you in France, it always gives me a headache.'

Constant's life was always touched by fantasy. His own description of himself was: 'The only Francophil English composer-conductor, the son of an Australian painter from St Petersburg who worked on the Trans-Siberian railway, who himself can play "God Save the King" literally by ear.' That 'literally' is literally true: Constant could hold his nose and, forcing his breath through a punctured ear-drum, produce a credible version of the National Anthem.

In 1951 I was at Edinburgh for the festival. I was looking forward to hearing Constant conduct, that evening, his own exciting new ballet, *Tiresias*, and to having supper with him afterwards. I was walking along Princes Street when I saw a news-bill which said: 'Constant Lambert dies in London.' He had died, aged forty-six, of undiagnosed diabetes.

Anyway, that encounter in Newcastle, and the development of our limerick game, made an agreeable break in the sombre wartime scene.

11

American journey

Soon, in October 1941, came a longer break, in sharper contrast to
wartime conditions in London — the third visit I had paid to the
United States. The journey there was remarkable enough: it took
twenty-three days in a Norwegian cargo-boat from Liverpool to
Halifax, Nova Scotia. This was because, having set out in convoy,
to dodge the German submarine blockade, we lost the convoy in a
storm — a terrific storm, lasting many days, upsetting our small
saloon like a poltergeist: bottles of sauce and packs of cards sailed
through the air, clock-faces and cutlery drawers flew open, tray-
loads of crockery slid to the floor. When the storm abated and we
were alone, idle upon a painted ocean, the captain opened his sealed
orders and we took an immense detour to the far north, lit at night
by the radiation of the Northern Lights, pursuing a wildly zigzag
course: one day they told us, 'We are 100 miles nearer England
than we were this time yesterday'. I recalled Churchill's simile of
hours that 'crawl like paralytic centipdes'. But it was a salutary
exercise in patience, self-control, and mutual tolerance: no radio
(except for occasional news in Morse), no sex, no drink (it ran out
quite soon). There were only three passengers: I shared a cabin
with an *Express* colleague, Charles Foley, and though he used to
leave his toothpaste uncapped and I had equally irritating tricks,
we never exchanged a cross word. The food could have been much
worse: lots of tinned fishy snacks, and the inventive chef (whose
name was Saga) produced, after several days of severe rolling and
pitching, 'a greyish glutinous confection called butter-porridge —
thickly sprinkled with cinnamon and inundated with raspberry
syrup'.

After the blitz in blacked-out London and after this purgatorial journey, New York was overwhelming, Broadway 'a blinding chasm of light'. For Pearl Harbour was nearly two months ahead, America was not yet in the war — though I thought I detected signs of a brink-of-war neurosis. To me, as a Briton, there was warm friendliness from people of all classes in New York. (There mightn't have been in the Middle West.) Among the people I like best in New York are the taxi-drivers, or most of them. On my first visit to America I had made friends with one driver, a Londoner by origin, named Alan, and saw a lot of him: I have always, everywhere, found such friendships not only enjoyable in themselves but productive of valuable copy. So now, in the first taxi I hired, the driver as usual shouted his monologue back through the open window: 'You from England? ... Gee, it must be terrible over there now ... Gee, I hope Churchill kicks the shit out of that Dutch bastard ... '

But I also attended an 'America-First' rally at Madison Square Garden — a frantic eleventh-hour demonstration by virulent pro-Nazis and many thousands of their dupes. The most famous speaker was Charles Lindbergh, once a pioneer transatlantic flyer. Walter Winchell had called him 'the trumped ace'. That night's chairman called him 'that brave spirit'. By now, I reflected, Mosley was in Brixton prison: Lindbergh was still at large. He was unimpressive to look at; his chin, in profile, weak, and double. After the hysterical enthusiasm which had greeted him, his speech was an anticlimax. Unlike some of the other speeches, it contained no word of disapproval of any aspect of the Nazi regime: it merely expressed regret that Hitler hadn't had his way in Russia sooner.

I came across some other friends of Hitler when I visited Yorkville, the German section of New York, one evening — a foolish thing to do, for anti-British feeling was running high there. Unobtrusively as I tried to behave, my nationality had evidently become apparent to some young drunks a few yards away — a slightly Teutonized version of American college boys:

They had been staring for some time. They now began tossing little round cardboard beer-mats in my direction. Several landed on my table. I reflected rapidly: would the prestige of the *Raj* be furthered by my implication in a tavern brawl?

Clearly not. I signed several of the beer-mats; said quietly to the waiter, 'I think those gentlemen were asking for my autograph'; and conducted a strategic withdrawal.

On Sunday, December 7th, I was as unprepared for a Japanese attack as the U.S. fleet slumbering at Pearl Harbour: I was enjoying a leisurely lunch at one of the best hotels in Chicago, with a charming Russian pianist, Prince George Chavchavadze. Just after lunch they caught me with a desperate telephone message: come at once to the office of the British Information Services. The chief of this Chicago bureau of the B.I.S., Graham Hutton, had gone to the country for a long weekend. I was roped in to help his assistant, William Clark (later Public Relations Adviser at Downing Street), cope with a flood of inquiries. The first thing he gave me to do was to telephone Colonel McCormick, the formidable proprietor of the *Chicago Tribune*, who had been conducting a sustained campaign for staying out of any European war, and against President Roosevelt's 'interventionism'. The Colonel came to the 'phone. I asked him what line the *Tribune* would now take. 'Full support for the President,' he growled.

There was full support for Roosevelt in Washington, too, when a joint session of both House and Senate declared that a state of war had existed since the Japanese attack. At midnight, in a snowstorm, I flew from Chicago to Washington to attend this session. Washington was a fantastic hubbub of traffic jams, armed guards, and diplomatic comings and goings. I couldn't get a room in any hotel, and for the next few nights had to sleep in a cubicle in a Turkish bath. There hadn't been time to arrange for a ticket for the press gallery of Congress (which held 100), and newspaper-men from all over the world were clamouring for tickets; I knew I had to get in. Security must have been less sophisticated then than it has become: wearing an innocent look and my English accent, I said to the Marine who barred my way: 'There's a ticket waiting for me inside – I have to collect it.' The good fellow let me through. I have used the same stratagem once or twice since then.

The scene was undoubtedly impressive. When the speeches were over, the voting began; each in turn cried 'Aye' as his name was called. There was only one 'No' – from a woman Representative well known as a pacifist. In the patriotic heat of the moment, some of those around me muttered angrily that she ought to be kicked out, silenced, punished in some way for daring to differ. I pointed out that that was exactly what Hitler would do to her — probably send her to a concentration camp.

If it be said that that is also what the British Government did, by detaining Mosley and Captain Ramsay, a Tory M.P., under Regulation 18B, I would say that they did rather more than say 'No', and that M.P.s who opposed the war or Churchill's way of running it, did so with complete impunity. Ramsay's case was very different: as he admitted to the judge in the course of his libel action against the *New York Times*, he deliberately, in time of war, used the machinery of the House of Commons — specifically, the Order Paper of question-time — to advertise the wave-length on which Britons could listen to Nazi propaganda broadcasts, in the hope that many would do so.

A few days later I was setting off for the west coast — my first and most exciting visit to California; exciting partly because the people living there were hourly expecting that the attack on Pearl Harbour would be followed by an attack on the west coast of the United States. I was looking forward to renewing my acquaintance with the redoubtable 'Hitch' — Alfred Hitchcock — who had kindly invited me to stay at his house in Bel Air, Hollywood. So I set off from Washington by air — to be grounded in a snowstorm, after midnight, at Wichita, Kansas. The passengers clustered disconsolately in the airport lounge, awaiting news of the weather. The news was bad. The airline offered to send us on to the coast by train — a train which stopped fairly frequently and so took thirty-six hours to get there.

I had got together with three people — two girls and a man — who looked more interesting than the other passengers, and we agreed to go on by this train rather than take the doubtful chance of being able to fly in the morning. The girls were Hollywood film actresses named Carole Landis and Linda Darnell; the man, whose name escapes me, was looking after their publicity; he was charming and amusing, as were they — Darnell being the younger of the two. The train was already full before it reached Wichita — full mostly with naval recruits and reservists rushing to join their ships at San Diego and other naval stations. We could not get private sleepers—only bunks separated by curtains from the corridor. By day we managed to get a 'drawing-room', in which we sat playing cards; they taught me gin-rummy. Landis had a sharp and entertaining laugh; her favourite expletive was 'Oh, mother!' At meals in the dining-car, it was amusing to see how the sailors treated these two stars—with no reverence or fan-worship at all, but simply as public property. Sometimes they ribbed them: 'Hi, Carole! That last picture of yours sure was lousy.' The girls took it well, as they had to. I talked for a time with a Texan aged about thirty-five, who had never been on a train before: he had always travelled by car or air, skipping the railway age.

At some stop on the way, Carole sent a wire to her home in Hollywood ordering a car to meet her at San Bernardino, about sixty miles before Los Angeles. She had decided that she would drive me to Hollywood; the other two stayed on the train; there was no chauffeur. It was an alarming predicament, especially as she seemed inclined to linger on the way; but I said that we must press on, as 'Hitch' would be worried already at my being so late. (In reverse, with a different companion, this scene has been enacted so often in my life.) We did have one enjoyable stop—at a drive-in café, where she said I must listen on the juke-box to a hit number which typified America. It was 'Chattanooga Choo-choo.'

I spent several weeks at Hitch's comfortable house, meeting Joan Harrison, sister of my Lancing friend, and Dorothy Parker, who was too drunk to sparkle as wittily as she was supposed to. (The only phrase I remember her using was 'Hollywood—this garden of dung.') When I was shown round the M.G.M. studios, I was invited to lunch with Mr Louis B. Mayer; I refused—a foolish and priggish gesture. I did have lunch one day with James Cagney, who asked me a lot of questions about British politics: he was distinctly 'progressive' and much more interested in politics than in films.

I also was less interested in Hollywood than in other aspects of life in California. On Hitch's advice, I explored and wrote a piece about the tatty coast near Los Angeles:

Everything around Hollywood feels essentially ephemeral. Within a few miles, the process of rapid decay has set in.

Much of the coast near Los Angeles is astonishingly unlike what you expect California's sun-bathed shore to be. It is no Riviera. It is more like the coast between Brighton and Worthing, but even grislier — a slatternly string-out of bungalows, drug-stores, petrol-stations, spaghetti-shacks and other 'good teas', pin-table saloons, 'motels' mostly in need of a coat of paint. (Motel is a portmanteau word for motor-hotel, but it's not the kind of place to which you usually bother to take a portmanteau: it is a congeries of cabins in each of which a notice asks customers not to clean their shoes with the towels.)

The most surprising feature of this banal eldorado begins at an unsuccessful place ironically named Venice (where a midwinter bathing-beauty contest had to be abandoned the other day on account of inclement weather). This feature is oil-wells. Rising above the smugly symmetrical viridescent palm-trees for many miles as you drive along the coast, the derricks have a black, incongruous beauty of their own. Thousands of them are massed on the skyline like a cobwebby forest of gamps or immense litters of baby Eiffel Towers. Interspersed among them are market gardens, mostly run by Japanese; these were pulled in by the FBI last month, but most of those who were American citizens were allowed to return to their businesses.

It is only fair to add that when you get away from this shoddy shore, the country is spectacularly lovely to drive through. Whole fields of poinsettias make crimson splashes across the purple hills. The road climbs steeply; as it swerves through a sandy cutting you catch a breathtaking panorama of lush valley below, snow-capped mountains beyond. Giant cactus writhes by the roadside.

The only human habitations are the squatters' or roadmen's cabins, or occasional country clubs; the only evidence of contemporary civilisation is the electric pylons, each bearing the intimation 'Jesus saves'.

Since I found it necessary to explain the word 'motel', it was clearly not yet current in Britain. From these American visits I often introduced, in my dispatches to the *Express*, neologisms or news of inventions that had not yet reached Britain. Nylon was one; frozen food another.

The most boring Christmas I ever spent was that one in Hollywood. This was no fault of Hitch's: he and his wife had long been committed to a family party somewhere else, so I stayed indoors and watched the rain descending all day with tropical ferocity, as in the film of *Rain*. I had managed to go to midnight Mass on the eve. The tall, handsome priest, whose wife was entertaining the congregation to coffee afterwards, showed interest when I mentioned St Mary's church in Pimlico. 'I know the district well,' he said. 'I used to be on the cathedral staff.' It took me a few moments to work out that he meant, not St Paul's but, of course, Westminster Roman Catholic cathedral; the presence of the smiling, pleasant wife meant that he had given up his Roman orders and transferred his allegiance to Anglicanism — to the Episcopal church of the U.S.A. Had she, I wondered, been one of his penitents, or even a nun?

On the whole, I was happiest in Los Angeles when I could get away from the artificial atmosphere of Hollywood. Even the squalor of much of downtown L.A. was a bit more like real life. I began to frequent an underground dive, a 'taxi dance', chiefly frequented by Mexicans:

The typical customer's attire at this joint would be an undervest, a long, light blue coat, striped trousers, and gym-shoes. I found their sallow, squat, high cheek-boned, melancholy faces far more 'inscrutable' than those of Orientals, and as difficult to distinguish from each other; but not disagreeable.

Perhaps because all the stories they told about themselves were obviously untrue, they refused to believe I was an English newspaperman. Flatteringly, they assumed I was something from Hollywood — perhaps a talent-scout. When I insisted, they would say, grudgingly, 'But you haven't always been a newspaper man, have you? I mean, you've been something better, too?'

A uniformed cop (a champion weight-lifter of Portuguese-French ancestry) controlled the bar, chucking out drunks every few minutes. For this he gets a dollar an hour from the place. I sat with him one evening at a corner of the dance floor, which was lit only dimly and indirectly by the garish neons above the bar beyond. Suddenly he flashed his torch in the face of a young man dancing with a girl. The youth looked round. 'Take your hat off,' bawled the cop. I remarked I didn't think that that would have mattered much at a dump like this. He replied, grimly, 'If a guy's any kindova gentleman, he'll take off his hat when he's dancing with a woman.'

It was some time before I disclosed to this cop that I was English. 'I couldn't figure what it was,' he said, 'but I could tell you had a kindova odd brogue.'

Other customers included two rather bogus Texas cowboys on the bum, who insisted on playing guitars and yodelling, and argued that beer was improved by the addition of salt; and a New Zealand sailor, straying far from his ship, who attracted a curious circle of Mexicans. 'He talks English as good as us,' they said in surprise.

This sailor was in London some six months ago. When he heard I was in Fleet Street, and returning there shortly, he said, 'Oh boy, I can tell you that you'll find it wiped flat.' I expressed a doubt. 'I'm telling you, boy,' he said, 'I've been there. Fleet Street, Regent Street, all round there — flattened out like a pancake.' This irritated me so much that I went off alone to a dance-club so exclusively Negro that I was my own Livingstone.

I next went to supper at a Chinese restaurant. The place was empty. The waiter brought me a delicious chop-suey with a sweet nobbly biscuit, which, when broken, I found contained two pieces of paper bearing the texts, 'You will be vigorous and go ahead with your plans,' and 'Kindness from those of whom you least expect it'.

I then observed, to my dismay and embarrassment, that the waiter (who should, of course, have been 'impassive') was weeping. I asked what was the matter. He explained that his parents were in Hong Kong and he didn't know what had become of them, and that his wife had just died of a haemorrhage, despite five transfusions. He then produced two bulky albums of Chinese family snaps, at every one of which he was good enough to insist I should look.

Exhausted by the kindness promised me by one of my biscuit's texts, and feeling little of the vigour foreshadowed in the other, I went home, paying only one more call on the way — at the world's largest bowling palace, which has fifty-two sound-proof alleys. (Bowling is a nation-wide craze among American youth.)

In the cocktail-bar here, a man came up to me and said, 'Excuse me, but can you tell me if David Garrick's tomb in Westminster Abbey has been damaged?' I said I wasn't sure, I thought it was all right. 'I only ask,' he added, 'because my name is David Garrick, and I am his last surviving direct male descendant.'

I omitted to ask him further details about himself: one's faculty of surprise becomes atrophied in California.

My visit to this astonishing State ended with a few days in San Diego — a great naval port with a bar on every street-corner and several dozen sailors in every bar. Every sailor was ready and willing for anything, and in need of a few bucks: my expense account became exorbitantly swollen, but Lord Beaverbrook, I reflected, would strongly approve of my spreading good-will towards Britain in the United States Navy.

But I had been in America for five months: it was time to go home. The return journey was made by bomber. These Liberator bombers, flying east across the Atlantic for delivery to the R.A.F., were used also to ferry official passengers to Britain. (No commercial airlines were operating in wartime.) I was lucky to get a lift in one of them. My fellow-passengers included the Dutch Foreign Minister, Dr Van Kleffens, a Free French general, an American colonel, and several British servicemen (one, a naval commander, I called W.). We were given an elaborate briefing on the rigours and hazards ahead: it would be very cold, our oxygen masks might ice up: no alcohol for twenty-four hours before the flight, 'no beans, cabbage, etc'; no smoking and no sleeping. (The last, in a flight lasting nine hours, proved difficult.) We were warned not to talk to the press, and lent flying suits, helmets and parachutes. During the flight I counted the articles of apparel that I had on: twenty-one, including four pairs of socks.

The first part of the journey was from Montreal to Newfoundland. Here, at the lonely, frost-bound spot called Beaver Centre, we waited five days. I shared a room with a Canadian soldier who was in acute need of consoling friendship: one sign of this is the warmth and tightness of the embrace; another is the speed, explosiveness, and creamier consistency of the ejaculation. He gave me his brass shoulder-flash as a souvenir. Another soldier had just been in trouble for getting drunk and turning on the fire-hose in his dormitory. He explained that he'd wanted to do some ice-skating before going to bed.

Now and then, across the frozen waste, one could hear a train honking. Trains ran twice a week: they carried, among other things, Beaver Centre's laundry, to be washed at a town several hundred miles away.

At last we were off. After that severe briefing, none of us had expected comfort, but the conditions were indeed stark:

Till some height had been made, all the passengers had to huddle together as far forward as possible in the bomb-bays. Then we went up to the 'living compartment'; settled down in two rows of seats facing each other, as in an old-fashioned bus, and about as close. The noise was considerable, not intolerable. It wasn't cold enough to wear gloves yet. The going was smooth. We read magazines.

The altimeter had mounted steadily. After some time the flight engineer came back to give us our oxygen-masks. This was a faintly distasteful reminiscence of the dentist's. The rubber mask sits comfortably enough over nose and mouth. A bag which expands and contracts with each breath hangs below the chin. A snaky coil of rubber tubing is plugged into the wall behind each passenger.

We made a strange spectacle sitting there in two rows, helmeted, masked, attached as though umbilically to the grey metal shell about us: the still-unborn monstrous brood of some mechanical mother.

Soon the oxygen was distinctly exhilarating ...

For a time W. and Dr Van Kleffens and I played the word game in which each player adds one letter, the object being to avoid finishing the word. Van K. betrayed a profound and subtle knowledge of English. Among the words he helped to construct were *streptococci*, *dabchick*, *presbyopic*. The game ended abruptly when I challenged an unseemly bluff by W. Bombers rarely carry the Oxford Dictionary.

It was also now becoming more uncomfortable. My notes became fragmentary:

'Ice forming in bag—hard granules like little rocks. Hands still not cold—paper I write on feels icy.'

We were well supplied with packets of sandwiches (with dainty paper napkins!) and vacuum flasks full of hot coffee. We got them out from under the seats. Although, as I say, my hands still felt fairly warm (I suppose on account of the dryness at this altitude), the flasks were coated with ice, the sandwiches frozen into solid slabs.

Occasional snacks helped to keep us awake when we were too tired to read any more. On the whole, it was an extraordinarily easy flight, not fulfilling at all the forebodings of extreme discomfort. The only trying part was that we were not allowed to sleep: there might be some danger that a sleeper would interrupt his own oxygen supply. Passengers had to watch each other, prod any who showed signs of dropping off.

Nor, of course, could we move about much (there was an extra oxygen tap beside the primitive toilet). The least restless of us was the American colonel, who sat motionless at the end of the compartment, his mask-bag filling and emptying with the utmost regularity. Dr Van Kleffens scribbled me a note: 'The colonel is what you might call a beautiful breather.'

This was, on the whole, the most rewarding and fascinating of the visits I have paid to America—largely because it covered the periods immediately before and after Pearl Harbour. But it was also an anxious and, in some respects, a depressing moment: for some months the news of the war had been consistently bad. The loss of the *Prince of Wales* and the *Repulse*, and the fall of Singapore —both due to folly at or near the top—were serious shocks. There had been many talks with American friends, passionately pro-British, and with other British correspondents in the United States, whose main theme had been: 'What has gone wrong? What can we do about it?'

When I landed at Prestwick on that grey wintry morning of March, 1942, I had not the faintest idea that in three months' time I should be seeking to become and actually becoming a Member of Parliament.

12

Going to Westminster

The Parliament that I joined in June, 1942, was to some extent enfeebled by three factors: the war, the necessity of wartime coalition, and its own old age.

Because of the war, many of the younger M.P.s were away in the Forces, returning occasionally to take part in some debate of special interest to them. This unusual arrangement had been agreed at the beginning of the war. It led to some first-rate first-hand accounts – uninhibited if they were in secret session – of what the war was really like for the serving soldiers. I remember particularly a challenging speech by William Anstruther-Gray,[1] a young Tory who was later to be Deputy-Speaker, in a secret session on tanks. When he was called to speak, Sir James Grigg, the Secretary of State for War, got up from his seat on the Front Bench to go out to keep a luncheon appointment.[2] He sat down again quickly when this young Coldsteam Guards officer in khaki, straight from North Africa, said, a bit sharply: 'Will the Secretary of State please stay and listen to this for a few minutes? I've come back to tell him something, and it's important he should hear it.'

This was indeed the more important because no *Hansard* record was kept of these secret debates; for the same reason, I cannot be sure that I am quoting Anstruther-Gray correctly. We were strictly admonished by the Speaker that even the rough notes that we might have made must be destroyed. Only one man was above the

[1] Now Lord Kilmany.
[2] At that time, because of the nightly bombing, the Commons met from 11 a.m. to 4.30 p.m.

rules made for others – Winston Churchill. He kept not merely the notes but the complete text of his secret session speeches, and got permission from the post-war Parliament to publish them as a book (of which he kindly sent copies to the M.P.s who had served in the wartime House).

The second factor that made this House seem, sometimes, lacking in fire was that all Parties were combined in the coalition government under Churchill, and every debate was therefore to some extent a sham fight. It was only towards the end of the war, when victory was in sight and we began to discuss post-war reconstruction, that the Coalition started coming apart at the seams: it had been formed *only* to cope with the external enemy. (The first major breaches in the Coalition, on the Tory side, were on 'peacetime' issues – catering wages and equal pay for women teachers. Both were occasions of big back-bench Tory revolts. In the latter case, the Government was actually defeated: next day Churchill made his rebels eat their words; Quintin Hogg, now Lord Hailsham, made a plaintive speech saying that Churchill didn't seem to realise that he was causing embarrassment to some of his most loyal friends. He realised it very well: he was rubbing their noses in it.)

The third factor, the age of that Parliament: it had been elected in 1935; the General Election that should have occurred in 1940 was deferred because of the war. So Parliament was now 're-freshed', as they say, only by the products of the by-elections caused by M.P.s' deaths or resignations. Coalition involved a Party truce: this meant that when an M.P. died or resigned, the seat would go automatically, without a contest, to the Party that he belonged to. Contests occurred only when this arrangement was challenged by Independent candidates. Which brings me to the strange chance and unexpected result of the by-election which I contested at Maldon, Essex.

When I had gone to America in the previous autumn, I had given up the lease of the mews in Kensington and stored my furniture. When I returned from America I found a convenient flat in Great Ormond Street, Bloomsbury – a conversion in what had been a fine house; in the eighteenth century, I was told, it had been part of the French Embassy; it still had a noble staircase. My flat was on the second floor – two rooms and a bathroom; tall

Georgian windows. The rent was about £90 a year. Because of the bombing, flats were easy to find, and cheap; and later this was a 'protected' tenancy.

One evening in May I came back to this flat fairly late from the *Express* office, or from some function or a pub-crawl. I turned on the radio and heard, on the news, that an M.P. had died — Sir Edward Ruggles-Brise, M.P. for Maldon, the constituency in which Bradwell, my home village, was situated. It sounds too pretentious to say that this seemed like a 'sign'; but I thought of all those worried talks in America and asked myself 'Shall I have a go?' I also recalled a recent public meeting at which I had spoken with several other journalists, calling on the Government to lift the ban on the *Daily Worker* (a ban which seemed particularly absurd now that Russia was in the war). After the meeting one of the other speakers, Tom Hopkinson, editor of *Picture Post*, told me of a group of people he was in touch with who were helping to promote progressive Independent candidates for Parliament: would I be interested in standing? It was not a definite offer; he was just sounding me; and I hadn't given the matter much thought at the time. (I may say that during the time I was M.P. for Maldon I always had the greatest courtesy and friendliness from my predecessor's son, Sir John Ruggles-Brise, who became Lord-Lieutenant of the county.)

There was something else, too. On the carpet in front of my gas fire was stretched out, naked, the slender, rangy form of my Canadian soldier friend, S. I must have betrayed some interest at the brief news item (which, of course, meant nothing to him). I must even have said something to the effect that I might stand for Parliament myself. I remember that he hooted with laughter and said some such words as 'You'd never do it — and, if you did, you'd never make it.' Perhaps this challenge fortified my recollection of Tom Hopkinson's approach. We went out to eat at Olivelli's, a delightful Italian restaurant, frequented by music-hall performers and censors from the Ministry of Information, which existed underground in Store Street. My mind was full of Maldon.

Next day I went to see Beaverbrook to ask for time off to fight the election. He greeted the idea with harsh scepticism. It was totally untrue that, as was hinted in some quarters — indeed, by Churchill himself — I was a 'Beaverbrook candidate'. I was much too far to the Left for him to risk backing me: the only candidates he had sponsored, years before, had been of the Right. Also, though he was out of the Government at the time and to some extent at odds with Churchill, he would not, I think, have endangered by so overt a snub his position as Churchill's favourite crony. So Beaverbrook made light of this quaint new-found ambition of mine and said that I must still do a certain number of Hickey columns during the campaign. (I was single-handed in the job at this time.) The only advice he gave me was 'Buy yourself a hat! British electors will never vote for a man who doesn't wear a hat.' I didn't, and they did. Beaverbrook was almost always wrong in his political judgment.

I knew nothing at all about the techniques of electioneering. The man who taught me how to do it was one of the group whom Tom Hopkinson had spoken of — Richard Acland, himself an Independent M.P. of the Left, formerly a Liberal, later the founder of Common Wealth. Despite his almost George Washington reputation for Christian integrity (a well-founded reputation it is too), Acland is no starry-eyed dreamer: I know of no one better versed in the tactics and technique of modern electioneering — and he could lecture key workers and helpers on how to do a job while at the same time infecting them with enthusiasm for it. The first lesson he gave me was on the use of the loud-speaker car: never speak while the car is moving (the voice fading into inaudibility is irritating); and when you give an open-air talk, always start by apologising for using the amplifying equipment and offer to switch it off if anyone is sick or trying to sleep. (They always think 'what a nice thoughtful man!')

One evening I paid my first visit to Braintree, the largest town in the constituency, where there was the most solid concentration of Labour votes. Although Labour Party members were supposed to be bound by the Party truce, I naturally hoped that many of them would rather vote for a Socialist than for the stuffy and colourless Tory — Mr Reuben Hunt, a local ironmaster and chairman of the finance committee of the County Council — who had been selected as official Government candidate. So indeed it turned out; but on this first evening I worked very quietly, moving from pub to pub in a solitary (and sober) crawl, sounding publicans and customers (none of whom knew me) about the impending election, saying who I was when instinct prompted me to do so.

It was not until some days later that I had a really lucky break in Braintree. Russia was then an admired ally. An Anglo-Soviet bookshop was to be opened in the Braintree market square. All three by-election candidates—the official man, myself, and another Independent—were invited to attend the opening. I was the only one of the three to turn up, and was asked to speak. Apart from any effect that this may have had in impressing the fact of my existence on the local dignitaries and electors present, this was my first contact with one who was to become both my most active and useful local supporter and a personal friend—the late Father Jack Boggis, then sub-dean of Bocking, near Braintree. He found himself unable in conscience to support the Tory candidate: as he was secretary not only of the Anglo-Soviet friendship society, but also of the Braintree local Party—a post he was now obliged to resign—his support meant a great deal to me. He became secretary of the local committee formed to assist my candidature.

Similar committees were set up at other towns and villages in the constituency. In order to lessen the concentration on the candidate's personality which is one of the embarrassments of Independent candidature—and to provide some sort of democratic machinery, such as an ordinary M.P. has in his local Party—we announced that if I were elected, the *ad hoc* campaign committees would be the basis of a new, non-Party Maldon Constituency Association, whose task it would be to engage in political education generally and in particular to organise meetings at which I would report back regularly on Parliament. This association was in fact formed after polling-day, and flourished usefully for three years. Its doctrinal basis was broad: members signed a statement of belief that was (without using the word) Socialist in general outlook— that, for instance, 'production should be for use rather than for profit'. At the end of the war the Party truce ended. Political Parties began to function normally again, and there was less need for such an association as this (or for Independent M.P.s).

But there had to be some exploitation of such personal advantage as there might be in the fact that I was a widely read columnist. Slogans were devised which now make me wince: one was 'the local man with the national reputation'. Since I did not attack

Churchill himself but the deadheads around him who were allegedly obstructing the war effort, it was the *Daily Telegraph* reporter covering the campaign who suggested the slogan that most annoyed the Tories: 'A candid friend for Churchill'. We used the techniques of modern publicity, and got people like Vernon Bartlett and Hannen Swaffer, whose names were known in the press and on the radio, to come and speak. Bernard Shaw sent a postcard; this impressed even those electors who did not quite follow the somewhat tortuous argument by which he sought to prove that 'the official Party candidates are breaking the truce and are entirely out of order' (because, in his view, the truce ought to have meant 'dropping the Party system and voting for the ablest candidate').

I have fought eight general elections since then, the last five of them at Barking; but I have not enjoyed any of them so much as I did that by-election campaign. It was fought in golden summer weather; most of our meetings were in the open air, in this loveliest and most unspoiled part of Essex. The big constituency embraced ancient villages like Finchingfield and quiet waterfronts like that of Burnham-on-Crouch; and Maldon itself, a favourite subject of such artists as Wilson Steer. At the King's Head in Maldon the splendid elderly landlady, Mrs Massingberd-Mundy, rallied all sorts of unexpected help. Dorothy L. Sayers, who lived at Witham, lent furniture for our committee-room there. (She thought better of it later; when I asked her in 1945 to help again, reminding her that we had been to Mass in London together, she replied that I appeared to be inviting her to commit inverted simony.) Another famous detective-story writer, Margery Allingham, lived at Tolleshunt D'Arcy: though personally friendly, she thought it wiser to leave everything to Churchill and not 'disturb people'.

But people *were* disturbed. I had never expected such enthusiastic support. A young R.A.F. man in uniform, Reg Clarke, volunteered to help, and eventually became my agent; he is now editor of the *Essex County Standard*. (It was in 1945 that we had Group-Captain Peter Wykeham-Barnes, 'terror of the Sicilian railways', and his father-in-law-to-be, J. B. Priestley, on our platform at Witham.)

The eve-of-poll meeting is the climax of a campaign. In our scattered division (since divided) we had to have at least five of them — at Burnham-on-Crouch, Maldon, Witham, Silver End, and Braintree, in that order. By the time I got to Braintree it was getting on for ten o'clock and nearly dark. This was my first personal experience of that awe-inspiring phenomenon, a really big crowd pressing eagerly, closely, round an open-air platform. The market square was filled, crammed tight: at least 6,000 people, the police said. Acland and Swaffer had been speaking. The crowd was excited, but less hilariously so than at an ordinary peacetime election; for the war was still going badly, and only a few days earlier had come the worst shock of all — the unexpected fall of Tobruk. So the crowd's mood was grave; it could be stirred to anger. When I spoke, I had just had reported to me the answer given by the Tory candidate that evening, when he was asked why things were going so badly in North Africa. He had replied: 'Because we've sent too much help to the Russians.' As I have said, this was the Anglo-Soviet honeymoon period. I told the crowd what my opponent had said. There was roar of astonished fury and the local Communist branch secretary, Harold Quinton, an honest and decent man, got up and testified fervently that he would have to support me. I expect he got into trouble for it: the C.P. line — ironically, as I felt — was to back the Churchill Coalition against all Independent candidates. At that moment I think we felt pretty certain that we had won; and so we did, by a two-to-one majority, despite the 'experts' who were still prophesying next morning that I would forfeit my deposit. That was what Beaverbrook had told Brendan Bracken, the Minister of Information, and others lunching with him that day, on the basis of the best available advice he could get from Maldon; this was before the days of the Gallup and other poll forecasts.

In Volume IV of *The Second World War*, Winston Churchill writes of his return from Washington in June 1942:

> We approached the Clyde at dawn ... In an hour we were off to the south. It appeared that we had lost a by-election by a sweeping turn-over at Maldon. This was one of the by-products of Tobruk.

In my own opinion, this is too simple an explanation. Tobruk may have had some last-minute effect, it may have contributed something to the turnover of votes; but before the news of Tobruk came through, those helping me were already confident that we were winning.

Next day the *Express* commented a trifle sulkily on my victory, in an 'Opinion' leaderette:

> Mr Driberg, who writes the William Hickey column in this newspaper, has won the Maldon by-election as an Independent. It should, of course, be made clear that the *Daily Express* has no share, no part in his triumph.
>
> On May 25th this column stated:
> *The Daily Express* does not support his candidature but, of course, members of the *Express* staff are permitted, and encouraged, to exercise their rights as private citizens.
> We do not agree with Mr Driberg's politics.

I retaliated in my column:

> The writer of this column is not responsible for the views expressed in any other part of this newspaper. He disagrees with many of them anyway.

It was a strange relationship between a newspaper and one of its staff. It may have been an uneasy one for the editor. But I was allowed to write a column describing my feelings when I went to take my seat in the House.

This is always an ordeal, but particularly after a by-election. After a General Election an untidy queue of M.P.s shambles slowly towards the Clerk and the Speaker, to take the oath, sign the book, and shake hands. After a by-election the new M.P. has to go through these motions alone, walking up the floor between his two sponsors and bowing the requisite number of times, while the assembled House scrutinises him critically and may raise the growl of a cheer. And doing all this was even worse in wartime, when we met in the far grander surroundings of the Lords chamber (the Commons having been destroyed by bombs in 1941). My two sponsors were Acland and Bartlett (himself an Independent who had won a famous by-election at Bridgwater). I was glad to know that in the gallery were three people whose presence there I valued: my brother Jack, Jeannie Hunt, and (in another part of the gallery) my Canadian friend S. Afterwards Jeannie said: 'How your mother would have loved to see this day!'

I found that I knew, or was known by, a surprisingly large number of Members on both sides of the House; I had often been there for a drink with Frank Owen and others, including Nye Bevan, with whom Frank had shared a flat. There were many friendly welcomes: on the Tory side, I think they didn't quite know what to make of me. One Tory, Ronald Tree, a wealthy Anglo-American who was Bracken's Parliamentary Private Secretary, gave me dinner one evening in his spacious suite at the Ritz. 'I honestly find', he said, 'that this is the cheapest way to live in wartime.'

One Tory M.P. who was no stranger to me was Henry ('Chips') Channon, now more famous for his gossipy diary, published, in discreet extracts only, in book form. Chips, of American origin, was a social figure at least as glittering as Lady Cunard. He had a large house in Belgrave Square and a lot of money—the latter, I suppose, largely through his marriage to Lady Honor Guinness, daughter of Lord and Lady Iveagh. (Gerald Berners said that Chips could now have a coat-of-arms: the motto must, of course, be *'Nil sine honore'*.) The Iveaghs, who were great benefactors of Southend, controlled a safe Conservative constituency there and, in effect, gave it to Chips as a wedding-present. Moreover, when his marriage broke up, these generous in-laws stood by him. He kept the Southend seat, and in due course it passed to his son Paul, while the latter was still an Oxford undergraduate. It must be the only hereditary pocket-borough left. But Paul Channon has worked hard as an M.P. and junior Minister: he has inherited his father's love for baroque architecture as well as his seat in Parliament and his habit of marrying Guinnesses, but not his other sexual tastes; and has indeed lived down his father's reputation, which he found as embarrassing as the stuffier Tories found it shocking. For Chips was one of the better-known homosexuals in London, and he was rich enough to rent almost any young man he fancied—a handsome German princeling, a celebrated English playwright. His seduction of the playwright was almost like the wooing of Danaë by Zeus: every day the playwright found, delivered to his door, a splendid present—a case of champagne, a huge pot of caviar, a Cartier cigarette-box in two kinds of gold ... In the end, of course, he gave in, saying apologetically to his friends, 'How can one *not*?'

Chips told me that the M.P. he found most sexually attractive on our side of the House was Sir Hartley Shawcross. I am sure he never did anything about it; when he told me this he was speaking of the Attorney-General. I admired Hartley's brains, and he once came to speak for me at Burnham (where he dived into the Crouch to rescue a girl swimmer who seemed to be in difficulties); but I could not bring myself to see him, even remotely, as bedworthy. Anyway, only a few hours after I had been introduced to the House, when I was still wandering about in a daze, and lost, Chips kindly showed me round the most important rooms – the Members' lavatories. This was an act of pure, disinterested, sisterly friendship, for we had no physical attraction for each other.

Nowadays a new M.P. seems to find it necessary to make his or her maiden speech soon after being elected. This is more difficult after a General Election at which a large number of new Members come in than after a by-election, since the Speaker can usually accommodate only one or two maidens in a day's debate: they break any continuity the debate may have, since maiden speakers tend to waste a lot of time in formal tributes to their predecessors, to the scenic beauty of their constituencies, or to the sterling worth of their constituents. One who did not bother with all this and also eschewed the other convention, that a maiden speaker should not be controversial – and made in consequence the best maiden speech I ever heard, on the very afternoon on which she had taken her seat – was Bernadette Devlin (now Mrs McAliskey).

But back in the early 1940s the tempo of this aged House was still as it had been in Edwardian times. Old Members advised me that I should wait six months or so before making my maiden speech and in the meantime ask one or two questions, to 'get the feel' of the place. I did not wait that long, but I hadn't quite the guts to do what I probably should have done – ask the Speaker to call me, as he would have been more or less bound to, in a major debate that took place a few days after I had been elected: this was on the highly controversial and indeed startling motion 'That this House has no confidence in the central direction of the war'. This was a direct challenge to Churchill and was obviously relevant to the Maldon by-election (despite that 'candid friend' slogan); and if I had had something worth saying, or not, I would have received maximum publicity.

However, as all the histories of the war record, the debate was ruined in its opening speech, by a pompous Tory fool, Sir John Wardlaw-Milne, who provoked a storm of incredulous laughter by suggesting that there should be a 'supremo' of all the Armed Forces and that he should be—and he named the most notoriously stupid member of the Royal Family—the Duke of Gloucester. The debate never recovered from this monumental *gaffe* (so perhaps it was as well, after all, that I didn't speak in it); and at the end, in hasty confabulation with Acland, Bartlett and one or two other of the more reputable Independents, I decided to cast my first vote against the motion and for the Churchill Government. This may sound very up-stage, but, apart from ridiculous reactionaries like Wardlaw-Milne, there were several Independents—some of the extreme Right, some mere shoddy demagogues, people like the ex-Tory playboy Alec Cunningham-Reid and the self-advertising trade union official W. J. Brown—whom we did not care to seem to be associated with. An Independent has to be rather careful about such things: he has to weigh every vote he casts slightly more scrupulously than the Party M.P. who can honestly, in most divisions, accept the guidance of the Whips. (On Acland's advice I had promised the Maldon electors that I would vote only when the subject was one that I knew something about and/or cared conscientiously about.) But it took me some twenty-five years of Parliament to learn that one can't always control, and mustn't mind, who else is in the division lobby with one: when the Common Market debates came along, we of the Left often found ourselves in the same lobby as Enoch Powell.

Enoch Powell, whose views on race I detest, and still more his manner of expressing them—'the river Tiber foaming with much blood'—utters more beautifully constructed prose than any M.P. of my time: Churchill, by comparison, was a windbag; Nye Bevan was more riveting and magical, but the words poured from him like lava and occasionally dwindled into aposiopesis. I got to know Enoch Powell fairly well only once—at Christmas, 1973, when he and I were guests in the home of Reggie Paget, M.P. (now Lord Paget). I am glad to say that we did not talk politics at all: it would have been a barren argument. Instead, he was much occupied with a theory, which he had just expounded in an article in *The Times*, about the social status of Jesus Christ and his family. According to Enoch as I understood him—and it is a doctrine, clearly, comforting to Tory voters – the Holy Family were not really of the working class at all, but at least of the superior artisan class; and the traditional pictures of a poverty-stricken occasion were misleading. The hotel was rather full, and was not perhaps of five-star quality, but the visitors from Nazareth were settled in quite tolerable, almost bourgeois, comfort; and the manger was used simply because they had travelled without a cot and it was the best cradle-shaped object around. This exegesis kept us going for the best part of the night.

Reggie's house is near the border of Leicestershire and North-amptonshire, and Enoch had been invited there for the hunting; there was a meet of the Fernie Hunt at the house on Christmas Eve. Reggie mounted Enoch on a powerful grey called Zebedee. They started off well, but soon Enoch, who was a bit out of practice, was thrown. He remounted and pressed on, but the brute threw him again. He returned to the house, white and shaken. The press had got hold of his presence and a spokesman for the Hunt issued a statement: 'It was very courageous of him, but he isn't quite up to Leicestershire standards.' Enoch returned to London to attend the Nativity Mass at St Peter's, Eaton Square – formerly just above middle-stump, now going a bit higher since a new young Vicar, of working-class origin, has gone there; I believe the dowagers adore him. Enoch shocked me by saying that, since it is now too big for its regular congregation, he favoured the demolition of this church, with its imposing classical portico – a perfect architectural climax to Eaton Square – its replacement by a small modern building, and the sale of the site. In this respect I am more conservative than he. But I hope he is right about our becoming a racially mixed society: such a mixture is more fun, and potentially more productive of talent, than a Nazi-like, static, artificially perpetuated, monochrome 'race' (even could that be achieved). I shan't live long enough, alas, to see a Black, or an Indian, Speaker.

Our host, Reggie Paget, was one of the most idiosyncratic M.P.s: certainly the only Labour M.P. who was at one time Master of a good Hunt. (He was joint-Master of the Pytchley.) He used often to enjoy a day's hunting at home and then drive to Westminster in time for the 6 o'clock division. His hope is that he will die of a fall in the hunting-field, as his father did before him. He is personally a charmer, rich, generous and amusing, and politically a mass of contradictions and almost always at odds with his Labour colleagues. Nominally a Socialist, he backs rebel white Rhodesia. Once a fervent campaigner for the abolition of capital punishment, he proposed a year or two ago that, for every I.R.A. bomb exploded fatally in Britain, an I.R.A. detainee in Ulster should be taken out and shot. I have always found his company delightful so long as one keeps off politics. In the Commons he made some of the fiercest attacks I have heard on the leadership of Harold Wilson. When he retired from the Commons in 1974, Wilson at once made him a peer.

Before I had made my maiden speech, I put down a few questions to Ministers pretty quickly. This is an educative process: one takes one's question to the Table Office, and all too often one finds that it is not in order and can't be printed. This is not because the Clerks in this office are against one; they are really on one's side and will often help to redraft the question so as to get it into order —the essential principle being that a question must be to a Minister about something for which he is, as a Minister, responsible. (The only non-Ministers who can be questioned orally are the Second Church (Estates) Commissioner and the Chairman of the Kitchen Committee.) Thus, the first question I essayed was ruled out: I had been incensed by an anti-Soviet speech made in the country by Lady Astor and tried to ask some Minister, I forget which, about it. But there was — luckily for them all — no Minister responsible for Lady Astor or her vapourings. Looking back on later experience, I think I might have managed it with a question to the Minister of Information, Brendan Bracken, innocently asking him to take steps to counter anti-Soviet propaganda in general, and then, having advised him privately what I was going to say, asked a supplementary question about 'the disgraceful outburst by the Noble Lady who sits for the Sutton division of Plymouth'; and, as things were, he would have had to agree in deploring such remarks. Or I could have taken the extreme step of asking the Home Secretary, Herbert Morrison — then called the Minister of Home Security — to lock the Noble Lady up in Brixton under Regulation 18B, along with her fellow-M.P. Captain Ramsay. But then there was another rule barring questions disparaging other M.P.s ...

In the event, my first question was about a Communist whom I had known in Spain named Jock Cunningham; he was now serving in the British Army, and had got into some trouble.

As it turned out, Bracken was the Minister in charge of the debate in which I did soon make my maiden speech: it seemed a suitable opportunity, since I was a journalist and the debate was about information. My speech was unremarkable, but there was one incident during it which I don't think had happened before or has happened since. The Deputy-Speaker (Sir Denis Herbert) who was in the Chair, interrupted to rule me out of Order when I raised the question of the ban on the *Daily Worker* and had begun to urge that it be lifted. This seemed to me strictly relevant to the debate, and I still think he was wrong, apart from his unusual action in interrupting a maiden speech. A few years later I would have argued with him, but naturally at this time I was much too over-awed to do so.

When I say I would have argued with the Chair, of course you never argue with the Chair: that is totally forbidden. Yet this is one of the favourite field sports of experienced M.P.s. What you say is something like this (after you have been severely slapped down by the Speaker): 'On a point of order, Mr Speaker. I am most grateful to you for that ruling, and naturally I accept it whole-heartedly. But I wonder whether, for the guidance of the House, you would be good enough to clarify it a little further in this respect. Do you mean that, for the rest of this debate, you are not going to allow any reference to the matter that I was seeking to raise——' Mr Speaker (tapping the arm of the Chair): 'Order, order. Perhaps the Honourable Member will come to the point.' The recalcitrant M.P.: 'Further to that point of order, Mr Speaker. Perhaps you will allow me to complete my sentence. I was asking you whether you proposed to rule out, for the rest of the debate, the sort of matter that I was seeking to raise, because I must put it to you, Mr Speaker, with the utmost respect, that when you were not in the Chair Mr Deputy-Speaker allowed a number of references of precisely the same sort to pass unchallenged, and——' Mr Speaker: 'Order, order. Perhaps the Honourable Member will now continue his speech, and I will let him know if and when he is out of order.' This would, I think, be taken as a tactical victory for the back-bencher; but, as I say, in 1942 I couldn't have attempted any such ploy. This game of hunt-the-Speaker must always be played with extreme courtesy and suavity. (Bob Boothby doesn't agree that this is the only way to play it: he says that there are *two* possible methods of handling the Speaker — '*either*' as in my illustration, 'lick his arse *or* give him hell.') Baxter at the *Express* once said to me: 'You have an air of deference which is very useful to you.' I have used it to the full, though it is really only a projection of my lifelong shyness; in Commons proceedings I used to vary it with bursts of anger, often genuine.

One of the more enjoyable of these incidents occurred during the 1945–50 Parliament, when a Leeds solicitor named Major Milner, who was Chairman of Ways and Means, was in the Chair and had ruled out of order something that Geoffrey Bing had said. Picking the word carefully, I said that the Chair's ruling was 'regrettable'. He jumped at the bait and rebuked me for having, as he thought, criticised the Chair. I rose on a further point of order and, putting on my most disgustingly, hypocritically solemn and lugubrious voice, said that none of us would ever dare to criticise the Chairman, coming as he did from 'the great conurbation of Leeds', and that in using the word 'regrettable' I had merely meant to suggest that I was sure that he, Major Milner, must *regret* as much as we all did that he felt obliged to deprive us of the pleasure of hearing the rest of my honourable friend's speech.

This kind of sport must seem to people outside Parliament a childish waste of time, but it keeps the Chair, so to speak, on its toes, and it was good practice for the filibustering — another theoretically impermissible practice — that we used to engage in when in Opposition, in the legitimate attempt to prevent the Government from getting through Bills that we disapproved of. Harold Lever once spoke for three hours in a debate about fish; he had to stop then, because his trousers had begun to come down. Tony Crosland, who had lately become M.P. for a fishing constituency, Grimsby, and had actually mugged up some serious points, was infuriated by the frivolity of our efforts to prolong the debate. But fish is a splendid subject for a filibuster. It is difficult for the Chair to prevent one from bringing in Rupert Brooke's poem on fish, Prunier's, Wheeler's, the interesting sex-life of oysters (who change their sex once a year) or Loch Ness. In cases like that, a 'commando' of only half-a-dozen resourceful Opposition back-benchers could keep the House up all night; the rest of their comrades could go home, but the Government Whips had to keep at least a hundred of their Members there, since that number is required to carry a closure. The Tories used to call us 'the midnight hags'. And at 3 o'clock in the morning a little light relief, on the lines of the Milner incident — lasting only a couple of minutes — is welcome.

So I gradually learned my way through the maze of procedure. Although I was an Independent, I usually found myself speaking and voting with the Left-wing Labour M.P.s, already led by Nye Bevan, who formed a kind of unofficial opposition within the framework of the Party truce. The two most memorable clashes of this period (unlike the Tory revolts, not about post-war issues) were on Ernest Bevin's Regulation 1AA — which was designed to make unofficial strikes illegal; and if he had ever dared to try to use it, it would have been as futile as the Industrial Relations Act would have been a generation later — and on Greece in the winter of 1944. On these issues, and on Herbert Morrison's action in releasing Mosley from jail, there was a substantial anti-Government vote, in which Bevan, Shinwell, Frank Bowles, Seymour Cocks and other Labour M.P.s were supported by such outsiders as Acland, D. N. Pritt, K.C., and myself. During the division at the end of this debate, I was walking through the lobby with Pritt and said to him in disgust after listening to Morrison's speech: 'That kind of thing makes one feel we've lost the war.' Pritt replied: 'Oh I don't know — it merely makes me feel we've lost Morrison, which is much less worrying.'

I also remember, in the debates on R. A. Butler's celebrated Education Bill, voting for an amendment, moved by a gentle, elderly Quaker, Edmund Harvey, whose purpose was to defeat the proposal for a daily act of worship in schools. (After the war I was successful in persuading the Labour Government to abolish almost all compulsory church parades in the Forces: anything in the nature of official or 'national', and compulsory, religion has always seemed to me deadly and self-defeating. Even compulsory chapel for small boys at school must have put thousands off church-going for life; in this I was personally an exception, largely because of the music.)

One day, while still quite new, I complained to Nye Bevan of the paucity of really black-and-white issues. Partly because of the

Coalition, so much seemed blurred. 'The House of Commons,' he said, 'is a fretwork, not a Passion play.'

I do not propose to do what some political autobiographers have done — quote great chunks of my own speeches at length. That has always seemed to me both vain and boring to the reader — partly because speaking and writing are different arts: a speech which sounds well in the House doesn't usually read well; and vice versa. This, in turn, is because the modern style of parliamentary debate is a conversational style, with interruptions and rejoinders — the well-known 'cut and thrust' — not the orotund Ciceronian style of former times. Anyway, anybody who, improbably, wanted to check some point I make here can always look it up in the annual general index of *Hansard* — an invaluable reference book, consulted even more infrequently than *Hansard* itself.

For one year I led a curious double professional life, going to the House regularly and then going to Fleet Street to write a Hickey column. I could not have afforded to give up journalism, even if I had wanted to: at that time an M.P.'s salary was only £600 a year, the whole of which I made over to my Maldon supporters to rent and keep going an office in the High Street there. But, since I spent so much time at the House, inevitably the column became loaded with parliamentary items; and, since I was now an M.P., Beaverbrook took a more critical interest in the column and told the editor, Arthur Christiansen, not to let me 'get away with all this left-wing propaganda'.

Anyway, the war was at its height; so there was plenty to write about without upsetting the old man unduly; and plenty of non-war subjects, too, such as a row at the Zoo, on which I sided with the Secretary, Julian Huxley, and a 'rebel' group of younger Fellows. More directly related to the war was a paragraph about the death of Alexander Woollcott, the American writer. He had died while taking part in a radio discussion programme. An immediate report suggested that his last words had been a repetition of the hackneyed charge that the German people were responsible for Hitler. This surprised me, for I had known of Woollcott as a civilised and intelligent man, so I took steps to check the story — and found that what he had actually said was: 'The German people are just as reponsible for Hitler as the people of Chicago are for the *Chicago Tribune*.'

This twofold occupation in London went on for one year, till the summer of 1943. Almost every weekend, certainly three out of four, I was at Bradwell—which was in a 'restricted area': one had to have a pass to go there—and touring the constituency, giving 'report-back' meetings in village halls; more often, in fine weather, on village greens. At Bradwell I lived in a small house by the waterside, with Jeannie Hunt to look after me, my own house being now the officers' mess of the greatly expanded local R.A.F. station. One night—I can't remember why—we had to put up the crew of a bomber which had crash-landed; one of them had to share my bed, another wet his bed—a misfortune probably due as much to the nervous tension of his job as to the quantity of beer he had drunk. This R.A.F. station was for fighters, not bombers. It was not hit by enemy bombs as often as it might have been because an ingenious replica of it, with alluring lights, had been constructed a few miles up the Blackwater, and this proved an effective decoy. On many evenings, later in the war, I used to sit on the broad window-sill in the bar of the Green Man watching the V1s, or buzz-bombs, coming in over us from the North Sea, moving quite slowly and making that unmistakable chug-chugging noise.

Occasionally I managed to get a weekend in Sussex, at Tickerage Mill, the home of Dick Wyndham, who before the war had given and well into the war was still giving the best weekend parties I have ever attended. Some of those who were often there were Cyril Connolly, John Rayner, A. J. A. Symons, Curtis Moffat, Peter Quennell and Constant Lambert, with assorted wives and girl-friends. Before the war, Constant would come down late after conducting at Covent Garden, still in white tie and tails, and by the light of many candles we would drink and play Lexicon till dawn. Dick had a superbly stocked cellar. On the sideboard before dinner would still be ranged that battery of perhaps half-a-dozen magnum decanters of château-bottled claret. Glancing at his visitors' book one day in 1943, I found on the first page, dated January 1929, the signature of Oswald Mosley—and beside it scrawled, also in his writing, the comment: 'My God, won't this book fetch a lot one day!' I wonder who has the book now.

Then, in June 1943, came another sharp break in my life. I had been in Parliament for only one year, but on the *Express* for fifteen years. One day, when I was about to go to the country for weekend

speaking engagements – I was booked to speak in Braintree market
square on the Saturday – Trevor Evans, the industrial correspondent and always one of the kindest and nicest people on the paper,
happened to mention a rumour that Sir Andrew Duncan, the
Minister of Supply in the Churchill Government, was planning to
retire from politics and return to private industry. I checked, and
found that this was not merely a rumour; it was a firm intention.
In my speech I denounced this as a grave scandal: apart from Sir
Andrew's knowledge of war production secrets, which might be
highly profitable to private industry, it seemed wrong for a leading
Minister to back out of his job at this critical moment in the war.
(I didn't mention that Beaverbrook had done the same.) I made
sure that the press had copies of this passage in the speech, and the
Sunday Times ran it on the front page. The leak must have caused
something of a commotion in Government circles (and perhaps
some embarrassment to my employer, who would have some irate
telephone calls). On Monday Christiansen sent for me and sacked
me forthwith, on the grounds that I was using outside the office,
for partisan political purposes, information which I had obtained,
presumably in a confidential conversation, in the office. I think that
he was, at least arguably, justified in this action; I also think that
the strain of combining Parliament and constituency work with a
daily column (with paper rationing, not quite so everyday as in
peacetime) would probably have led to my departure from the
Express fairly soon. They gave me six months' money in lieu of
notice; I can't remember how much this was – not much by present-
day standards – but then money was worth more in those days.
I think that, when I left the *Express*, I was earning, in pay and
expenses, about £50 to £60 a week. Later Beaverbrook asked me if
they had given me enough; I foolishly said Yes. He also said, truly
or not, that he had opposed the sacking and had told Christiansen
to get me back. About ten days after the sacking, Christiansen did
ask me to return, on my own terms, for by that time several other
people had had a shot at doing the column; the mistake was made
of trying to do it just as I had done it, and in my style, instead of
letting another 'Hickey' (if they had to keep the absurd name)
develop his own individual style. But 'style' in that sense, as a
personal attribute, was something alien to Beaverbrook's thinking.
While I was still doing Hickey, I had the greatest difficulty – it

took months of argument, memoranda and pleading—in persuading him to allow the signature to be slightly different when I was away on holiday—though it must have been puzzling to the reader if, apparently, the same columnist contradicted one day the views he had expressed the previous day. Eventually it was agreed that, when I was away, the column should be signed, dynastically, William Hickey II. To Beaverbrook a column was a slab of printed words: he knew if he liked it or not, but not how it happened. '*Le style, c'est l'homme même.*' (The best aphorism on style that I know is by George Sampson, the Cambridge scholar: 'Style is the feather in the arrow, not the feather in the cap.')

I did not return to the *Express*. Apart from the general principle of not back-tracking, I had at once had an approach from Bill (now Sir William) Richardson, the editor of *Reynolds News*, a fairly left-wing Sunday paper belonging to the Co-operative movement. Here, after a few preliminary articles, I did for many years, under my own name, a column which was similar to 'Hickey' in some respects but was much more uncompromisingly political. It had the advantages of requiring my services only once a week instead of daily; it supplemented and complemented my work as a left-wing M.P.; and, from 1945 onwards, it helped to consolidate my new position as a member of the Labour Party.

A pause for recapitulation seems to fit in here. I never like using the word 'career' of myself. I don't think I have had one, if the word implies an evolving pattern directed, perhaps by ambition, to a planned and foreseeable climax. My adult life, as I hope this book shows, has hinged on a series of chances—the Sitwell introduction to Baxter, the Maldon by-election, the move from the *Express* to *Reynolds News*—each leading to a new phase lasting some years. Except in the case of Maldon, none of these developments occurred as a result of my own initiative: I am naturally lazy, and when I get into a position in which I am reasonably comfortable, I tend to stick there. While I was still working regularly for a newspaper, to a remarkable degree my political and journalistic lives interacted: I would not have won Maldon as an Independent if I had not been known as the *Express* columnist; I would not have been a Labour M.P. if I had not first been an Independent M.P. for three years (but I am coming to that); and in 1949, after I had been writing my column in *Reynolds News* for six years, and had been a member of the Labour Party for only four years, the Party conference unexpectedly elected me to the National Executive Committee of the Party. This can only have been due to the *Reynolds* column; I would not otherwise have been widely enough known in the movement (except for occasional newspaper reports of rows that I was involved in in the House). I was re-elected to the N.E.C. every year from 1950 to 1972. *Reynolds News* was transformed into the Tabloid *Sunday Citizen* in 1962; in 1966 the managing editor, Eric Wright, fired me (over lunch at my favourite restaurant, the Gay Hussar) because they couldn't go on paying fifty guineas a week for my small column; and in 1967 the *Sunday Citizen* died. In recent years I have worked as a freelance, sometimes contributing the 'London Diary' to the *New Statesman*, and doing many book-reviews, some for that remarkable monthly, *Books and Bookmen*. In February 1974, I retired from Parliament. It has, I suppose, been a sort of 'career'; but I still don't like the word.

'Yes, but,' a reader may say (and it has often been said to me), 'you were in Parliament for a long time and seem to have done reasonably well. How is it that you were never made even a junior Minister?' The answer is simple: both the Labour Prime Ministers with whom I served, Attlee and Wilson, knew of my reputation as a homosexual and both were deeply prejudiced puritans – though Attlee had been at a public school, Haileybury, at which homosexual practices flourished in or soon after his day. So this 'career' perfectly illustrates a twofold theme of this book – that it is possible for a practising homosexual to do an adequate job in public life, but that if it is known that he is homosexual he will be subject to discrimination.

Back in 1943 and 1944 I had no anxiety about my future in politics. Now and then I discussed it quite casually, with friends in the smoking-room of the House – people on the Right as well as the Left of the Labour Party. I had not thought out in detail what was likely to happen at Maldon when the Party truce ended, as it would at the end of the war. Ellen Wilkinson was sympathetically eager that I should get into the Labour Party as soon as I could (bearing in mind my pledge to my constituents); John Parker, M.P. for Dagenham, whose neighbour I was to become at Barking in 1959, suggested that as a step towards joining the Party I should join the Fabian Society, which I did; Fred Bellenger, a right-wing house-agent who became in the post-war Labour Government Secretary of State for War — one of Attlee's worst appointments — said, in a sneering voice: '*You'll* never be a Labour M.P., Tom.' A few years later, through my election to the N.E.C., I was one of those on whose endorsement his candidature depended.

The General Election of 1945, immediately after the end of the war in Europe, was unlike others in that many constituency Parties, on both sides, had been caught unawares and had for various reasons not selected their candidates. In other cases, candidates had been selected and were in the Forces overseas: special arrangements were made to bring them home at once for the campaign. At Maldon the Constituency Labour Party faced a peculiar difficulty: the prospective candidate, Morris Janis, had been selected some time before; but he unfortunately was overseas and could not be brought home quickly, for he was a prisoner in a Japanese P.o.W. camp. Meanwhile the constituency had been represented in Parliament by an Independent, manifestly of the Left, who had captured the seat from the Tories, had served the constituents more actively than was customary, and was in consequence 'popular'. There were various considerations in the minds of delegates to the crucial meeting of the General Management Committee of Maldon Labour Party: first, there were only a few weeks to go to the rushed polling-day, and a decision had to be reached that day. Then there were a few — to whom, perhaps, I already seemed too Left-wing — who felt that they ought to be loyal to the chosen candidate, in the hope that he might yet be released from prison camp just in time, or even fight the campaign *in absentia* (not a realistic hope, this, since he would have been unable to sign the necessary papers). But the strongest feeling among the delegates appeared to be that I should be, so to speak, drafted. At the meeting they made embarrassing speeches praising my three-year record, in Parliament and in the constituency, and urging their colleagues to agree that I should be selected as the official Labour candidate.

There was just one snag: even at that late date, I did not particularly *want* to join the Labour Party. This may seem strange: I have since then been national chairman of the Labour Party, and

I now believe it to be, with its mass membership in the trade unions, the only instrument through which there can be in Britain an advance towards Socialism; but at that time I still retained much of the youthful impatience which had taken me into the Communist Party; the Labour Party seemed to me rather stuffy and bourgeois. So I was as torn in mind as the delegates were — and I decided, in my genuine doubt, to put myself in their hands. I was called on to speak, and said that various courses were open to them and to me: either I could continue as an Independent with their friendly support, and this was what I would like best (I realise now that this was 'not on', since every major Party claims the right to run its own candidate in every constituency); or they could choose some other candidate, already an experienced member of their Party, and I would stand down (for I would not split the Left-wing vote); or, if they insisted but with some reluctance on my part, I would agree to be their candidate. They opted over-whelmingly — I am not sure, but I think unanimously — for the last course.

Re-reading this, I realise that it may look as though my speech was cunningly slanted to achieve the result that did follow. This is not so: I was honest in preferring the first of the three courses, but, knowing it only from outside, I underestimated the intense loyalty of Labour people to the Party, as Party, which is one of the great strengths of the Labour Party; I found their response moving and accepted the decision with humble gratitude.

The enforced absence of Morris Janis, which was extremely bad luck for him — quite apart from what he may have been undergoing in the Japanese camp — made this another of those cardinal chances that have determined the course of my life. Had he been available, the Maldon Party could not have made the offer to me; if by some aberration they had, I could not have accepted. Standing down at Maldon, I would either have reverted to full-time journalism or, just possibly, found another constituency; as I have indicated, there were quite a few going at that moment. But I had formed so strong an attachment to Maldon, and knew so many of the people there, that I wouldn't have liked another seat so well.

By the platform at the G.M.C. meeting, in the wings, stood a mild little man whom I had not noticed until he stepped forward with some papers for me to sign. This was Wilf Young, the Party's admirable regional organiser; he told me later that he had been anxiously keeping his fingers crossed, and 'sweating', in case the decision went the other way. The first form that he gave me to sign was an application for membership of the Party: I became, probably, the only Labour M.P. who had actually joined the Party at his adoption meeting. (There may have been one or two others at this exceptional election, when dozens of serving officers, knowing little about politics, flocked to get candidatures in the Party that looked like winning. Some became junior Ministers in Attlee's Government; most of these are now safely where they belong, in the Tory Party). I have often recalled this meeting when, sitting on the N.E.C. platform at Party conference, I have heard passionate speeches from delegates demanding that nobody should be allowed to be a Labour candidate till he has been a member of the Party for at least ten years.

The result of the 1945 General Election is part of history. Here I need only briefly record that at Maldon the campaign was largely a repetition of the 1942 by-election campaign, with national and local supporters backing, this time, an official Labour candidate (and with another message from G.B.S.). But this time the Conservatives put up a much more sophisticated candidate — a sharp young barrister named Melford Stevenson. Having defeated him, I feel rather like the old Irish mother who gives a son to the Church: in his case, it was the Bench, for he became the distinguished Draconian judge who has imposed controversially heavy sentences on Cambridge offenders. His successor as my Tory opponent, Aubrey Moody, I did give to the Church: after his second defeat, in 1951, he went to Mirfield and studied for the priesthood: he is now Vicar of Feering in what was the Maldon constituency. He is a great charmer, with a charismatic smile and a beautifully vague manner. The Maldon Tories (whom a great local friend of mine, Dr David Cargill, described as 'snobs, spivs, and counter-jumpers') didn't really take to Aubrey: he was too gentle for them, and too apt to be friendly with political opponents — 'too nice to be in politics', some said. He had considerable private wealth, and had been in the Coldstream Guards. He described to me how, at the fall of Tobruk, he had stood by the road and watched the German tanks sweep in; and how the German officer standing on the foremost tank had stared at him but had made no move to take him prisoner. 'Perhaps,' said Aubrey in his quiet, ingenuous voice, 'he recognised me from Baden-Baden.'

There was one episode, in the year before the 1945 election, which stands out in my memory; it was not without elements of drama. In the House and in my column I had on a number of occasions expressed detestation of racialism, drawn attention to instances of it, and urged action to check it. Early in 1944 a number of us became aware of a serious incidence of anti-Semitism among the Polish Armed Forces stationed in Scotland — not surprising in view of the long history of this disease in Poland, but unacceptable in our own country, in the Forces of an ally in what was thought to be a war against Nazism and for democracy. One day I received an urgent message: would I go that night to meet some Jewish soldiers from Scotland at a hall in Whitechapel, in the East End of London. I went to the hall: its blackout was imperfect, so we had only the light of one or two candles and a hand-shaded torch; and by this dim light I could just make out a large number of men in khaki. About a hundred of them had gone absent without leave from their units and had come to London to protest about the intolerable persecution to which they were being subjected by Polish soldiers, supposed to be their comrades. One after another stood up and gave his testimony: each had experience of some such threat as 'When we land in Europe I'll have one bullet for a German and one for you.'

For the opening of the Second Front — D-day — though none of us knew exactly on what date, was approaching; and this, I think, was why the campaign to save these Jewish soldiers was one of the shortest political campaigns that I have ever engaged in; the War Office didn't want trouble among the Allied Forces just as they were getting poised for the invasion.

We campaigned both in and out of Parliament. For the National Council for Civil Liberties, who ran the extra-parliamentary side of it, I wrote a pamphlet, *Absentees for Freedom* (they were not, technically, 'deserters'). We held a big meeting at the Stoll opera-house in Kingsway, at which Eleanor Rathbone, Michael Foot and I spoke and more than £1,000 was raised in the collection. (This may have been because the C.P. were backing us: they were always good at organising collections.) In the House we pressed the

Government hard, in questions and in debate; at first we got the usual futile answers: assurances, which we knew to be worthless, had been obtained from the Polish commanders ... Then, suddenly, the Government gave way: the Jewish soldiers were to be transferred at once to the British Army. The odd thing was that we had pursued this matter in the House against the advice — the almost lachrymose pleading — of the official spokesmen of the Jewish community in Britain. They felt that any publicity about this might lead to more anti-Semitism, perhaps directed against their own flock. They may have been right from their point of view, and they may have been making private representations to the War Office, but I felt afterwards that, if I had listened to them, those Jewish soldiers would still have been suffering bullying in Scotland or been killed by Polish bullets in Normandy.

Some weeks after this surprising, and heartening, success, a green card was sent to me at the House: a small deputation of Polish-Jewish soldiers had called to say thank-you (a courtesy that M.P.s rarely get from their regular constituents). They were flourishing in health and spirits, and looked smart in their new uniform, with British Army flashes on the shoulders. They had brought a thank-offering — a bottle of fine old brandy, almost unobtainable at that time. 'Where on earth did you get it?' I asked. 'Ah,' they replied, 'we have a cousin in the trade.'

13

War correspondent

During Parliament's long summer recess in 1944, I took advantage of my accreditation as a war correspondent – from *Reynolds News* now, not from the *Express* – to go to the Western Front and see what was happening there. It was D-day + 77 – i.e., mid-August – when I crossed the Channel, from Southampton to a Normandy beach at Arromanches. This meant a few days' wait in Southampton, then severely wrecked, sordid, and overcrowded with men of the Allied Forces; I found a few former comrades from the C.P. among the seamen. The pubs were suffering from a shortage of beer and a shortage of glasses, so that what beer there was had to be drunk – warm, brackish, watery – out of jam-jars, often someone else's unwashed jam-jar.

The ship I crossed in was the *Princess Josephine Charlotte*, an old Ostend cross-Channel steamer. She had the best sick-bay I had ever seen in a ship that size, with a seven-bedded ward and brilliantly lit operating theatre – presumably because, on the return journey, she would be carrying casualties. By some freak of red-tape, the Admiralty, while supplying a hypodermic syringe, firmly refused to supply needles to go in it. Looking at the account of this crossing that I wrote at the time, I see that I had caught, from Auden or somebody, the 'catalogue' trick, tiresome unless strictly controlled: there were 500 Guardsmen on board, reinforcements for the Guards Armoured Division, mostly sleeping the night on deck; and I noted that sleep smoothed out the mask of discipline and revealed their diverse human characters – 'the brutish, the coltish, the vacant, the knowing, the spotted cherub, the dark horse, the hard-bitten, the joker'.

After various adventures with the British and American forces and after some blissful nights in newly liberated Paris, where I found Harold Acton in R.A.F. uniform, an American correspondent, G. K. Hodenfield, and I personally liberated Liège (as I proudly noted, the third largest city in Belgium). We rode into it in a jeep at 5.30 p.m. on September 8th, 1944, and were instantly swamped by cheering, kissing, flower-throwing crowds – and discovered that we were well ahead of the first of the American troops: the Germans had only just left. In the hotel we went to, which had been the Gestapo H.Q., the beds were still warm, the waste-paper baskets full of German débris – German newspapers, razor-blades and benzedrine tablets. At 9 p.m. we heard the B.B.C. announce that Allied Forces were 'pressing on a broad front towards Liège'.

Brussels was fairly shocking. I was not surprised that it was said to have demoralised more armies in history than any other capital. Luxurious black-market restaurants were filled with war profiteers, who had sold to the Germans whatever they needed, now feeding champagne and steaks to British officers. At least the Resistance organisations, especially the 'White Army', were doing their best to catch some of the humbler collaborators:

Night after night they go on their rounds, combing the multitudinous cafés and bars of Brussels.

I was in a café last night when a rather dreary, youngish man began to talk to me. He had a Resistance brassard on his arm and a Soviet emblem in his buttonhole. He asked the usual questions about England, and seemed anxious to go and work there.

Suddenly and quietly, two men – a tall young one and a short older one – came in and stood by him. They exchanged a few words – and the younger hit him sharply on the chin, while the elder held a pistol to his chest.

He cowered with his face to the wall, his hands up, while they went through his pockets. They found that he had no right to be wearing the brassard. He had been recognised as a Rexist, they said. They took him away.

Outside a café which is being raided, two Resistance cars draw up facing each other, twenty yards apart, and turn on blinding headlights, so that no one can slink out of the café without being seen.

Almost as tough, and more gruesome, was the revenge administered to collaborators and suspects at Antwerp. They were detained, awaiting trial, in the lion-house at the Zoo there:

The lion-house is a large one — much larger than that in the London Zoo. A harsh top-light from the glass roof beats down on the cages, in each of which are half-a-dozen or more men and youths. They pace up and down as though they were the original tenants; or lounge against the thick bars which form the front of their cages, hats pulled over their eyes; or lie huddled apathetically on the loose straw which is their only furniture. Because of the straw, they may not smoke.

Amiable marble-whiskered busts of defunct dignitaries of the Zoo beam down on them.

They were unimpressive types, varying from the brutish to the imbecile. They would have looked at home in a British blackshirt procession. One, I was told, had betrayed 17 of his patriotic fellow-citizens to the Gestapo.

The most respectably-dressed was an editor and publisher, with a weak, pink, Liberal face.

Two cages were full of women: one had a pekingese dog with her.

A wax-pale, blond boy of 23 stretched desperate hands to me between the bars. He had only been a member of a Nazi organisation for two months, he insisted, and only because he was so poor — because the pay was good and there were extra rations.

All that will be fairly sorted out and checked at his trial.

I remarked to the White Army officer who showed me round that these seemed to be small fry, that there weren't any obvious millionaires, any prominent industrial collaborators, behind these bars.

He admitted that many such had escaped, having more facilities for escape — some to Germany. He added with pride, however, that the Burgomaster of Antwerp himself had been one of the earliest occupants of a cage.

On the day of the disastrous airborne operation at Arnhem — Sunday, September 17th, 1944 — I was with the British armoured forces as they swept up a long, straight road into Holland to try to join the paratroops; this, had the plan not been betrayed to the Germans, supposedly by a Dutch spy, would have been the greatest land-air operation since D-day. Here I caught up with the Guards Armoured Division, including, no doubt, some of the men I had crossed the Channel with. Their tanks advanced along this straight main road, hindered rather than helped (or so it seemed) by the deafening, intensive barrage put over by our own Typhoons, some of whose rockets hit our forward tanks. The woods on each side were still full of live Germans: the Devons had the tricky task of clearing these woods:

The top floor of a battered house made a good observation post for a Gunner captain. He had been there for several days, with Germans only 50 yards along the road — 'the leading man of the 2nd Army', they called him.

From his window we could see the infantry advancing across the meadows towards an ominous wood, reported to contain an S.S. battalion. Cows, grazing peacefully, seemed not to notice the incessant shell-fire at all; one suddenly rolled over and lay grotesquely dead. (Pigs, more cannily, get down in slit-trenches when the noise starts: it is disconcerting to find one in a trench beside you.)

Along the road the tanks rumbled forward in stages. Sometimes they would stop for ten minutes, and there would be time for a smoke. As the Typhoons and their rockets roared and howled above us, showers of empty shells and ammunition-clips came tinkling down like shrapnel.

I walked through a wood that the Typhoons had torn up. It was a plantation of young firs cut by a straight track running diagonally from the main road. Every third or fourth tree seemed to have been hit. The shattered trees, and their white fresh splinters, made a crazy angular pattern in the sombre plantation.

By the path lay a young English officer, his left arm torn out, his head battered. A German sniper a few yards away seemed to have been killed by blast; his uniform was in shreds, his body curled up in horrible contortion, his greenish fingers clutching the air stiffly.

Towards dusk, under an ominous sky, we came out on an open common or heath; and here was a heartrending spectacle indeed — a dozen or more of our great tanks dotted about, stuck motionlessly on either side of the road, all blazing furiously. The trouble about Shermans seems to be that they do catch fire ('brew up', the phrase is) rather easily; and the fire is so fierce and quick that some of the crew are usually trapped. 'Sergeant-major ——'s dead, sir,' a man standing on one of these burning tanks called out to the Guards officer I was walking with.

The aplomb of these young officers is miraculous. In the most unpleasant and noisy predicaments they behave as if they were strolling into Trumper's in Curzon Street for a hair-cut. With all sorts of ugly objects hurtling around, they wear berets, not tin hats. They have the *sang froid* which conceals a courage that is none the less real.

All the time, wretched straggling files of German prisoners were being prodded along, at the double, towards our rear. (My Scottish driver, Andy M——, couldn't resist taking charge of one lot of them.) The Germans looked done for and absolutely terrified; they were subjected to a good deal of rough badinage as they trotted past. Several of our chaps told me of 'dirty tricks' that some of the Germans were alleged to have been up to — pretending to surrender, for instance, and then tossing a grenade. These stories may have been exaggerated; but men who have just seen their friends killed horribly are not in a tolerant mood.

Later the same night I saw many parties of prisoners, huddled in stables, or kitchens talking in low voices while their guards played cards. Most of them, I noticed, had been furnished with cigarettes. The English are not good haters.

As night fell, the fires blazed up more luridly or died smouldering away. To complete the misery of the scene, a fine but heavy rain began to fall, soaking everyone and everything, pulping into the mindless earth the note-books and letters from home and snapshots of girls scattered everywhere from the pockets of the dead men.

Some nights I slept in the vehicle that had been allotted to me; I think it was a Land-Rover. One night I got a room in a window-less, lightless, waterless, blitzed hotel at Eindhoven. It always amused me to note small, incongruous details: here, for instance, on my bedside table was a copy of Dorothy L. Sayers' *Nine Tailors* belonging to Cricklewood Public Library.

Some years later the editor of *Reynold News* asked me to under-take an unusual mission which took my thoughts back to that episode in Holland. One of the paper's local contacts in the north country had discovered, working underground in a coalmine, a man who, as an airborne soldier, had been shot down and severely wounded at Arnhem: he had lost an eye and both arms. Astonish-ingly, he was able with artificial arms to do a job down the pit. This man, whose name was Andrew Milbourne, had one am-bition – to return to Arnhem, visit the graves of his comrades in the war cemetery there, and meet and thank the Dutch family who had befriended him when he lay almost dying. The editor said that if I would escort this man to Arnhem, look after him (for he still needed some attention) and write the story, the paper would hire a small aircraft to fly us there for the weekend and back. It was one of the most moving and rewarding newspaper jobs that I have ever done. Looking after him for only a few days and nights, I realised in a small way something of the patient devotion with which his wife must be caring for him all the time: cutting up the food on his plate, helping him to dress and undress and bathe, swabbing out the socket of his blind eye ... He had had to show a lot of patience, too, and was learning to be more and more independent of others' help. I liked him and thought highly of him, and wrote an intro-duction to a book *Lease of Life*,[1] in which he described his experiences. He had learned to type with his claw-like artificial hands, and later got a highly suitable job in the Ministry of Pensions at Newcastle.

Seven months later, in April, 1945, I went on another mission to Europe, not as a correspondent but as an M.P. – as a member of the parliamentary delegation which went to inspect Buchenwald concentration-camp just after the American forces had overrun this camp and Belsen. It is easy to use words like 'unforgettable'

[1] Museum Press, London, 1952.

and 'incredible'. I simply know that of all the experiences of my life — and there have been some unpleasant and beastly ones — this was by far the worst.

One Friday morning — usually a quiet day in Parliament — I was sitting relaxed on one of the red benches, half-listening to the start of the day's business, when the Speaker got up and read a telegram which he had received from General Eisenhower. (A similar message had been sent to Congress in Washington.) It was a pressing invitation to Parliament to send without delay — he meant, before all the bodies were buried — a delegation of M.P.s to see what the Americans had uncovered in Buchenwald. Such a delegation is always an all-Party one. The members of it are chosen by the Whips, in consultation with the Speaker. I don't know why I, an Independent, was included; possibly, because with my journalistic experience, I could be expected to draft quickly an accurate and readable report. There were ten members of this delegation, from both Houses of Parliament; the leader of it was Lord Addison, a veteran doctor of medicine.

We left next morning by air. Eisenhower, looking spruce and fit — very different from the flabby old President of later years — received us hospitably. We drove on at once to the camp and were, so to speak, thrown in at the deep end. We spent many hours talking to the inmates (some of whom could speak English, while some of us could speak German), assessing their state of health, listening to their stories. The Americans had been there for a week or more, clearing the camp and giving medical treatment, but prisoners were still dying at the rate of thirty-five a day. We were photographed standing beside a cart piled high with dead prisoners:

The bodies were scraggy and tiny, the flesh turning patchily green and mauve, the eyes filmed and staring, the feet sticking out stiffly at odd angles, some of the young mouths fixed in an eternal scream. A tiresome little breeze blew dust from the cart into our faces.

But I found the dead — hardly human as they were, like waxen Tussaud figures — less moving than the emaciated living, whom one wanted so desperately, and could do so little, to help. They lay crowded together on their scraps of quilt, their eyes enormous, lustrous, and pleading in their shrunken faces — little tadpoles or grasshoppers of men with big bullet skulls and match-stick limbs.

These wasted bodies are the answer to anybody who is foolish or wicked enough, as some are, to try to mitigate the Nazis' criminality by pretending that it was only in the last few weeks before the camps were uncovered that 'some disorganisation', attributable to military reverses, had caused food shortages. These extremes of physical debility could only be the result of many months of deliberate starvation, applied as a ruthless economic as well as ideological policy to those who were no longer healthy enough to work.

There was something else more sickening still:

Worse than any sight or sound was the smell that overhung the whole place, even after a week's intensive cleaning-up: a stuffy, sweetish-sour smell, not unlike the ordinary prison smell plus death and decay; a stench, compounded of excrement, dirty blankets, disinfectant, and decomposing flesh, which seemed to seep pervadingly into every channel of our heads and cranny of our clothing and to linger in everything that one took away from the camp.

I had always been — and still am — sceptical about 'atrocity stories'; in all wars they are invented and spread, by the British no less than by everyone else, as part of the war effort. But the *penchant* for tattooed human skin of Frau Ilse Koch, wife of the Nazi Commandant of Buchenwald, was no myth: such was the volume of evidence that we felt obliged to accept even this fantastic horror:

Frau Koch, I was told, was always quite nice and ladylike about this business. She would never let them stage actual parades of tattooed men. However, if one of the doctors or guards happened to notice a prisoner with a good specimen of tattooing, they would mark him down and later kill him (painlessly, with an injection).

We brought home with us pieces of some of the lampshades that she had had made from the tattooed skin.

It was an exhausting and horrifying day that we spent in

Buchenwald. I think that the shock was the greater for us because of the sudden contrast with the comparative comfort of even wartime London. That night we were accommodated in an hotel in Erfurt. Usually, when M.P.s are on an overseas delegation and have had a tiring day, they relax light-heartedly in the evening, and there is a certain amount of frivolity. That was not possible in this case; and it was not easy to eat the rather high hamburgers they served for dinner.

A curious sequel to this visit was that, of the ten members of the delegation, almost all fell ill, in one way or another, quite soon: one went down with laryngitis, one who had been (before the war) strongly pro-German had a severe breakdown and retired from Parliament not long afterwards. The one woman member of the delegation, Mrs Mavis Tate, who had borne the experience with calm fortitude, died two years later; it was said that she had never completely recovered. The two of us who seemed to take it best were the two who could to some extent treat the whole thing professionally: Addison, who could look at it as a medical problem; and myself, making copious notes and thinking of the treatment I would give it as a journalist. I am now the only survivor of that party.

As I had anticipated, I was called on to write the official report of our visit; it was agreed unanimously and signed by all the members of the delegation, and published almost at once as a government White Paper. It was written, I think, in reasonably good plain English. One paragraph in particular impressed my old Oxford friend Brian Howard. (Some might not regard this as the highest recommendation; his own biographer reckoned his life a failure and Evelyn Waugh, who modelled Anthony Blanche on him, called him 'mad, bad, and dangerous to know'; but Auden paid him the signal honour of dedicating a major poem to him, and one person, an ex-A.B. named Sam, who nursed him through tuberculosis, loved him.) He insisted on reading this passage aloud, rather dramatically, one night at the Gargoyle Club. It was a paragraph describing the dysentery hut:

This hut was about 80 ft long by 24 ft wide; estimates of its normal sick population varied from 700 to 1,300. Four, five or six men, including those who had undergone operations (performed without anaesthetics by prisoner doctors on a crude operating-table at one end of the hut, in full view of the other patients), had regularly to lie in each of the small shelf cubicles. Here, too, there were no mattresses. The excreta of the dysentery patients dripped down from tier to tier. If the living were strong enough, they pushed the dead out into the gangway. Each night the dead were thrown into a small annexe at one end of the hut, and each morning collected and taken in carts to the crematorium or, if required as specimens, to the pathological laboratory of the Nazi doctors.

That was a few days after I had got back and the White Paper had just been published. Dylan Thomas was also at this club that night, and questioned me closely about Buchenwald. After listening intently, he said: 'They ought to send poets there.' If he could have gone, the ghastly experience might have inspired some powerful poetry.

In the summer of 1945, the war in Europe was over, the war in the Far East was still dragging on. The General Election had been won by Labour, but the official result had not yet been announced when I went for a few days to the Potsdam Conference. (The counting of the votes was delayed for a few weeks so that the ballot papers from troops overseas could be included.) At Potsdam, in the hall in which press briefings were held, the Russians, in accordance with their custom, had put up enormous portraits of Stalin, Churchill, and Truman. I caused an incredulously derisive stir by asking whether a similar large portrait of Attlee was being prepared to replace Churchill's when the election result was announced. At about this time I received an urgent invitation from Frank Owen, who was editing *SEAC* (the South-East Asia Command daily newspaper), backed officially by Command H.Q., to come out there as a war correspondent, to write about the troops in Burma, who were beginning to feel themselves, in a familiar phrase, a 'forgotten army'.

Then, on August 6th and August 9th, the atomic bombs fell on Hiroshima and Nagasaki, and Japan surrendered. The Supreme Allied Commander in South-East Asia (SACSEA) was Admiral Lord Louis Mountbatten (now Earl Mountbatten of Burma). He was given very little warning of this literally epock-making event: during the Potsdam Conference he happened to be briefly on leave in Paris, and Churchill, hearing he was there, said 'Send him here'. When he got to Potsdam, Churchill and Truman, each in turn, took him into an empty room, shut the door, and in strict confidence told him about the bomb and the collapse of Japan that it would inevitably cause. He was aghast: he had made elaborate plans for the invasion of Japanese-held Burma and Malaya and the defeat of the Japanese in land-fighting (which he believed to be, for various reasons, the correct policy). Now all those plans would have to be scrapped – but, having been told about the bomb in confidence, he would be unable to tell his staff the reason for scrapping them.

So I got to Mountbatten's H.Q. – in a series of huts ranged across the beautiful Botanic Gardens at Kandy, in Ceylon – just as a kind of peace was breaking out in Asia as well as Europe. The most welcome immediate consequence was the liberation of thousands of British prisoners-of-war from Japanese camps throughout this area. This was in itself a massive problem: there was not enough shipping-space to send all these ex-P.o.W.s home at once, or even soon; they were in a high state of emotional excitement but also suffering from malnutrition and beri-beri, septic prickly heat and other tropical complaints; they had to stay in the camps – there was nowhere else to put them – and be subject to some discipline. Conditions in such camps were foul. In a camp hospital ward that I was visiting, I stood for a moment with my foot resting casually on the edge of a low bed. 'I should mind your foot,' said the patient – and lifted the side of his mattress to disclose the loathsome traffic of not one or two but swarming hundreds of bugs.

They still felt the effects of the brutal and wasteful Japanese policy of withholding Red Cross food-parcels from prisoners. At one camp, Kranji, they built a wall from unopened tins and cases of Red Cross food.

Soon Mountbatten had to leave Kandy to go to Singapore for the Japanese surrender ceremony. He took me with him in his comfortable white-leather-padded Dakota. An A.D.C. and the Supremo's batman were with us, the batman to serve meals en route. Mountbatten is what is known as a perfectionist: he tends to become obsessed with detail and therefore, perhaps, not to delegate sufficiently. On this journey something was wrong with the lock of the lavatory door: the A.D.C. heard about little else till we arrived at our first stop. By Mountbatten's choice we went by a roundabout route, so as to be able to visit as many P.o.W. camps as possible on the way. We spent several nights at Rangoon, and this was where I first appreciated Mountbatten's political acumen and his understanding of the new nationalist forces rising in Asia. We attended a dinner given by Rangoon's Orient Club at which a Japanese officer's dagger was presented to Mountbatten by Aung San—approximately, the Tito of Burma, the outstanding Resistance leader; unlike some of the older Burmese politicians, honest and incorruptible; a slight, boyish figure with a surprisingly strong, deep voice; physically and mentally agile, with an irrepressible sense of humour and a gift for cynical wisecracking which he exercised impartially at the expense of his Burmese friends and of the British. At this Orient Club dinner the elder statesmen of Burma, with their dainty pink or mauve headdresses, sat at the top table: they had been crass enough to put Aung San at a lower table, at the far end of the room, and his name was not in the printed toast-list on the menu. Mountbatten insisted that Aung San should be called on to speak, even threatening that if Aung San did not speak he, Mountbatten, would not speak either. Aung San's was the speech of the evening. In the course of it, while paying tribute to the conciliatory spirit shown by Mountbatten in their conference at Kandy, he said (in fluent English):

The principles of an Act may be all right when the Act is passed; but principles are liable to be undermined by the rules framed under the Act; and the rules again undermined by directives; and the directives by the whims and fancies of the persons executing them ...

From the time of this visit, from the first of many meetings with Aung San, Burmese independence, and the transfer of power to Aung San and his People's Anti-Fascist freedom movement, was a cause that I was committed to and pressed on the Government in many Friday morning sessions in the House. There were only a few M.P.s who took an interest in this: one of them was Woodrow

Wyatt, who later moved to the Right, left Parliament, and became a successful owner of provincial newspapers and a *Sunday Mirror* columnist. But it took an awful lot of prodding to induce Attlee to move (as Nye Bevan used to say when he came into the smoking-room for a drink after a wearisome Cabinet meeting, 'We'll never get anywhere till we get rid of this fellow Attlee'); and eventually it was Mountbatten who saw Attlee and persuaded him that it was necessary — militarily necessary — to fix a date for Burmese independence. As Leader of the Opposition, Churchill was stertorously opposed to this instalment of the liquidation of the Empire — partly, we supposed, because it was his father who had annexed Burma.

Another obstacle was Sir Reginald Dorman-Smith: he had been Governor of Burma before the war, retained this post nominally throughout the war, after the Japs had kicked us out, and was restored to it after the war. He was a blimp of the old school, bitterly mistrustful of Aung San and out of sympathy with Mountbatten's progressive ideas. I spent a long and fascinating evening dining and drinking alone in a private room with Mountbatten and Dorman-Smith, listening while they argued. Each time one of them went out of the room to pee, the other would say to me, 'Take no notice of what he's saying — he's just a hopeless reactionary' (or 'an irresponsible radical', as the case might be). I have no doubt that Dorman-Smith was one of those advising Attlee against giving way to our pressure.

At last, in 1948, Burma was independent. The first Burmese ambassador to Britain was a young man whom I had known throughout these years as a poor student living in one room in Hampstead (and as the London representative of the Burmese anti-Fascist front). His name was Maung Ohn: we called him 'Maung' even after he had acquired the more honorific prefix U. When he became ambassador his government bought him a grand car: he exchanged it for a smaller one, more suitable, he said, for the envoy of a poor country. And in the house which they bought for an embassy, he lived simply, making his own bed, eating austerely. He was a Buddhist and a Marxist, and one of the gentlest and most sincere people I have known. After London U Ohn was transferred to the Moscow embassy.

Aung San came to London in 1947 for talks about the details of the transfer of power. On the night before he returned to Burma I spent several hours with him in his hotel suite. He was depressed and seemed full of foreboding – undefined, though he saw clearly the difficulties ahead. He told me that he was by now convinced that it would be better for Burma to be a member of the Commonwealth; but he was not sure that, even with his great prestige and popularity, he could convince all his colleagues, and the Burmese people, that this would be the wisest course. A very few months later came news of an appalling tragedy: Aung San and all the ablest of his colleagues had been assassinated; assailants had burst into the room where they were meeting in cabinet and had mown them down with machine-guns.

Some years later, after U Ohn had left London, his successor gave a splendid reception, the purpose of which was to confer Burmese honours on Mountbatten and other friends of Burma. I learned privately that it had been the intention of the Burmese government to award honours also to one or two back-bench Labour M.P.s, including myself, who had helped Burma towards independence. Their embassy was advised through diplomatic channels that, as a routine courtesy, their list of honorands should first be shown to the Foreign Office: they were surprised, but I was not, when the list was returned with the back-benchers' names struck out.

After Rangoon we moved southwards towards Singapore, stopping several times on the way at camps in which British P.o.W.s, though now free, were still living. Mountbatten's technique on these occasions was brilliant. The men would be lined up formally in honour of the Supremo. He would jump up on a truck, followed by his wife, Edwina (who was there by virtue of her position as Dame Grand Cross of the Venerable Order of St John of Jerusalem); would order the men to break ranks and gather round; and would then give them a talk, ten or twelve minutes long, in which he would put them completely 'in the picture' – the picture both of the latest general news of war and peace and of their own prospects of repatriation. When he mentioned Labour's victory in the General Election, there was usually a cheer. This was not unexpected. Earlier that year, General Bill Slim – like Mountbatten, one of the senior officers whom the ordinary soldier had some respect for – had been in England and had gone to lunch at 10 Downing Street. Churchill asked him how the troops were going to vote. 'Ninety per cent Labour,' said Slim. 'Oh,' grunted Churchill, 'and what about the other ten per cent?' 'They won't vote at all.'

After several of these brief halts, we stopped for a night at Penang; and here, for the first time since we had left Kandy, Mountbatten had to put on evening kit for a dinner that was given in his honour. This was the occasion of a major domestic crisis. Like all royalty, Mountbatten is extremely knowledgeable and punctilious about orders and decorations and the correct wearing of them; and he had a good many rows of them. Some hours before the dinner it was found that his batman had forgotten to pack the miniature decorations which are worn, instead of the full-sized ones, with evening dress. The storm raged for some time – and then an A.D.C. checked, after much telephoning, that the miniatures had been found in the Supremo's quarters at Kandy and that there was just time before the dinner for an R.A.F. aircraft to fly them from Kandy to Penang.

At Singapore I was put up at Government House, whose huge bedrooms were crammed with 'top brass'. I was not quite up to major-general status, so I had to share a room with ten brigadiers. There was, of course, only one bathroom for each bedroom, so one had to queue for some time to get a bath. One day the Mountbattens gave a cocktail party, at which he introduced me to a man who ought to have qualified for that *Reader's Digest* series on unforgettable personalities – the Bishop of Singapore.[1] This was only days after his release. I arranged to meet him later; he told me the full story of his imprisonment (asking not to be made to seem a hero or a martyr) and I wrote at some length about him for *Reynolds News*:

> The Bishop was not detained immediately after the capitulation of Singapore in February 1942. He was therefore able to organise an underground supply of money for those already interned, so that they could buy food without which they would certainly have starved.
>
> On March 28th, 1943, he was interned; the Japanese seem

[1] Leonard Wilson, later Bishop of Birmingham.

to have thought that he was a key man in an espionage and sabotage organisation (which did not in fact exist).

The black date, at any rate, was 10/10/43 – 'the double tenth'. On or about that day, fifty-seven internees, including the Bishop, were removed from Changi jail to the Y.M.C.A. and other 'Gestapo' centres in Singapore. The Bishop remained in the Y.M.C.A., under frequent interrogation and torture, for $7\frac{3}{4}$ months.

I spent an evening with him, to hear about it. He is a man of 43, vigorous and broad-shouldered, with a fine head, a strong, eager, sun-burned, humorous face, and a black beard.

He described to me in detail his first three days of interrogation.

On the first night he had to kneel and was beaten about the shoulders for the space of two hours, 'but not severely'.

On the second day he had to kneel for a longer time, under a table, his hands strapped behind him and a triangular, sharp-edged rod fixed in behind his knees; the Japanese stamped and jumped repeatedly on his thighs, on which scars still show lividly.

On the third day he lay strapped on a table, face upwards, head hanging down over the end of the table. For many hours on end, guards in relays – seven men in all – flogged him from the waist downwards with threefold ropes. When he fainted they revived him and continued flogging. 'Naturally,' he says, almost casually, 'I was a complete wreck for days afterwards.'

They threw him back into his cell. 'Everything seemed to be disintegrating,' he said to me. 'You felt as if your mind didn't belong to you and as if your legs didn't belong to you.'

Yet the Bishop never once answered a question to the satisfaction of his captors. 'If it is possible to say this,' he added, hesitatingly,' without appearing a prig of various kinds – on the third day of this torture, by the grace of God, I overcame most of my fear.'

It was physically impossible not to cry out. Once, he confesses, he 'cried out most blasphemously, saying that this was worse than crucifixion'. But he never cursed those who were torturing him.

This astonished them. 'All the others swear at us,' they said. 'Why don't you?'

He explained that, in spite of appearances ('I was a little sarcastic about it'), he believed them to be God's children, brought up in wrong conditions.

'Why does God not save you?' they asked.

'He never does save you from pain,' he replied. 'He gives you courage to bear it.'

So he used to pray aloud, while they tormented him: 'I know, O Lord, that they are doing what it is their duty to do. Help them to see that I am innocent.'

His longest period of interrogation lasted for seventeen hours continuously.

Only one of his guards—a Buddhist—never ill-treated him. Another, who used to jeer at him when he was being tortured, secretly put a bottle of witch-hazel in his cell and whispered to him in Greek (having, apparently, once studied Christian theology), 'O heavenly father ... '

Even some of the most brutal had moments of macabre amiability. (One of the curious and rather frightening things about the Japanese, differentiating them from the Nazis, is their unpredictability: they have been well likened to naughty children bullying a puppy and then, a few minutes later, fondling it.) So on the Bishop's birthday, November 23rd, they entertained him to a formal and sumptuous dinner-party. Going through his belongings, they came on photographs of his children—and stuck them up in his cell, to please him.

'They used to roar with laughter at my rather simple jokes,' he says, 'about how many bugs I had caught ... or when they were torturing me and I said "I suppose you call this Bushido for Bishops". But you never knew where you were with them: as Gilbert said, in *The Yeomen of the Guard*, "It may draw a tear, Or a slap on the ear ... "'

As bad, in a different way, as the actual torture must have been the monotony of ordinary life in a cell too small for its twenty occupants, who were not allowed any books, bedding, soap, towels or handkerchiefs; and not allowed to talk. In the cell there was one pedestal W.C.; the water flushing into the pan was their only water for all purposes, including drinking. Nearly all the internees suffered from enteritis or dysentery.

This lavatory water was once used for a strange purpose indeed—for the baptism of a 35-year-old Chinese railway employee. He had been impressed by the behaviour of the Christians in the cell; the Bishop, convinced of his genuineness by his unselfishness and lack of greed ('until you're really hungry you don't know what greed is'), instructed him night after night, in the small hours, in whispers, and christened him at the W.C. very early one morning, with Chief Justice Worley as sponsor.

What aggravated the monotony most cruelly was that the Japanese allowed them to sleep only between 10 p.m. and 8 a.m. (with bright lights still burning overhead); all day they had to sit on the floor in an approved posture, hands on knees ('like this,' said the Bishop, squatting on the floor of his study).

If anyone rested a hand on the floor, he or she was at once knocked on the head with a bamboo stick.

To the Bishop, this timeless purgatory was an opportunity. He 'managed to work out a routine' of prayer, meditation, and reminiscence.

From the window he could see a corner of a Wesleyan chapel; each morning he recited Wesley's hymn, 'Christ whose glory fills the skies,' and grew 'more and more cheered' by it. In the afternoons he went methodically through the years of his life (leaving out school-days, which he didn't enjoy); it was, he says, 'a wonderful opportunity for true repentance and true thanksgiving'. In the evenings he repeated as many as he could remember of *Hymns Ancient and Modern*.

He also learned by heart—whispered to him by another internee, A. W. Ker, now dead—more than 2,000 lines of Keats. Ker had never cared much for poetry until he was sent to Changi; fortunately, while there, before being transferred to the Y.M.C.A., he had memorised a good deal.

Conditions at Changi—a 'show' camp for visiting Japanese big shots—were considerably easier, at any rate until the 'double tenth'. It was there, for instance, that the Bishop was able to organise P.T. classes. The internees and P.o.W.s heard gratefully (and the Japanese didn't understand) his 'One — two — three — four, lift — up — your — hearts ... '

It may be said, generally, that the camps in which the Japanese kept either P.o.W.s or internees were about on a level with the Nazi concentration camps; far worse, of course, than the Germans' military camps.

On another day I was walking round Changi jail with the Mountbattens when a voice called me by name. It was a friend I had known before the war, Paul Miller.[1] He took me to the hut in which several prisoners had written and edited the camp magazine, *Exile*. The editor was Alan Roberts; the 'business manager' was Jack Wood; the artist who illustrated the magazine was Ronald Searle, later celebrated both as a serious artist and as the creator of the formidable girls of St Trinians. At a glance I could see the quality of their work, and I called out to Mountbatten that there was an interesting story here. He said at once: 'Tell 'em to get in the second jeep and come to Government House.'

Even at that moment Government House was pretty luxurious, certainly by comparison with what these men had been through; Searle, for one, had worked on the notorious Burma–Thailand railway. We arrived — the three magazine staff, Miller and I — just at cocktail time. It was good to see them sink into deep armchairs and be given strong dry Martinis by elegant A.D.C.s and servants. (It was lucky that they didn't get instantly drunk.)

They also wanted things to read. I lent Miller William Plomer's slim volume of witty ballads, *The Dorking Thigh*; unlike most people who borrow books, he sent it back some years later.

Dinner was at a long table, bright with candles in silver cande-labra (but the food was only the best that could be done with rations). The table seated about forty people — all senior officers, in impeccable white evening gear embellished with 'gongs'. The four young men in their shabby prison garb were treated as guests of honour: Mountbatten and his wife sat in the middle of the long table, facing each other, and one of the four prisoners was placed on each side of the host and hostess. Towards midnight the four began to wilt: it had been almost too strong a contrast to the years

[1] Now a Canon of Derby Cathedral.

of hardship, starvation and torture. Since they were supposed to be back in camp quite early in the evening, Mountbatten wrote a chit which they could show at the guard-room, authorising their late return, and sent them back in a jeep. It must have given them intense pleasure to say to an incredulous sergeant of the guard 'It's all right, sarge—we've been dining with the Supreme Commander'—and then, as he began to explode, show him the obviously authentic chit.

This incident, I thought, showed the best side of Mountbatten's character—his lack of pomposity, his curiosity about people, his keen sense of the effective gesture, perhaps of public relations. I found him and his wife an unusual and interesting couple: both were extremely good at their jobs—so much so that there was almost a kind of competition between them. At breakfast they would compare the total numbers of British prisoners in the camps whom each of them had spoken to and shaken hands with. This may have been because (as he himself told me) when he first wanted to marry Edwina Ashley, who had inherited a fortune from her grandfather, Sir Ernest Cassel, the match was strongly opposed by his mother, Princess Victoria, Queen Victoria's grand-daughter: she warned him that everybody would say that he was marrying this heiress for her money. So, having been in youth something of a playboy, in company with his cousin the Prince of Wales, he devoted himself to showing that he could succeed by his own efforts—which he certainly did, his chosen career being the Navy; and in the course of proving that point, he fulfilled his other strongest ambition, to avenge his father's memory by becoming First Sea Lord. (His father, Prince Louis of Battenberg, had been hounded out of this office, in the First World War, by vulgar xenophobia.)

Beaverbrook, who had for many years an inexcusably malicious vendetta against Mountbatten, used to claim that this was simply legitimate criticism of a man holding public office (though whether a serving naval officer can be so described is arguable): he cited in particular the disastrous Dieppe raid in 1942, for the failure of which he wrongly blamed Mountbatten. In my biography of Beaverbrook[1] the passage dealing with this was vetted thoroughly

[1] *Beaverbook: A Study in Power and Frustration,* Weidenfeld & Nicolson, London, 1956.

by Mountbatten and by Vice-Admiral Sir Charles Hughes-Hallett, M.P., who had been Naval Commander and had won a D.S.O. in the Dieppe raid; but, like the rest of that book, it also was mutilated by Beaverbrook's lawyers under threat of libel proceedings; so that, although I believe that it approximates to the truth, it does so in rather more veiled language than I would have liked to use. For instance, shortly after the Dieppe raid, Beaverbrook and Mountbatten were at dinner with the American states-man, Averell Harriman, at his London flat. Beaverbrook drank a good deal and became aggressive, eventually hurling at Mountbatten the extraordinarily personal reproach (which I was not allowed by the lawyers to quote verbatim) 'You murdered my Canadians in order to wreck my Second Front campaign' – for he had indeed been engaged in such a campaign. As recently as 1974 Mr Harriman, visiting London, confirmed to me this account of his dinner party.

The other issue on which Beaverbrook claimed the right to attack Mountbatten publicly was India. Up to a point, again, this was legitimate (though Mountbatten could argue that, as Viceroy, he was only carrying out the policies and directives of the British Government). To Beaverbrook, the unreconstructed imperialist, Mountbatten was 'the man who threw away India'.

Both Dieppe and India were undoubtedly public issues – but they were merely fresh material for a vendetta which had begun some years earlier, before the war. (The lawyers did not like the word 'vendetta': it had to be changed to 'feud'.) My source for this information is Frank Owen, who saw a great deal of Beaverbrook at this time. According to him, the vendetta's origin was in an incident involving Beaverbrook's beloved friend, the Hon. Mrs Richard Norton, a beautiful woman who sincerely loved him; her touching last letter to him is quoted in A. J. P. Taylor's official life.[1] Devoted though they were to each other, he used her roughly; such was his wont with women – particularly aristocratic women, some of whom he seemed to delight in humiliating (perhaps in revenge for the snubs which he had suffered when he first arrived in England and was called a 'little Canadian adventurer').

So each morning Jean Norton would ring him. He would ask

[1] *Beaverbrook*, Hamish Hamilton, London, 1972.

her what she was doing that evening. If she said she was doing nothing he would say that she was to come round after dinner and play backgammon. If she said she had a dinner engagement, he would almost invariably say 'Break it. Come to dinner.' Her friends began to get used to her breaking engagements in this way. Both the Mountbattens remonstrated with her—and on one occasion Mountbatten said: 'Look, it's Edwina's birthday next ——day. You have *got* to come to dinner. You mustn't let Max run your life like this.' And when the day came Mrs Norton refused to break the engagement. Beaverbrook raged violently— and from then on (except for brief periods of détente) Mountbatten rarely received a favourable mention in the *Express*. I say that there were exceptions, because Beaverbrook, when criticised for the vendetta, for example by A. J. Cummings of the *News Chronicle*, used to produce a sheaf of *Express* cuttings containing favourable or neutral mentions of Mountbatten. But most of the references to him were hostile: it was generally recognised that there was a real vendetta. Taylor in his book—which is in the main markedly hagiographical—says of the whole affair: 'It is difficult not to feel that more lay behind. None of Beaverbrook's friends could discover what it was. Something about Mountbatten touched Beaverbrook on a raw nerve.'

I have dwelt on this matter at length because, like the business of the white list, it throws a glaring light on the irresponsibility of a press owned by individual millionaires. It is not Mountbatten's wounded feelings that matter (though he is as entitled to justice as anybody else): what matters is the withholding from the readers of information that they are entitled to have, or its presentation in a form warped by private bias. It is fair to say that nowadays many newspaper proprietors do not allow their personal caprice and prejudice to dictate editorial policy, as in the heyday of Beaverbrook, the late Lord Rothermere, and Northcliffe.

As I say, Beaverbrook used to deny the existence of this vendetta. He privately summed up the Mountbattens' characters, as he imagined them, in a bleak chiasmus: 'Mountbatten is vain, not clever. The woman is clever, not vain.'

Before leaving South-east Asia I paid a brief visit to Vietnam— then called French Indo-China—and was in Saigon when the

French, in the small hours of 23rd September, raided the Town Hall, where the leading Viet-Minh nationalists were sheltering. This provocative action, in breach of an undertaking given to Mountbatten personally by the French commander on the spot, was, in effect, the start of a war in which the Vietnamese people had to fight and defeat first the French, then the Americans, for some thirty years.

At the time, through friends in London, I had contacts with the Viet-Minh and their leader, Ho Chi-Minh (who had been in the Town Hall but had been warned of the French raid and had escaped into the country). I had told Mountbatten this and had offered to get in touch with Ho Chi-Minh and try to mediate (if the French could be induced to see any sense at all, which was doubtful). Mountbatten felt that, as I was an M.P., he must pass my offer on to Whitehall; this he did, with a recommendation that the attempt be approved. But I could not wait indefinitely: I felt that I must be at Westminster for the opening of the new Parliament, the first in history with a clear Labour majority – and I, though not a new M.P., was a new Labour M.P. So, reluctantly, I left Saigon and South-East Asia and came home to London. Mountbatten wrote and told me that the authority for my approach to Ho Chi-Minh had come through on the day after I had left.

Objectively considered, Mountbatten's policy was a left-wing policy, but, since he was a military commander, he was always careful not to take an explicitly political line and to show that whatever policy he proposed was justified in terms of military necessity or expediency. He wrote me a number of letters at this time, of great historical interest, mainly deploring the blind obstinacy of the French and Dutch governments, who refused to realise that the days of their empires were over. Though I could not quote them publicly, these letters often provided useful material for speeches and questions in the House.

In subsequent years, seeing them in England, it always seemed to me that Edwina was the more Left-wing of the two: she showed an instant strong sympathy with any Asian nationalist who was being oppressed by some American-backed right-wing regime.

In 1947, when his period as Viceroy of India was coming to an end, Mountbatten, who was back in England, asked me to come and see him. He wanted me to sound my Burmese friends about the title he was proposing to adopt on receiving an earldom. He wanted to be Earl Mountbatten 'of Burma': did I think they would object? (I inquired: there was no objection.) He also told me, under a pledge of secrecy, that his nephew, Prince Philip of Greece, who was serving in the British Navy, was about to adopt the style of Lieutenant Mountbatten — and that this change would shortly be followed by the announcement of his nephew's engagement to Princess Elizabeth, the heir to the throne. He added that Prince Philip had never been to the House of Commons, and asked me to take him there and introduce him to a few of the younger Labour M.P.s. This was arranged: Philip came and lunched at the House, and among the colleagues whom I invited to meet him were John Freeman and Donald Bruce (now Lord Bruce); I think they were favourably impressed — as he said afterwards he had been by question-time, for which I got him a ticket.

14

Russian escapades
I: With Guy Burgess in Moscow

I have never kept a diary – possibly because I used to write a daily newspaper column – but I have stacks of small engagement-books, dating back many years, which occasionally remind me of people or places.

Glancing through a pre-war one recently, I was surprised to see the name of Guy Burgess, for I had and have no recollection of ever having met him before the war. The first meetings with him that I recall were when he was working for the B.B.C. at the House of Commons and chose me, several times, to do the programme called 'The Week in Westminster'. In those days this was simply a fifteen-minute talk by one M.P. describing, as impartially as he could, the parliamentary events of the past five days; it went out on a Saturday, if possible live. The M.P. doing it used to lunch and go over his script with the producer, Guy Burgess: this was obviously an easier process if the M.P. was a professional writer; others required rather more coaching.

Books have been written (one of them by me) about the defection to Russia in 1951 of two senior members of the Foreign Service, Guy Burgess and Donald Maclean. There is no point now in going over the whole of that business. It was in 1956 that the two men reappeared briefly at the National Hotel in Moscow, read a prepared hand-out to a few invited correspondents, and vanished again without answering any questions. At that time I was temporarily out of Parliament and therefore working more or less all the time as a journalist (and earning much more money than I could as an M.P.). It occurred to me that, as I had known Burgess in London, I might be able to go to see him in Moscow and get the full story of his and Maclean's disappearance. I told this part of it in a small book, which was serialised in the *Daily Mail* and, through the formidable bargaining skill of my literary agent, the late Jean Leroy, brought me more money than any other single story I have written.

What I could not tell then was what it was like to see Guy again when I went back to Moscow to go through the proofs of the book with him. (There is a picture of us doing this in the book, which may possibly still be found in the libraries.) Maclean I did not see: Guy told me that he had strongly disapproved of Guy's arrangement with me (though I had no doubt that it had the approval of their employers). The text of the book could not be changed: I had written it, a chapter a day, for a month, and presumably Guy had shown each chapter to his Soviet colleagues or superiors. But we had more time to talk privately now: he had lately moved into a new flat in Moscow, for which I had sent him a good deal of Scandinavian furniture from London, and I was also able to spend a weekend at his *dacha*, in a country village about an hour's drive (by official pool car) from the city; this I had not been allowed to do before, because the village was said to be in a restricted area. According to Guy, this did not necessarily mean that there were defence plants there — merely that a number of important people had houses in the neighbourhood.

The *dacha* had been allocated to him some time before. It had been taken over by the State because the Party official who had built and occupied it had been removed for embezzling Party funds. It was the largest house in the village and for this reason, and because it was State property, it was guarded constantly by four secret police, who lived in a cottage in a corner of the extensive grounds. This, at least, was the explanation that Guy gave me of these somewhat rigorous security measures: I do not know if he believed it himself, but I was not in a position to disprove it. He knew by certain means (I had better not, even now, say what they were) that these guards had to report, about once a fortnight, on his conduct and movements and on any visitors he might have. One of the guards became quite friendly with him, and told him that there was one room in the house, a small study, which was not 'miked'. As they were sitting in this room when the guard said this, and as he went on to make disparaging remarks about his own superior officers, Guy was inclined to believe him; but it could have been a trap. We did not, in any case, use this room when we wanted to talk privately; we thought it wiser to walk in the garden. (At his flat in Moscow we used to stand by a large radiogram and talk against the loudest possible music.)

The village of Guy's *dacha* was a small and pretty one, with an English-looking duck-pond and a typical onion-domed Orthodox church. Walking round it on the Saturday afternoon, I asked if there wasn't a bar we could go to in the evening, as one would go to a pub in England. Guy looked worried. 'There is one,' he said. 'But I can't go there now. Donald [Maclean] was staying here, and he had one of his drunken fits and wrecked the bar. There was a hell of a row about it. That was before he had his last cure.'

Then I worried him still more by saying that I thought I would go to the church in the morning: it would be interesting to see how many people – in particular, young people – still went to it. Guy said: 'I don't know which secret policeman will be on duty in the morning, but I don't think he'll like it. He'll probably feel he'll have to escort you, in case there are any hooligans around.' I pointed out that I had never, in any country, seen a village more tranquil and hooligan-free, and in the morning insisted on going to church, unescorted. (There were rather more people there than there would be in a comparable English village, but few young people.) The guard on duty saw me out of the big gate in the high wall surrounding the grounds, saluted, and locked it behind me – so that when I got back from the church I could not get in and had to go round to the corner of the grounds by the guards' cottage and shout to them to let me in.

Their reports on Guy's conduct would no doubt have included references to his drinking habits. These varied considerably. In Moscow he was alert in the morning but often, by the evening, getting a bit sozzled on vodka. At the *dacha* he kept only wine – usually a Georgian white wine – and drank no vodka. He led a solitary life there, occasionally talking to the friendly guard or to his elderly, devoted woman housekeeper, and doing a great deal of reading, chiefly of classic English literature. Occasionally he would sit down at a decrepit upright piano and strum a tune: at his request, I had got him a copy of the *English Hymnal*, and he would pick out with two fingers the hymns he had known at Eton, tears running down his cheeks. (As has been recorded before, he used to wear an Old Etonian tie in Moscow.) Many of his books were still in store in London. Some of them I retrieved and shipped to him, together with the furniture for his new flat. One book I gave, at his request, to the library of the Reform Club. It was Margot Asquith's autobiography, given to Guy by her, with marginal notes which she had scribbled, identifying some of the characters not named in the book — for instance, her first lover.

Naturally, I asked what his job in Moscow really was: his ostensible (and actual) work for the Foreign Literature Publishing House was hardly full-time. He recommended Western authors whom he thought worth translating into Russian, and was proud of having persuaded them to start on Graham Greene (not surprisingly, with *The Quiet American*), and, I think he said, E. M. Forster. Apart from this, he said, he sat on various committees concerned with international affairs, particularly Western policy, and wrote memoranda which, he claimed, were read at the highest level but one. That was when I first saw him. When I saw him again, some months later, the Suez crisis had occurred, and he said that he knew that his memoranda were now read at the highest level.

This was for an interesting reason. It is difficult to look back now and realise how almost universal was the belief that, after Eden's collapse, the next Prime Minister of Britain would be R. A. Butler. Apart from the Westminster commentators, that was the forecast communicated to Moscow by the Soviet Embassy in London. Only two men I know of — Randolph Churchill in London, Guy Burgess in Moscow — prophesied correctly that Macmillan would be the successor. Churchill had a special source of information in his father, whose dislike of Butler was well-known. 'How on earth did you get it right?' I asked Guy. 'Oh,' he replied, 'from a study of the life of the great Lord Salisbury' — and, indeed, I remembered his saying that this Victorian statesman had been, to him, one of the most fascinating figures in modern political history.

I don't know how much of a handicap it was to him that he was not a fluent or correct Russian speaker: 'Kitchen Russian' was all that he said he could manage.

Guy's life in Moscow was somewhat restricted socially. He took me to spend an evening with two British Communists, a man and his wife, working there: it was a pleasant evening of serious talk, a good supper, and a splendid television performance of *Swan Lake* by either the Bolshoi or the Kirov ballet, but it hardly competed in excitement, for someone of Guy's temperament, with his much-publicised wild parties in London.

As we walked back from their flat, Guy said, doubtfully: 'Tell me ... Are they as nice as I think they are?' I said: 'Yes, I like them both very much, but I don't think you'd ever have met them – or, at least, bothered to cultivate their friendship – if you'd still been in London.' While I was there we also saw, once or twice, the late Ralph Parker, a well-known British journalist who had been Moscow correspondent, successively, of *The Times* and of the *Daily Worker*. I had the impression that Guy did not care for Parker much. Indeed, he expressed mistrust in what was, for him, an odd remark: 'We all think he's an agent, but we can't make out whose side he's on' – adding that it was regarded as suspicious that Parker had his car serviced by a corporal at the American Embassy.

Especially after seeing the ballet on television, I said that I would like to see Ulanova dance: she was to appear in *Giselle* at the Bolshoi theatre (not my favourite ballet, but the chance of seeing her might not recur). Guy got tickets easily enough, but at the last moment was kept late at work and could not go with me. I took a taxi to the theatre, paid it, got the tickets out of my pocket – and was immediately surrounded by a clamouring ring of people, mostly young, holding out sheaves of rouble notes. Whether they wanted the tickets for their own use, or for black-market sale, I couldn't tell; but, as I had one to spare, I gave it to the first man who spoke, to his astonishment refusing the roubles that he tried to thrust on me. Evidently he was not a black-market tout, for he turned up in the seat next to me. Then, greatly to my embarrassment, I heard a rustle and felt a movement: the roubles I had rejected outside had been thrust into my coat pocket. The only thing to do was to go and spend them with him, in the interval, in the theatre's champagne bar. This was not a lively encounter: we had no language in common, and the Soviet 'champagne' was too sweet.

On my return visit to Moscow, with the proofs, I also had more time to go out and meet people. (While I was writing the story, I had had no time to see anyone but Guy.) Because of the circumstances of these visits, I had not paid the customary courtesy calls to sign the book at the British Embassy; but one evening, at a spectacular open-air cocktail party at the Indonesian Embassy, I met an old friend of Guy's, the celebrated Oxford don Isaiah Berlin. He had heard that I was seeing Guy, explained that he could not do so himself because he was staying with the British Ambassador, but said: 'Give Guy my warmest love, and tell him that none of us are speaking to Goronwy.' This was a reference to Goronwy Rees, who has more recently dealt with the matter in a serious book but had at that time earned some notoriety by selling his reminiscences of Guy, a former friend, to the *People*, where they appeared in sensationalised form. When I reported Berlin's comment to Guy, he was pleased, but did not himself take such a censorious view of Rees's behaviour, simply saying: 'He probably needed the money. He always did.' Only one instalment of the series really annoyed him — one, headed 'Unholy Love Drew These Men Together', in which it was alleged that his and Maclean's identity of political views had been inspired or fortified by homosexual association. 'The idea,' he said, half in anger, half-amused, 'of going to bed with Donald! It would be like going to bed with a great white *woman*! It would be like going to bed with——' and he mentioned a justly famous, but formidable, actress. (I told this anecdote, years ago, to someone who printed it; but, at this point, he inserted the wrong name, choosing, in order to avoid libel, an actress who was dead.)

Berlin was not the only reputable friend in England who remembered Guy with affection. In particular he valued the admirable letters he received from Harold Nicolson. In some respects Nicolson — a most charming companion — was a timid man. I remember having an argument with him when he was a Governor of the B.B.C. and he had said that, though an agnostic himself, he would 'never agree to the broadcasting of a single word that might upset the simple faith of a child'. I considered this grossly unfair to atheists (and was even more horrified when, later, the B.B.C. did allow an argument for humanism to be put in the course of a religious programme — but only in a script read by an actor and written by an Anglican canon!). Harold Nicolson – the story of whose happy marriage to Vita Sackville-West has since then been told by their son Nigel – was also extremely cautious in referring to, or indulging, his own homosexual tendencies. He told me, whimsically, of an incident in a provincial hotel bedroom, where a waiter who had brought him tea – 'a *ravishingly* beautiful youth' – lingered for a few moments and then said, awkwardly, 'Can I ask you a question please?' Harold, his hopes raised, said 'Yes, oh yes!' Instant deflation followed, for the boy blurted out: 'Can you get me a job with the B.B.C.?' Harold also told me once that, in old age, while potency may fail, desire does not – an axiom which I have found only too true. So, in all the circumstances, I thought it notably courageous of Harold Nicolson to keep up this correspondence with a man whom all the media were black-guarding as a traitor and 'pervert'.

Neither the British nor the Soviet secret services need feel disturbed by my reference to the private and, we believed, unmonitored talks I had with Guy. We traded no national secrets. We gossiped about life in London: he gave me messages for former lovers. The theme that he constantly reverted to – with other, later visitors also – was the possibility that he might some day be able without danger to come home to England: for a holiday visit, he insisted, perhaps once a year, to see his ailing mother and his old friends. Couldn't I, he asked, get some sort of safe-conduct for him? I always gave him the same answers, then and later when we used to talk by telephone. (It was easy and quick to get through by phone from Essex to Moscow, where one had to ask for him by his Soviet name, Jim Andreyevitch Eliot, Eliot being not after T.S. but after George, for whose *Middlemarch* he had intense admiration.) First, I said, no British government would give a hypothetical assurance of that kind in advance. Second, in my view it would depend largely on the prevailing international climate: if there were a real détente some day, perhaps … Third, would the Soviet authorities let him go? (The last time we spoke of this, he said that he thought he had made some progress: they had given him permission to pay a holiday visit to Yugoslavia.)

He was certainly homesick for England; but, equally, there seemed no doubt that he would have wanted to go on working permanently in the Soviet Union – though the value of defectors to those they have joined must diminish gradually without refresher visits to their homeland. His general attitude there was exactly the opposite of that of most Western 'Kremlinologists'. They profess their deep regard for the Russian people, coupled with loathing for the system which oppresses them: he positively admired — almost idolised — the Soviet system, but often found Russian people 'maddening'. An exception to this was his office colleague Vladimir (I never knew his other name), whom I met once or twice and found intelligent and likeable.

There was one other welcome exception. When I first saw Guy in Moscow, he was lonely — starved not only of congenial non-political company but of sex. I am glad to think that, by an extraordinary chance, I was indirectly responsible for filling this need and so making happier the last year or two of his life. Because of his position in Soviet official circles, he could not go in search of the sort of companionship that he used easily to find in London; and although Moscow is reasonably permissive in this respect, there are occasional spasms of puritanical repression. Nor, indeed, if Guy had dared to look for the solace he lacked, would he have known where to go to find it. In fact, it was close at hand, in the middle of Moscow: a large underground urinal just behind the Metropole Hotel, open all night, frequented by hundreds of questing Slav homosexuals — standing there in rigid exhibitionist rows, motionless save for the hasty grope and the anxious or beckoning glance over the shoulder — and tended only by an old woman cleaner who never seemed to notice what was going on. When I told Guy about this place, he decided to risk one visit — and was lucky enough to pick up a decent and attractive young man, an electrician in a State factory, Tolya by name: they formed a strong mutual attachment, and Tolya went to live with Guy in the new flat, where I had dinner with them. Guy made me promise not to publish at that time the photographs I took of them together in a Moscow park. Since I imagine that the association was known to the authorities, and not disapproved of, I hope that it can do Tolya no harm to publish one now. Perhaps Guy's masters felt that he was entitled to a little relaxation after his years of work for their cause.

They did not, however, approve of his bouts of hard drinking. When I went back to Moscow with the proofs of my book, my

London publisher asked me to have some photographs taken there for illustrations. Guy arranged for a photographer and said he would bring him to my hotel at three o'clock one afternoon. They were late for the appointment but, opening my door impatiently, I saw them coming along the corridor – Guy as drunk, one may say, as a commissar, reeling and chortling idiotically and then, when the photographer tried to do his job, making silly faces at the camera. It was impossible to get the pictures that day: I made Guy promise to be there again, with the photographer, at ten next morning.

At eight next morning he rang me, sounding his usual bright and brisk morning self. 'I'm afraid I shall have to be late again this morning,' he said. 'I've been "sent for" … about yesterday afternoon.' When he arrived, I asked what being 'sent for' had involved. He explained that, after the usual morning conference, his chief had asked him to stay behind and had then given him, by no means harshly, 'a bit of a talking-to'. He had been 'extremely nice' about it, said Guy – 'which, of course, made one feel all the more of a shit.' In short, he summed it up, his chief had behaved 'exactly like the best type of English public-school housemaster.' Since this, like other passages in this book, may excite furious, incredulous, or hilarious protest, I emphasise that these comments are not mine: I simply record, verbatim, what Guy Burgess said to me.

When back in London during these months, I had from time to time gone to see Guy's mother. She was elderly and an invalid; I found her easy to get on with, and we could talk candidly about her son. His defection had, as may be imagined, caused her a great deal of embarrassment and actual suffering: herself, formerly, an active Conservative, she found that she was now boycotted by the other ladies of her local Conservative Association – even though her name was not the same as his, since she had remarried after his father's death. Throughout the long-drawn-out anxiety of the years after his departure, his stepfather had done all that he could to protect her from the importunacy of the reporters and photographers who dogged the approach to their flat in Arlington House. The most persistent of these were from the *Daily Express*, who regarded the Burgess-Maclean story as 'their' story, since they had first broken the official secrecy which had for a time concealed the fact that two senior diplomats had vanished mysteriously and that one of them (Maclean) was already under suspicion and observation. Before her health got worse, Guy's mother was able to spend a holiday with him in the Soviet Union, at a Black Sea resort. He warned her not to talk at all to the Western press. She flew back by the Scandinavian airline, and had to change planes at Copenhagen. The *Express* sent to meet her there. She refused to be interviewed, but could not stop them from photographing her or from following her when she got back to London. Her flat was besieged: later in the evening, when she thought that the siege had been lifted, she went to her club (one of those refined gentle-women's clubs). At last the *Express* had a scoop: they managed to obtain from a club employee the fag-end of a cigarette that the old lady had been smoking. An enlarged picture of this was published triumphantly – and, horror of horrors, it showed that she had been smoking a *Russian* cigarette!

Such an incident is worth recounting merely as an illustration of the essential triviality of the mass-circulation British press. The Burgess-Maclean defection was a matter of legitimate public interest, and the *Express* deserved some credit for bringing it to light: the persecution of Guy's mother, and the photographing of one of her discarded cigarettes, shows how low able journalists and photographers can fall in the desperate attempt to go one better than their rivals. This scoop mentality infects all who have worked for the capitalist press – including, of course, myself, for the thought of getting an exclusive story was one of my motives for embarking on this venture: I am afraid that it amused us some-times, on our way to dinner at the Prague or the Peking or the Aragvi, to walk past a bar full of Western journalists many of whom had spent months trying to find my companion.

At any rate, his mother, though devoted to Guy, had no illusions about his character. She could hardly have any, after all the press 'revelations' about his drinking and his homosexual practices – the latter being irrelevant, since those who seduce to treason have at least as often been glamorous females like Mata Hari, and their prey the most committed heterosexuals. Nor is there any evidence either that Guy's services were obtained by the use of homosexual allurements, or that Nunn May, Pontecorvo, Fuchs and other modern defectors had ever cast lustful eyes on a boy. However wrong their actions may have been – and I personally always made it clear that I disagreed with what Guy and Maclean had done—they were inspired by genuine opposition to the (as they thought) incurable evils of Western society and, especially, American policy in the Far East. This is, as Dick Crossman once said, an age of treason, and in such an age—as in the religious wars of the sixteenth and seventeenth centuries—conscientious traitors may be found on both sides.

So I was able to tell Guy's mother, who always longed to hear details of his life in Moscow, about the incident with the photographer and his subsequent carpeting. She thought for a moment and then said—remarkable words on the lips of an elderly, normally 'patriotic', Conservative lady: 'You know ... I think that Soviet discipline is *good* for Guy.'

As I have said, these matters could not be included in my published story, because they were subsequent to it in time. One other curious exchange deserves to be recorded. When the book was about to go to press—it was a rush job—and only a few days before serialisation in the *Mail* was due to begin, I was telephoned to by Admiral Thomson, the well-liked liaison man between Fleet Street and the secret services. Jolly as always in manner, he told me that the text of the book would have to be submitted for 'vetting'. (As in all countries which profess pride in the freedom of the press, this happens in Britain, too—and no publisher, except perhaps, nowadays, *Private Eye*, dare resist the pressure.)

Proofs were submitted. The vetting was speedy. Only one passage had to come out. It concerned resistance—to me, surprising—by Ernest Bevin to Foreign Office and State Department pressure by extreme Right-wing officials who were urging him to agree to the active promotion of anti-Soviet revolts in Eastern Europe. Guy Burgess, who had been private secretary to Hector McNeil, Minister of State at the Foreign Office when Bevin was Foreign Secretary, knew about this and described Bevin smacking his desk, crying 'I won't 'ave it!' and declaring, correctly, that such risings would be futile, would lead to a lot of people being massacred, and would impair East–West relations still further.

The top people at the Foreign Office, however, are skilled in handling their Ministers. (They preferred Bevin to Eden because Eden knew too much himself about foreign affairs.) One of them, now dead, was the subtle and reactionary Ivone Kirkpatrick. They eventually induced Bevin to agree to just one Eastern European rising, a small 'token' one, in a country which wasn't thought to matter much—Albania. Agents, arms, and propaganda were sent in, and a lot of taxpayers' money spent on making a 'good show' of it. Everything happened as Bevin had predicted: a few bishops, priests and other resistance leaders were hanged, and some thousands of their dupes exiled to camps; the revolt was a flop.

It would be interesting to know whether the memory of this bloody incident was one of the reasons why Albania's orientation switched from Moscow to Peking.

I tried to reason with the Admiral. After all, I pointed out, I had written my story in Moscow, and Guy Burgess had cleared every chapter, including this passage, with his office, so the Russians already knew about it. What possible harm could there be in telling it now?

'Good heavens, old boy,' said the Admiral, with a light laugh. 'It isn't the Russians we worry about. It's *the British public* we don't want to know about it!'

II: Lunch in the Kremlin

During these visits to Moscow in 1956 I twice had the opportunity of long talks with Khrushchev, then still in power. These were arranged through Guy Burgess's office—a detail which confirms that he had a certain status in the Soviet bureaucracy. On each occasion I was alone with Comrade Nikita, as Khrushchev was called—alone except, of course, for an interpreter. The interpreter was the same one on both occasions, a pale, fair young man named Mikhailov, highly expert at his job, as I imagine he had to be. Unless one knows another language very well—and I know only a few words of Russian—I always find it preferable to have a serious conversation through an interpreter. You can tell, by watching the face of the other man, whether the interpreter is conveying correctly what you are saying; you even know if he has left out some qualifying clause, and can remind him of it; and, while he is translating your last question or statement, you can be observing the facial reactions to it and thinking what to say next.

The first of these two encounters was, and was known to be, 'on the record' — so that I could publish as a newspaper interview what Khrushchev said. I was working at the time for *Reynolds'*, and the interview was so long — it lasted four-and-a-half hours — that it was published in two parts, on successive Sundays.

In these memoirs, as I have said in the introduction, I have kept to a minimum the reprinting of anything already published: the most boring part of such books usually consists of material rehashed (or not even rehashed, just quoted straight) and, when they are by politicians, extracts from speeches reported in *Hansard*. In this case, however, the interview with Khrushchev took place so long ago, and the circulation of *Reynolds News* was so small, that it seems just worth reprinting a good deal of it. Almost at the start, I found myself defending the Right-wing leadership of the Labour Party. I agreed personally with some of Khrushchev's criticisms of the then leader, Hugh Gaitskell, and my other colleagues on the National Executive of the Party, but I thought that these criticisms went much too far; I also realised that the room (an office at the headquarters of the Communist Party of the Soviet Union) would certainly be miked, so that whatever I said could later be used in various ways. In any case, I was more interested in discussing the affairs of Soviet Russia, for this was soon after the XXth Congress of the C.P.S.U., at which Khrushchev had made his astonishing speech denouncing 'the errors of Stalinism'.

The interview went on:

After our argument about the British Labour Party I turned to the subject on which I was really more anxious to question him — the present situation in the Soviet Union.

I mentioned two words that have been much in the air since the historic XXth Congress of the C.P.S.U. — the words 'decentralisation' and 'legality'. As part of the general current process of decentralisation, the All-Union Ministry of Justice has been dissolved, and its powers transferred to ministries in the various Republics of the U.S.S.R.

I had heard it said that this would prevent a repetition of those breaches of legality which have now been condemned, and I asked Mr Khrushchev if he thought this was so.

KHRUSHCHEV: 'We think that this decision will help to prevent violations in future, and improves the work of justice in the Soviet Union, because the Soviet Union is composed of sovereign republics, with their own economies and cultures.

'Justice concerns the people, and the people live in the Republics: the Soviet Union itself is an abstract concept; there is no territory of the Soviet Union as such. Therefore legislation should be legislation by and for the Republics. The Soviet Union itself can simply provide co-ordination, to guard against contradictory legislation. For this purpose, the supervision of the procurator is enough, with an All-Union special commission.'

DRIBERG: 'To what extent is there uniformity of punishment in the various Republics? Could there be capital punishment for murder in one Republic, and not in another?'

KHRUSHCHEV: 'It is quite possible. Every national Republic has its own criminal code. Even now, there are some differences. But there is some co-ordination.'

I mentioned one minor respect in which decentralisation did not seem to be occurring adequately as yet. The Soviet authorities set great store by visual education through large satirical posters. A few days earlier I had seen a number of these — satirising drunkenness, nepotism, and other anti-social vices — at a crowded country fair in Uzbekistan. I took a photograph of one of the posters, and a youth standing by pointed to it and spoke to me.

My interpreter explained that he was asking what the poster meant: like most of the people there, he was an Uzbek; Uzbek is the official language of Uzbekistan; yet the explanatory captions on all these posters were in Russian, which most of the people at the fair could not read.

'That shows,' said Mr Khrushchev, 'inadequate organisation by our propaganda services.' He added that he was 'amazed by the silliness' of such a mistake.

I next raised the question of the Supreme Soviet, as compared with the British House of Commons, as a forum for the criticism and questioning of ministers.

KRUSHCHEV: 'The character and procedure of the two assemblies are different. The Supreme Soviet is not in session all the year round, but only for definite, and comparatively brief, times. There would hardly be time for an hour of questions each day, as in the House of Commons.

'We were present at your question-time when we were in London. I like it. It *is* a democratic feature of your Parliament. To some extent I think it raises the blood-pressure of the ministers. It is democratic and interesting.

'Probably we ought to find some way of introducing a similar procedure in the Supreme Soviet. I cannot now say exactly what it would be like, but something of the kind is not excluded.

'Nevertheless, your question-time is a bit theatrical, because of your two-party system: it is chiefly the Opposition that asks questions, while Government M.P.s mostly support their leaders.'

DRIBERG: 'To some extent that is so, but it is not entirely true. At question-time the House of Commons is less rigidly divided in two than at other times: it is much more the House as a whole *vis-à-vis* the Executive. If there is some case of injustice to an individual, it will be taken up at question-time by that person's M.P. whether he is Labour or Conservative.'

I added that I had been told that the most effective forum of democratic criticism in the Soviet Union was the ordinary Party meeting. I had wished to attend one of these, but was told that it might be difficult to do so, as non-members were (naturally) not usually admitted. Could Mr Khrushchev help?

KHRUSHCHEV: 'I promise to speak for you.'

He went on to say that great importance was attached to party meetings, trade union meetings, 'and general meetings of the workers at which every question can be raised.' At one time they used to have evenings of questions and answers.

Workers had the right to question their factory managers or trade union officials: no question was barred, and if the answer wasn't known it had to be given at the next meeting.

I asked if these valuable meetings were no longer held. Not so often as before, said Mr Khrushchev, but they were 'not rejected'. Formerly they had been compulsory; now they were voluntary.

DRIBERG: 'If they are voluntary, isn't there a tendency on the part of managers and officials to avoid organising them? If question-time in the House of Commons was voluntary, very few ministers in the British Government would insist on having it.'

He agreed that bureaucratic human nature was the same the world over—'but we have a great medicine against bureaucracy in the mass correction of our Party, and it is compulsory on leaders and officials to answer every question.'

This sometimes wastes a lot of time, he said, because there are some people who are never content with an answer and go on fussing and nagging at everyone.

He told me of two of his own personal experiences during a recent visit to the Ukraine.

An old woman had complained to him ('she was a nervous and garrulous type') that she couldn't get a satisfactory answer to her problem, though she had been round to every official in turn.

There is a law that, if a collective farmer stops working on the collective, he loses his private plot of land (which varies in size in different districts). This woman had two sons, both of whom had formerly worked on the collective; now they had gone to work in a factory, and had accordingly been deprived of their plots of land. But they, and their mother, could still go on living at the collective; and they still had the much smaller portions of land that non-members were allowed.

The mother, however, was not satisfied with this. She wanted her sons' former plots of land back as well.

KHRUSHCHEV: 'After I'd looked into it, I had to tell her that I thought she'd been given the correct answer first time. So now she's not satisfied with me, either!'

DRIBERG: 'At least you can be sure that she won't vote against you.'

KHRUSHCHEV: 'Yes—besides she's not in my constituency!'

Next he told me of the complaint of another woman, the wife of a mining engineer. Her husband had been sent to jail for three years because a worker in a pit that he was in charge of had fallen and died. The woman said it was the worker's own fault, because he hadn't bothered to wear a safety-belt.

But her husband had been convicted for negligent supervision.

KRUSHCHEV: 'In this case I could not take sides. I asked the higher judicial authorities to investigate it.'

DRIBERG: 'Had the man the right of appeal to a higher court?'

KHRUSHCHEV: 'Certainly. I'm afraid I do not know if he had exercised it – I think perhaps I came on the scene before he had had time to.'

I then turned to the subject of the Soviet press. I said that I had gathered that the newspapers were full of criticism of individuals and institutions.

KHRUSHCHEV: 'Yes, and this must make our enemies abroad think that we are in a terrible state, and are about to collapse, when they read our papers full of nothing but criticisms. Still, year after year goes by, and we survive!'

DRIBERG: 'And if there were no criticism in your papers, people abroad would say you had not a free Press. Besides the criticism at Party meetings and elsewhere, the Press is also a valuable medium for raising questions and grievances?'

KHRUSHCHEV: 'It is most important, in the public interest, because it affects not only the person criticised but the readers, who can learn the proper lessons from it.'

DRIBERG: 'I am not quite sure how high criticism can go. I hope you won't mind my asking this, but has a newspaper the right to criticise you?'

KHRUSHCHEV: 'Yes.'

DRIBERG: 'They didn't criticise Stalin. At present, I know, they are particularly pleased with you and the other Soviet leaders for doing what Stalin failed to do – going round and visiting the various Republics'.

KHRUSHCHEV: 'You are quite right, we are getting a great response on these tours of ours.'

DRIBERG: 'But if at some future time, for some reason, an editor thought that you deserved criticism, would he print it?'

KHRUSHCHEV: 'So far as criticism of my work as First Secretary of the Central Committee is concerned, the Party organ will not criticise me because – like my own work – it is guided by the directives of the Central Committee. If my work is not according to the policy of the Party, then the Central Committee and the Party press will criticise me openly.

'If any member of the Central Committee is not doing his job properly, the Central Committee can expel him; and if this person insists on his mistakes, he will be criticised in the press; and if he still insists, he would be expelled from the Party. This is essential Party discipline.'

DRIBERG: 'If, in the past, editors had been more in the habit of criticising the leaders, isn't it possible that the errors of Stalinism would have been avoided, or might have heen corrected sooner?'

KHRUSHCHEV: 'Certainly—but such situations develop over a long period of time. They are like the Ukrainian funeral mounds: it was a tradition that, when a leading man had been buried, every passer-by should throw a handful of earth on the grave—and so, gradually, a great hill grew ...

'It was the same with Stalin's authority. His freedom from criticism grew out of his positive work for the Party and the people. Then, in the conditions of the time, his peculiar temperament transformed what had been positive and good into a negative force. Things have been put right again by the XXth Congress.'

DRIBERG: 'Are you satisfied that collective leadership is now so well established that there cannot be a repetition of the errors of Stalin?'

KHRUSHCHEV: 'I think so. But this is a matter of relations between people as well as the creation of a democratic framework. Our aim is to prevent any repetition of the cult of the individual, and to return to the Leninist position and methods. Lenin was very strict in this respect.'

To ensure accuracy (and no come-back) I took the precaution of getting Mikhailov, later in the day, to read through what I had written. So far as I can recall, he did not suggest any changes.

My second meeting with Khrushchev was also arranged through a colleague of Guy's, whom, not knowing his full name, I will call Nick; but it was more informal than the first and unexpected by me, and one aspect of it was mildly comic.

This visit to Moscow was not in connection with the Burgess book. The Russians had just made world news in the biggest possible way by launching the first sputnik into space. So far, no

Western journalists had succeeded in tracking down the sputnik scientists and talking with them: another Sunday paper, the *Dispatch*, knowing that I had good Soviet contacts, had commissioned me to try to do just that. It seemed an improbable errand. Apart from the intrinsic or routine difficulties of the job — getting a visa in a hurry to start with, and finding out, when I got to Moscow, where the scientists were — I was totally without the kind of knowledge that would be needed if I were to talk intelligently to these scientists. Moreover, I happened to have only the next weekend free; it was now Wednesday; and the paper would need the story by about six or seven o'clock on the Saturday evening. However, my agent Jean Leroy had once more brought off a coup, inducing the editor (who must, I thought, be out of his mind) to pay £1,000 and expenses if I could get the scoop. So I brought such pressure as I could on the Soviet Embassy to rush the visa and optimistically booked a flight to Moscow for the next day, Thursday.

Optimism indeed: though the visa was okay, Thursday's flight was delayed for twenty-four hours. Now I could not arrive in Moscow till the Friday evening, with just one day in which to get and transmit my story. Every journalist will realise how almost hopeless the mission seemed.

To my relief, Nick was awaiting me, with a caviare-laden buffet, in the hotel suite that had been booked for me. Although I had rung Guy Burgess from London to tell him of this visit, I had not known that his colleagues would be able to help. Nick was still not sure that he could, but he was going to try: he said that in the morning — Saturday morning, press day for an English Sunday paper! — I should stay in my room until he rang me with any news he might have.

There was nothing else to do. I waited with mounting anxiety in the Edwardian-baroque suite, with its quasi-classical statues, nineteenth-century pastoral landscapes, ornate electroliers, and hidden mikes. It was not until 11.30, when 'hope had grown grey hairs', that Nick rang. Miraculously, he told me of a double event: I was to meet the scientists in their laboratory at noon, and a car was on its way to collect me; and another car would call for me at 2.45, to take me to lunch in the Kremlin 'with an interesting person'.

I would not care to re-read or reprint now the interview with the scientists. I could, of course, ask only the simplest questions – such as how long did they think it would be before they could land men on the moon. (They said: 'About ten years, or a bit more.') Anyway, I was back in the hotel and writing my story by two o'clock, but I could not finish it, or phone it to London, before the car called to take me to the Kremlin luncheon, which I was naturally anxious not to be late for.

The car was, I gathered, a Foreign Ministry car – one of the largest kind of Soviet car, the Zil. It was furnished with a rich carpet, spread over the seat as well as the floor, and with semi-transparent green curtains which screened the windows from inquisitive passing eyes. A young official had been sent to escort me. I observed that the chauffeur was driving us down the central part of the wide streets, which I had thought reserved for ambulances, and asked my escort if there were some symbol on the front of the car which informed the traffic police that we were entitled to drive that way. His answer was beautifully and unchallengeably simple. 'No,' he said. 'But I think they assume that we would not do so if we were not entitled to.'

We entered the Kremlin by a back gate, over a kind of drawbridge. A guard stopped us. My escort leaned out of the window and murmured something, and he let us pass. I asked my escort what he had said: 'Was it a password, or something?' He replied: 'I simply said, "Mr Driberg is here".' Security arrangements of this kind seem much the same wherever you are. If you have an appointment at Buckingham Palace, your name has been given in advance to the policeman on the gate.

This interview with Comrade Nikita (for he, as I had suspected, turned out to be the 'interesting person' of Nick's phone call) took place in a much grander office than the one at Party H.Q. in which I had previously seen him. He was in a genial mood and I did not now have to spend a lot of time defending my colleagues. It occurred to me later that there were probably two reasons for this changed attitude. First, Suez had occurred, and – though Khrushchev no doubt still thought little of the Labour Party as a revolutionary force – he had to admit that he could no longer dismiss it as a mere appendage of the Conservative Party. Labour, in Opposition, had led the broad-based attack, in and out of

Parliament, on the Suez aggression. Second, since I had last seen him, Nye Bevan and Jennie Lee had spent a holiday with Khrushchev by the Black Sea, and had undoubtedly taught him something of the history of the British Labour Movement.

At any rate, we had a pleasant enough off-the-record talk. On Guy's advice, I asked Khrushchev if I could attend one of the regular factory meetings which, in Guy's opinion, were a good demonstration of grass-roots Soviet democracy. Khrushev said that he would 'try to get permission' for me to go to one, but couldn't guarantee it. (The permission came through.)

But time was wearing on. It was now four o'clock: I had been asked to lunch at three. I still had an afternoon of urgent work ahead of me. No book of etiquette known to me contains advice on how to say to the ruler of one of the two most powerful nations in the world: 'Sorry – we must stop talking now. It's time to eat.' But Mikhailov the interpreter somehow conveyed this tactfully to my host – who was in any case pleased that I should be writing about a triumph of Soviet technology.

He jumped up from his desk at once and led the way, his stubby figure waddling briskly, along a short passage into a fine oval room, of the eighteenth century, in which three places were laid at a large table: Khrushchev sat at one side of it, Mikhailov and I at the other. There were the customary courtesies in vodka – a brown-coloured vodka, made with pepper, he said, very good for colds – but again, appreciating that I had work to do, he was sensible enough not to press me to go on drinking: none of the rumbustious bibulousness of the legend. It was a fairly long luncheon – small helpings, but many courses. Both of us were so busy talking that we kept poor Mikhailov even busier: course after course, his plate was swept away with the food untouched. At last, I said to him: 'Please tell Comrade Khrushchev that he and I must stop talking for five minutes, to let you eat some lunch.' Mikhailov whispered back: 'It is all right. I knew that this would happen, so I had my lunch beforehand.' Anyway, I was able to finish my report, dictated it in good time by telephone to the *Dispatch* office, wired also a photograph of the scientists, and then went to the cosy domestic dinner, already mentioned, with Guy and Tolya.

During this period, we often, inconclusively, discussed the coincidental acts of criminal folly of which the West and the East were then guilty—Suez and Hungary. Guy was particularly puzzled by Anthony Eden's involvement. 'I can't understand it,' he kept saying. 'It's absolutely out of character ... Eden's *not* a warmonger: he's a man of peace.' I had the impression that he might have given an inaccurate appreciation of the situation; if so, he more than made up for it, soon afterwards, by his lucky guess about Eden's successor. Then, defensively, he would curse the West for having, by the actual attack on Suez, given the Kremlin 'an excuse', as he put it, for 'going back' into Budapest when the Soviet troops were already leaving.

Postscript

by Michael Foot

Before I had read the foregoing pages, David Higham who has edited them with such care and scruple (*presented* may be a better word than *edited*, since I can testify there have been no censorious excisions whatever – only a bare few on grounds of possible libel) asked me to contribute a section on one of the essential aspects of Tom's life upon which he had not started at the time of his death, a full section on his role as a sceptical member of the Labour Party. Too hastily I agreed, but any idea of such a complete project wilted as I read on. A lengthy recapitulation by another hand of dates and committee meetings and how a huge variety of duties were meticulously discharged (and Tom could be extremely meticulous) would be bound to read tediously after what has gone before. And yet he did lead another life, or several of them, apart from the one he himself has so heart-rendingly described. So I also attempt something more personal.

I first met Tom in the late 1930s, in his Beaverbrook-Stalinite heyday, and by that I mean when he combined his William Hickey column in the *Express* with the profession of the most orthodox Communist-Party-line politics. Frank Owen, at that time editor of the *Evening Standard*, and myself were among the other Beaverbrook wage slaves ('Do they call themselves wage-slaves?' Beaverbrook asked one of his editors on one famous occasion – 'If so, set them free!') We were always prepared to argue on all these topics, and Tom would dismiss us as a couple of Trotskyite deviationists.

Thanks partly to these divergencies and to other imperfect

sympathies, we did not at that time become particularly friendly. It was not until roughly the last ten or fifteen years of his life that our true friendship developed. Political proximity forced us together, and then gradually Tom began to pour out his heart — to me in small doses, and much more profusely to my wife, Jill. She comprehended long before I did how his ruling homosexual passion had condemned him to a life-time of deep loneliness; how excruciatingly he found it impossible to have satisfactory sexual relationships with those in his own social milieu — a hint of the story now elaborated in these pages. Of course there were indications before, but clearly Tom longed to tell what he could only tell properly in a posthumous autobiography. Doubtless, and perhaps unavoidably, its publication will be treated as a sensational event, but it will be read by all his friends with compassion and pity to mix with the interest.

His homosexuality truly was his ruling passion: no one, I believe, can read these pages and doubt that. But the fact makes the record of his other pursuits the more creditable and the more courageous. He was Member of Parliament for Maldon from 1942 to 1955, and for Barking from 1959 to 1974, and served on Labour's National Executive from 1949 to 1974. Mostly these duties, both to his constituency and to the national Party, were discharged with immaculate diligence, but there were one or two lapses.

In November 1950, he spent three months in Korea as a war correspondent at a time when the Parliamentary Labour Party sorely needed his assistance on three-line whips. He was bitterly condemned at a special meeting of the Party in one of its most vindictive moods, and was compelled to offer, to appease his eager persecutors, a near-grovelling apology. He did it in the iciest of tones. Some of us had feared that his detention in Korea, with all the accompanying rumours about other pursuits apart from his war correspondence, might end his political career. However, we managed to secure as his chief apologist before the wretched Party inquisition the services of Jimmy Hudson, a teetotal Quaker and the most spotlessly pure member of the Parliamentary Party bar none. Jimmy saved Tom for the moment. And quickly others rushed to his aid, some who thought they knew him best. His Management Committee 'recalled his exemplary and unmatched service to the Maldon Division.'

Alas, the Korean chapter is another which Tom as an auto-biographer never started upon—whether the inhibition was psychological, who can begin to guess? However, he lived to serve the Labour Party which he had joined with such suspicion and circumspection for another quarter of a century. And the service was truly of a different nature from that which it received from anyone else.

For Tom had one gift from the gods which he lavished on the cause of Socialism in general and the Labour Party National Executive in particular with a wonderful never-failing generosity. His singular god, by the way, was, as readers may now see for themselves, the one true Catholic, the strictest and most learned of Anglicans. No one could ever quite tell—or at least I could not—how much Tom's religion (a Christian agnosticism, he would call it in his later or latitudinarian moments) was the inspiration of his life or how much of it was a pose, useful for many necessary purposes, handy in the last resort for bashing lapsed Puritans, like myself, on the head.

However, Tom's god is a distraction from what I wanted to write; he has now intertwined that strand of the story into his life after his own fashion and inextricably. His gift from the gods was a splendid love and mastery of the English language. Whenever he took a pen in his hand, he became a perfectionist. All temptations, failings, inadequacies, were set aside. He knew what good English was, could weigh the value of every word, and had a nose for every form of falsity, bombast and misleading rhetoric. He could detect cant or humbug in an unwanted adjective or a misplaced comma. His own style indeed had a special precision and purity.

These talents were first used as a highly successful commercial proposition, as he himself has explained, when he wrote the original William Hickey column in the *Daily Express*, and of course any comparison with later products of that title must be banished from the mind at once and for ever. Not merely did Tom prove better than any journalist of his generation how good English could make good copy. He gradually turned the column into a genuine social criticism of the 1930s Establishment, under the admiring but suspicious and slightly dazed eye of Beaverbrook who had his own brand of criticism of the same institution, but who could never quite make up his mind whether Tom was a friend or an enemy.

But Tom was a Socialist — in those days, as I have said, almost an unreconstructed Stalinist. An explosion with Beaverbrook was bound to have come even if Tom had not gone off and won the election at Maldon in 1942 against the rickety Churchill coalition. He soon transferred his famous column to *Reynolds News*, and joined the Labour Party without shedding any of his Left-wing convictions. And in a few years again, much against the odds and much to the alarm of some of the Party leaders, he won a seat on Labour's National Executive Committee and held it quite securely for something like the next quarter of a century.

There he played a leading part in all the Bevanite and other Left–Right controversies which racked the Party over the ensuing period. But however deeply he engaged in these political disputes, he also managed to keep a watchful eye of mixed horror and solicitude on the flood of publications which poured from Transport House. He could not be held responsible for the final products; but what mountains of slush, stupidity and solecism he did remove by his labours! It was a devotion to duty which those who knew him in his other incarnations never dreamt him to be capable of. But his service to the Labour Party was beyond calculation, in every office of the Executive up to the Chairman, but most of all as the greatest of sub-editors.

How he endured such tedium and travail is not easily explained, except when it is appreciated how profound was his devotion to the Socialist cause. His own constituents, first in Maldon and then in Barking, knew it. People in other continents, Africans, Asians, West Indians, Cypriots and a host of others, came to know it. Down-and-outs, criminals, impostors of various types came to know it just as well. Which brings me, none too soon, to one at least of the various underworlds where Tom could find himself even more at home than in the Smoking Room of the House of Commons, the one refuge in the place which he found tolerably congenial. He led a series of erratic, wandering, often lonely lives of his own. And sometimes when he re-emerged, he could relate enthralling or foolish tales of his feats and adventures; he might even indulge in what he would rarely write, an absurd boast. At the next moment, he might lament his own inadequacies. But all these were no more than occasional spasms, or so he wished us to believe.

His autobiography tells us a somewhat different tale. Even if the proportions would have been altered had he been able to complete it himself, he must have written first — the chapters here — what he wanted to say most avidly. Clearly he could and would have written much more — for example, the pigeon-holes of several government departments, notably the Home Office, must be stuffed with huge Driberg correspondences, for once he took up some case of the victim of bureaucracy, he would fight the issue through to the end.

Remarkable as this autobiography is, one of the most honest I have ever read, I believe that most of his readers will conclude these last pages clamouring for more. But no one else can complete the portrait. And, to be sure, modesty has prevented him from illustrating in full measure the greatest of his qualities, the courage which he needed at so many sore moments and which would always re-assert itself. Somehow his brand of that shining quality reflected his Socialism and his love of language and his abiding love of all the other arts too. It encouraged him to shock and scandalise, to run terrible risks, to unloose his bitter contempt on the surrounding scene and those unlucky enough to encumber it. But that same courage incited him never to budge from his Socialist convictions, to defy the world if need be, to find his own road to hell or to heaven. Some of those whom he has left behind will miss him very much. The lonely Tom could be a marvellous comrade.

NOTE

Robert Graves permitted the publication of his letter only if I obtained Laura (Riding) Jackson's agreement. Mrs Jackson agreed only if I would include the following statement, in relation to the letter and comments on Robert Graves, Norman Cameron and herself. 'She regards Tom Driberg as having acted inexcusably towards her as a writer and a person, in the period of the described incidents. She views him as having violated kindness manifested toward him by her in blatantly disrespectful general talk, besides in attitudes exhibited to associates of hers. She denounces as perversely wrong the memoirs' allegations made against the two involved; and she protests as insolent and factually false the personal early and late life-picturings, there, of herself and Robert Graves; and she characterizes as despicable the memoirs' author's boast of his continuing to keep her letters filed under "Graves" – and as very unpleasantly hypocritical his posturing as one "ingenuous" in the matters in question. Finally, she wishes that it be recorded that she deplores the kind of material exemplified in the section of the memoirs presented to her as pseudo-inside report aimed at psuedo-literary appetites, and that she has consented, conditionally, to the publication of Robert Graves's letter, first, from reluctance to act by a mere power to suppress, but fundamentally, for a possible opportunity to provide some little counterweight to the literary-critical-biographical spuriosities increasingly loaded upon the literary market.'

DAVID HIGHAM

Index

Abdullah, Emir, 113
Acland, Richard, founds Common Wealth, 150, 181; teaches T.D. techniques of electioneering, 184, 188; sponsors T.D. to House of Commons, 185; and debate on central direction of the war, 188; supports Bevan, 193
Acton, Harold, 102, 205
Addison, Lord, 210, 212
Admiralty, 204
Aga Khan, 97
Aitken, Jonathan, 4
Alan, 167
Albania, 239
Albrighton, 126
Aldo, 80
Allingham, Margery, 183
American Telegraph & Telephone Company, 122–3
Amnesty, 61
Ancaster, Lord, 108
Anstruther-Gray, William, 178
Anti-Semitism, 202
Antwerp, 206
Arlanza, 35
Arnhem, 207, 209
Arnot, Olive Page, 150
Arnot, Robin Page, 150
Arras, 153, 154

Arromanches, 204
Ashdown Forest, 2
Asprey's, 90
Asquith, Margot, 78, 231
Astor, Lady, 153–5, 190
Athens, 72
Attlee, Clement, 66, 198, 199, 213, 216
Auden, W. H., 58–62, 65, 204, 212; *About the House*, 58
Aung San, 215, 216–17
Austria, 58–9
Avant-Garde, 58, 59
Ayrton, Michael, 164

Bacup, 21
'Baedeker raids', 157
Bagheria, 82
Barcelona, 117
Barking, 4, 183, 252
Barrington-Ward, J. G., 55
Bartlett, Vernon, 183, 185, 188
Battle of Britain, 155
Baxter, Beverley, 93, 100, 102, 192
B.B.C., 110, 228, 233–4
Beaton, Cecil, 93
Beaver Centre, 175
Beaverbrook, Lord, 40, 174; and references to Gordon Selfridge in the *Daily Express*, 96–7;

Beaverbrook, Lord – cont.
  and the 'white list', 97–8;
  kills 'Talk of London', 101,
  103; support for Chamberlain,
  103; starts William Hickey
  column, 104; habit of teasing,
  104–5; helps T.D. with his trial
  on indecent assault, 132;
  attitude to T.D.'s candidature
  at Maldon by-election, 180–1;
  at odds with Churchill, 181;
  critical interest in Hickey
  column, 194; on T.D.'s
  dismissal from Daily Express,
  196; vendetta against
  Mountbatten, 223–5; attitude
  to T.D., 253–4
Beebe, Lucius, 123
Beer, Ian, 52
Beerbohm, Max, 81–2
Beethoven, Ludwig van, 68–70
Begbie, Harold, 98
Bell, Birdie, 26–8
Bell, Herbert ('Bertie') Irving, 2,
  18, 26–9
Bell, Jockie, 18
Bell, John, 18
Bell, John of Blackethouse, 18
Bell, Laurence, 20, 21, 24
Bell, Margaret Irving, 18–21,
  24–8
Bell, Maurice, 24
Bell, Nora, 20, 21, 22–4, 25
Bell, Sybella, 19
Bell, William, 18
Bell, William the Redcloak, 18
Bell, Willie o' the Neuke, 18
Bellenger, Fred, 199
Belloc, Hilaire, 97, 98, 112
Belo Horizonte, 36, 37
Belsen, 209
Bentley, J. F., 54
Bérard, 66
Berlin, Isaiah, 233
Bernal, J. D., 147
Berners, Gerald, 186
Besant, Annie, 25

Betjeman, John, 5, 72, 102
Bevan, Nye, 186, 188, 193–4,
  216, 248
Bevin, Ernest, 193, 238–9
Bing, Geoffrey, 192
Blake, William, 77
Bligh, Eric, 22
Blumenfeld, R.D., 100–1
Boggis, Jack, 182
Bolshoi Ballet, 232
Books and Bookmen, 198
Booth-Clibborn, Augustine, 85
Boothby, Bob, 146, 192
Boulogne, 118
Bournemouth, 54; St Osmund's,
  55; St Stephen's, 54
Bowlby, H. T., 52–3
Bowles, Frank, 193
Bracken, Brendan, 184, 186, 190–1
Bradwell, 155, 195
Bradwell Lodge, 39–40, 41
Braintree, 181–2, 184, 196
Brazil, 35–8
Brent-Smith, Alexander, 48, 52
Brighton, 41, 46, 47, 50, 86;
  St Bartholomew's, 45
Bristol, 157
British Gazette, 72
British Information Services,
  Chicago, 168
Britten, Benjamin, 62
Broadclough Hall, 21
Brown, Arthur G., 69
Brown, W. J., 188
Bruce, Lord, 227
Brussels, 205
Buchanan-Jardine, Sir Jock, 19
Buchenwald, 209–13
Buchman, Frank, 98–100
Buckley, Christopher, 152
Buckley, Denis, 39
Budapest, 249
Bullingdon Club, 56
Bunting, Basil, 60
Burgess, Guy, 228–39, 245, 246,
  248–9
Burke, Thomas, 88

Burma, 4, 31, 213–27
Burnham-on-Crouch, 183, 184, 187
Burns, Robert, 145, 146
Butler, R. A., 193, 231
Butterfield, William, 89

Cagney, James, 170
California, 169–74
Camberwell House, 22
Cambridge University, 32, 33; King's College chapel, 127; Magdalene College, 126; Peckard Feast, 126–7
Cameron, Norman, 63, 64, 255
Campaign for Homosexual Equality, 148
Campbell, Sir Robert Neil, 3
Cardiff, 125
Cargill, David, 201
Cassel, Sir Ernest, 223
Cassels, J. D., 132, 134–41
Castlerosse, Lord, 104
Catholic Revival (Oxford Movement), 3, 44, 45
Caux, 100
Cecil, Lord David, 68
Cefalù, 85
Chamberlain, Neville, 103, 149, 154, 161
Chandra, Raj, 4
Changi jail, 219, 221–2
Channon, Henry (Chips), 186–7
Chaplin, Charlie, 98
Charlton, Father, 42
Chavchavadze, Prince George, 168
Cherkley, 40
Cherwell, 72–3, 82
Chesterton, G. K., 97–8
Chicago, 168
Chicago Tribune, 168, 194
Chittagong, 38
Christian Scientists, 154
Christiansen, Arthur, 132, 194, 196
Christie, Hector Lorenzo, 51

Churchill, Randolph, 231
Churchill, Sir Winston, 166, 188, 213; pubishes British Gazette, 72; turns down milk bar in the Commons, 154; direction of the war, 169, 187; secret wartime debates, 179; Coalition government under, 179; Beaverbrook at odds with, 181; T.D. a 'candid friend for Churchill', 183; on the Maldon by-election, 184; tells Mountbatten of collapse of Japan, 214; Burmese independence, 216; General Election, 1945, 218
Chutney, Jesus, 86
Clark, William, 168
Clarke, Reg, 183
Clifford, Alex, 152
Cliveden, 154
Cocks, Seymour, 193
Cocteau, Jean, 66
Cole, G. D. H., 71
Cole, Dame Margaret, 71
Common Wealth, 150, 181
Communist Party, T.D. joins, 50; General Strike, 1926, 70–2; Beaverbrook attacks, 105; Tom Wintringham excluded from, 147; attitude to World War II, 149; T.D. expelled from, 150; supports Polish Jews, 202
Comper, Sir Ninian, 47
Coney Island, 121
Connolly, Cyril, 59, 81, 195
The Constant Nymph, 90
Cooper, Father Henry, 61
Copenhagen, 237
Corvo, 101
Cosmo ('The Great Cosmo'), 85
Coventry, 157
Coward, Noël, 98
Cox, Geoffrey, 115
Cranwell, 95, 96
Crewe, Lord, 102

Cricklewood Public Library, 209
Cripple Ernie, 92
The Criterion, 58, 81
Crosland, Anthony, 192
Crossman, Dick, 238
Crowborough, 32; All Saints', 44: St John's, 42, 44, 46–7, 88; T.D.'s dislike of, 5; T.D's grandmother comes to stay at, 24, 25; T.D.'s mother in nursing home in, 41; T.D.'s parents settle in, 5; T.D. returns to after Oxford, 87, 88; T.D.'s revolt against, 50; T.D. sells Daily Worker in, 50
Crowford, George, 145–6
Crowley, Aleister, 83–6
Cummings, A. J., 225
Cunningham, Jock, 191
Cunningham-Reid, Alec, 188

Daily Express, Evelyn Waugh works for, 93–4; T.D. joins, 93–4; T.D.'s early career with, 94–104; 'Talk of London' column, 96, 101–4; white list, 97; Beaverbrook on style of name, 97; William Hickey column started, 104; T.D. as William Hickey, 104, 107–28, 152, 181, 185, 194, 196–7, 253–4; T.D. leads industrial action at, 150–2; references to Mountbatten, 225; Guy Burgess 'scoop', 236–7; T.D. sacked from, 195–7
Daily Mail, 85, 229, 238
Daily Mirror, 147
Daily Telegraph, 152
Daily Worker, 50, 180, 191, 232
Dali, Salvador, 67
Darnell, Linda, 169–70
Davies, Dai, 124
Davies, Gwyneth, 124
Dawkins, Professor, 71
Dean, Basil, 90
Delmer, Tom, 115

Devlin, Bernadette, 187
Diaghilev Ballet, 66
Dickinson, Emily, 42
Didinga, 30–1
Dieppe raid, 223–4
Dinka, 81
Dorman-Smith, Sir Reginald, 216
Douglas, Norman, 66, 164
Dresden, 162
Driberg, Amy Mary, feature in T.D.'s dreams, 1; T.D.'s feelings for, 2; marriage, 3; family background, 5–6, 18–19; sense of public duty, 5; settles in Crowborough, 5; beekeeping, 6–7; nostalgia for India, 10; relations with her mother, 19–21, 24–5; relations with her sister Nora, 22–3; estrangement from Bertie, 26–9; worries about Jim Driberg's welfare, 34, 35–8; visits Jim in Rio de Janeiro, 35–8; visit to Italy with T.D., 78–81; and T.D.'s desire to become a journalist, 88; knowledge of T.D.'s homosexuality, 132–3; death, 6–7, 41–3; will, 38, 42–3
Driberg, Colonel van, 17
Driberg, Jack Herbert (brother), 29–33, 42, 43, 185; Engato, 32; Lango, 30, 33
Driberg, James (Jim) Douglas, 29–30, 33–41, 42, 72, 100
Driberg, John James Street, T.D.'s memory of, 1–2; ancestry, 3, 17; at Lancing, 3; marriage, 3; in India, 3–4; gives evidence to East India Hemp Commission, 4; returns from India, 4–5; settles in Crowborough, 5; ill health, 5, 14; nostalgia for India, 10; mother-in-law's dislike of, 19–21; strong will, 21; death, 46

Driberg, Tom
  childhood, 2–15
  education: pre-school, 8, 9;
    the *Grange*: 10–14; a loner
    at, 11; subject to school
    mobbing, 11–12; sexual
    experiences, 12–14; *Lancing*:
    44–53; Uncle Bertie pays for,
    28; religious experiences,
    44–5; religious music at,
    48–9; meets Evelyn Waugh,
    49; awakening interest in
    politics, 50; stripped of
    offices and segregated, 51–2;
    sacked, 52–3, 54; chapel,
    54; writes for school
    magazine, 87; *Oxford*: 54–73,
    87; preparation for, 51, 52;
    free life at, 55–6; visits
    Hypocrites' Club, 55; student
    raids, 56–7; meets W. H.
    Auden, 58; meets Graves,
    62–4; development of literary
    and artistic interests, 65–70,
    72–3; 'Homage to Beethoven',
    68–70; General Strike, 70–2;
    writes for *Cherwell*, 72–3;
    vacations, 74–86; works
    as pavement artist, 75–8
  family background, 1–7, 17–43;
    mother features in dreams,
    1; memory of father, 1–2;
    godfathers, 3; father's
    ancestry, 3, 17; mother's
    ancestry, 5, 18–19; mother's
    death, 6, 41–3; aunts, 21–4;
    visits to Aunt Mary, 21–2;
    visits to Aunt Nora, 22–3;
    arranges Aunt Nora's
    cremation, 23–4; uncles, 24,
    25–9; brothers, 29–43;
    relations with Jack, 29–30;
    Jack's death, 32, 40;
    relationship with his brother
    Jim, 29–30, 34, 35, 38–9;
    Jim lives with, 38–40;
    Jim's death, 40

  homosexuality: earliest sexual
    experiences, 7–8; experiences
    at the Grange, 12–14;
    adolescent experiences, 15–16;
    and his religious nature,
    47–8; physical beauty and,
    50; experiences at Oxford,
    55, 71, 87; first essay in
    prostitution, 75–6; picks up
    down-and-out from
    Embankment, 75–7; holiday
    in Rapallo and Milan,
    79–80; Rupert Street vigils,
    88–9; cottage cruising in
    London, 88–9; experience in
    Palestine, 114; visits male
    brothels in America, 123;
    charges with indecent assault,
    129–44; effect on life as an
    M.P., 142–3, 198; narrow
    escape from arrest in
    Edinburgh, 144–6; brush
    with the police in
    Jockey's Fields, 147–8;
    advocates male brothels,
    148
  interests and causes: penal reform,
    3; Burmese independence,
    4, 215–16; liberalisation of
    the law on marihuana, 4;
    ecclesiastical committees,
    48; ballet, 66–7, 232;
    visual arts, 68; the raising of
    the ban on the *Daily
    Worker*, 180, 191; detestation
    of racialism, 188, 202–3;
    anti-Semitism in Polish
    Armed Forces, 202–3
  journalism and writing:
    poetry, 87; early desire to
    become a writer, 87–8;
    book reviews, 88, 198;
    mastery of English language,
    253; *Books and Bookmen*,
    198; *Cherwell*, 72–3;
    Daily Express: T.D. gets
    job at, 93–4; early career

Driberg, Tom – *cont.*
  with, 94–104; 'Talk of
  London' column, 96, 101–4;
  first scoop, 98–9; first 'by-
  line', 103; William Hickey
  column, 104, 107–28, 152,
  181, 185, 194, 196–7,
  253–4; reports George VI's
  coronation, 107–9; reports
  papal funeral and coronation,
  110–13; reports on Spanish
  Civil War, 115–18; interviews
  Fritz Kuhn, 119–21; reports
  on home life of a miner, 124–5;
  Hickey 'double', 127–8;
  leads industrial action at,
  150–2; war correspondent,
  152–3, 155–62; reports
  bombing of London and other
  cities, 155–61; the bombing
  of Hilda, 161–2; sacked from,
  195–7; *New Statesman*:
  88, 198; *Reynolds News*:
  starts column in, 197–8,
  254; war correspondent for,
  27, 204–9, 214–26; returns
  with Andrew Milbourne to
  Arnhem, 209; attends
  Potsdam Conference, 213;
  interview with
  Khrushchev, 239–45;
  Sunday Citizen: sacked
  from, 198; *Sunday Dispatch*:
  interviews Russian scientists
  for, 245–8; *Sunday
  Worker*: 74–5
    politics: awakening interest,
  50; early attitude to Labour
  Party, 50; joins Communist
  Party, 50; works for
  Communist Party, 70–2,
  74–5; helps Communist
  Party during General Strike,
  70–2; Beaverbrook attacks
  communist beliefs of, 105–6;
  expelled from Communist
  Party, 150; becomes M.P.,

  150, 178–88; wins Maldon
  by-election, 179–85; takes
  seat in Commons, 185;
  maiden speech, 187, 191;
  tables first questions, 190–1;
  becomes M.P. for Barking,
  198, 252; retires from
  Parliament, 198; joins
  Labour Party, 198–201,
  254; serves on Labour
  N.E.C., 198, 199, 252, 254;
  General Election, 1945,
  199–201; parliamentary
  delegation to Buchenwald,
  209–13; service to Labour
  Party, 254
    publications: *Absentees for
  Freedom*, 202; *Beaverbrook*,
  223–4; *Guy Burgess*,
  228–39; *Colonade*, 103–4;
  *The Mystery of Moral
  Re-Armament*, 99
    religious background and
  interests: family prayers,
  14–15; newly discovered
  interest in, 16; first High
  Mass, 16; mother's funeral,
  42; Sunday morning services,
  44; while at Lancing, 44–5,
  48–9; interest in the
  Romanized Church, 45–7;
  and his homosexuality,
  47–8; religious music, 48–9;
  liking for Westminster
  Cathedral, 54–5; gives
  University Sermon at
  Oxford, 59–60; interest in
  church ceremonial, 73;
  European Youth Conference,
  Lausanne, 99–100; attends
  papal funeral and
  coronation, 110–13; abolition
  of compulsory church parades
  in the Forces, 193; as the
  inspiration of his life, 253
    travels: Austria, 58; Burma and
  Malaya, 38, 213–26; France,

118–19, 152–3; Greece, 72; Italy, 78–81, 110–13; Korea, 252; Middle East, 113–14; Prague and Sudetenland, 118; Russia, 228–49; Scandinavia, 99; Spain, 115–18; Sudan, 30; Switzerland, 99–100; United States, 58, 99, 119–23, 166–77; Vietnam, 226; Western Front, 204–9
    other employment: film extra, 89–90; pavement artist, 75–8; works in Soho café, 90–2, 93
Driberg White, R. H., 17
Dumfries, John, 90
Duncan, Sir Andrew, 196
Dupré, Marcel, 55

East India Hemp Commission, 4
Échanges, 70
Eden, Sir Anthony, 231, 238, 249
Edinburgh, 144–6, 165
Edward VII, King, 109
Edward VIII, King, 106, 107
Edwards, Tickner, 6
Egerton, Wilfred, 141
Eindhoven, 209
Eisenhower, Dwight D., 210
Eliot, George, *Middlemarch*, 234
Eliot, T. S., 58, 93
Elizabeth II, Queen, 227
Ellesmere, Lord, 141
The Enchanted Garden, 79
English Hymnal, 48, 230
Epstein, Jacob, 102
Erfurt, 212
Essex County Standard, 183
European Youth Conference, Lausanne, 99–100
Evans, Stanley, 147
Evans, Trevor, 196
Evans-Pritchard, E. E., 32
Evening News, 39
Evening Standard, 105
Exeter, 40, 157

Exile, 222

F., John, 55
Fabian Society, 199
Fabre, John Henri, 6
Fagan, J. B., 67
Fairbanks, Douglas, Jr, 98
Faithfull, Marianne, 61
Farrer, David, 99
Fat Adelaide, 91
Feering, 201
Fernie Hunt, 189
Fettes College, 24
Figueras, 117
Finchingfield, 183
Firbank, Ronald, *Concerning the Education of Cardinal Pirelli*, 65
Foley, Charles, 166
Fonteyn, Margot, 66
Foot, Jill, 252
Foot, Michael, 202, 251–2
For Your Convenience, 88
Foreign Literature Publishing House, Moscow, 231
Forster, E. M., 231; *Where Angels Fear to Tread*, 79
Fothergill, John, 55–6; *An Innkeeper's Diary*, 56
Fox, Adam, 49
Fox, Mr, 123
Franco, General, 115, 118, 126
Freeman, John, 227
Friends of Spain, 126
Frisco's, 196
Fuchs, Klaus, 237
Fuck You, 59

G., Derek, 12–13, 34
Gait, Sir Edward, 3
Gaitskell, Hugh, 71, 240
Gargoyle Club, 212–13
Garrick, David, 174
Gaselee, Sir Stephen, 115, 126
Gask, 101
Gaunt, Hilda, 163
Gay News, 148

Gellhorn, Martha, 115
General Elections, 1935, 179;
    1945, 183, 199–201, 213,
    217; 1959, 198
General Strike, 70–2, 74
George VI, King, 107–9
Gerrard, Teddie, 34
Gibbs, 51
Ginsberg, Allen, 4, 60
Girouard, Dick, 90
Giselle, 232
Glasgow, 163
Gleneagles, 23
Gloucester, Duke of, 188
Glubb Pasha, 113
Goering, Hermann, 152
Gollancz, Victor, 105
Gorki, Maxim, 121
Göteborg, 99
Graham, Angus, 57
Grandi, Count, Dino, 108
Grange, 10–14
Grant, Lady Sybil, 102
Graves, Robert, 62–5, 255–6;
    Lars Porsena, 64; Mrs
    Fisher, 64–5
Greene, Graham, 231
Greenfield, Florence, 78
Greenwood Gate, 2
Gresson, Frank, 10, 11
Grey, Mary, 67
Grigg, Sir James, 178
Guards Armoured Division,
    204, 207
Guards Club, 89
Guildford, 44
Guinness, Bryan (Lord Moyne),
    57
Guinness, Lady Honor, 186
Gurdon, Basil, 47, 50

Haileybury, 198
Hailsham, Lord, 179
Haldane, J. B. S., 147
Halifax, Edward Frederick,
    Earl of, 103
Halifax, Nova Scotia, 166

Hall, Marguerite Radclyffe,
    The Well of Loneliness, 102
Hall Brothers, 56
Hansard, 179, 194, 240
Harcourt, Sir William, 67
Harper, Allanah, 70
Harriman, Averell, 224
Harris, Lady, 86
Harris, Sir Percy, 86
Harrison, Harry, 115
Harrison, J. F., 44
Harrison, Joan, 44, 170
Harvey, Edmund, 193
Hastings, 86
Hawksmoor, Nicholas, 61
Helen of Kirkconnel, 5, 18
Hemingway, Ernest, 115
Hemsley, 8, 9
Henry, 158–61
Herbert, A. P., 161
Herbert, Sir Denis, 191
Heseltine, Philip, 163
Hewart, Lord, 133
Hickey, William, 104; see also
    Daily Express
Hilda, 161–2
Hiroshima, 213
Hitchcock, Alfred, 44, 169–70,
    172
Hitler, Adolf, 99, 103, 120,
    149, 152
Ho Chi-Minh, 226
Hodenfield, G. K., 205
Hodza, 118
Hogarth Press, 68
Hollywood, 169–74
'Homage to Beethoven', 68–70
Hooft, Visser 't, 100
Hooker, Miss, 8, 9
Hooker, Mrs Stenson, 21
Hopkinson, Tom, 180, 181
Horner, Arthur, 125
House of Commons, M.P.s and
    public scandal, 142–3;
    war-time enfeeblement, 178–9;
    Maldon by-election, 1942,
    179–85, 197; Party truce,

179, 182, 193, 198; T.D. takes his seat, 185; T.D. tables his first questions, 190–1; T.D.'s maiden speech, 191; debating tactics, 191–2; filibustering, 192–3; Parliamentary delegation to Buchenwald, 209–13
Housman, A. E., 22
Howard, Brian, 72–3, 212
Hozier, Nellie, 33
Hudson, Jimmy, 252
Hugerl, 59
Hughes-Hallett, Sir Charles, 224
Hull, Robert H., 69
Hungary, 249
Hunt, Jeannie, 21, 42, 185, 195
Hunt, Reuben, 181
Hutton, Graham, 168
Huxley, Aldous, 93
Huxley, Julian, 194
Hymns Ancient and Modern, 48, 221
Hypocrites' Club, 55

Indian Civil Service, 3, 4
Ingersoll, Colonel, 91
I.R.A., 190
Islip, 62
Iveagh, Lord and Lady, 186

Jackson, Laura, *see* Riding, Laura
Jagger, Christopher, 61
James, Edward, 67, 90
James, Henry, 58
James, Mrs Willie, 67
Janis, Morris, 199, 200
Japan, 168, 213–22
Jardine, William, 5, 19
Jardine Matheson, 5, 19
Jay's, 89
Jerrold, Douglas, 126
Jerusalem, 113
Jervaulx Abbey, 51
Jesus Christ, 188–9
John, 114
Jones, Alan, 94, 101

Joyce, James, 68; *Ulysses*, 65–6
Joynson-Hicks, William, 102
Juliana, Queen of the Netherlands, 108

Kallman, Chester, 58, 62
Kandy, 214, 215, 218
Keats, John, 221
Kennedy, Harry, 150
Kenton, Lou, 115
Kenyatta, Jomo, 32
Ker, A. W., 221
Khartoum, 31
Khrushchev, Nikita, 239–49
Kirchstetten, 58, 61
Kirkpatrick, Ivone, 239
Kleffens, Dr van, 174, 175–6
Knox, Sir Alfred, 126
Knox, Ronald, 98
Koch, Ilse, 211
Korean war, 252–3
Kranji, 214
Krishnamurti, 25
Kuhn, Fritz, 119–21

L., A., 131–41
La Mora, Constance de, 115; *In Place of Splendour*, 115
Labour Party, T.D.'s early attitude to, 50; T.D. joins, 198–201; T.D. serves on N.E.C., 198, 199, 252, 254; T.D. condemned for absence during Korean war, 252–3
Lambert, Constant, 81, 102, 163–5, 195
Lancaster, Osbert, 72
Lancing, T.D.'s father at, 3; Jack Driberg at, 32; chapel services at, 44, 45, 48–9, 54; Evelyn Waugh at, 49; T.D. stripped of offices at, 51–2; T.D. writes for school magazine, 87
Landis, Carole, 169–70
Lang, Dr, 107
Lango, 30

Larkin, Philip, 17, 21
Lausanne, 99–100
Law, Andrew Bonar, 97
Lawrence, D. H., 102
Lawrence, T.E., 154; *The Mint*, 154
Leadbeater, Bishop, 25
Lee, Jennie, 248
Lenin, 245
Leonardo da Vinci, 80
Leroy, Jean, 229, 246
Le Touquet, 118, 119
Lever, Harold, 192
Leverson, Ada, 81–2
Lewis, Cecil Day, 62
Liège, 205
Lifar, Serge, 66
Life, 58
Lincoln Battalion, 121
Lindbergh, Charles, 167
Littlemore, 44
Litvinov, 108
Liverpool, 156, 166
Lloyd George, David, 108
Lockerbie, 23
London: Alhambra Theatre, 34; All Saints', Margaret Street, 89; Broadcasting House, 56, 157–8; Canada House, 78; Central Criminal Court, 132, 134–42; Eiffel Tower restaurant, 82; Gay Hussar, 61, 198; Hyde Park, 157; Jockey's Fields, Holborn, 147–8; Old Bailey, 132, 134–42; Olivelli's, 180; Queen Elizabeth Hall, 60; Reform Club, 231; Ritz, 186; St Alban's, Holborn, 25, 45; St Augustine's, Haggerston, 155; St Barnabas, Pimlico, 47; St George's, Bloomsbury, 61; SS. John & Elizabeth, St John's Wood, 32; St Mary's, Pimlico, 89, 149, 172; St Paul's Cathedral, 157; St Peter's, Eaton Square, 189; Savile Club, 67; Savoy Grill, 94; Savoy Hotel, 34;

Washington Hotel, 82; West London Magistrates Court, 132; Westminster Cathedral, 54–5, 172
London Hospital, 33, 41
London Mercury, 65
London School of Economics, 31
London Zoo, 194
Long, Franco, 61
Long, Graham, 61
Loos, 33
Los Angeles, 170–1, 172–4
Louis of Battenberg, Prince, 223
Loveday, 85

M., 156
M., Andy, 208
McCawry, Mother, 91, 92
McCormick, Colonel, 168
MacDonald, Ramsay, 50
Macey, Mr, 7
Mackenzie, Compton, 46; *Thin Ice*, 146
Maclean, Donald, 228, 229, 230, 233, 237, 238
Macmillan, Harold, 60
McNeil, Hector, 238
Madrid, 115
Maeterlinck, Maurice, 6
Magnasco Society, 82
Malaya, 214
Maldon, by-election, 1942, 179–85, 197; General Election, 1945, 199–201
Manchester, 148
Manners, Angela, 33
Manners, Lady, 33
Martin, Kingsley, 88n, 89
Marvell, Andrew, 77
Mary, Queen Consort of King George V, 108
Massingberd-Mundy, Mrs, 183
Mauritius, 5
Mayer, Louis B., 170
Messel, Oliver, 102
Mikhailov, 239, 245, 248
Milan, 80

Milbourne, Andrew, 209; *Lease of Life*, 209
Miller, Paul, 222
Milner, Major, 192, 193
Mirfield, 201
Mitford, Nancy, 72, 102
Moffat, Curtis, 195
Molson, Lord, 49
Monkman, Phyllis, 34
Mons, 33
Montreal, 175
Moody, Aubrey, 201–2
Moore, Beaufoi, 135–41
Moore, John, 139
Moorehead, Alan, 152
Moral Re-Armament (M.R.A.), 98–100
Morrison, Herbert, 190, 193
Morrison, Ian, 152
Moscow, 228–49
Mosley, Sir Oswald, 125, 126, 167, 169, 193, 195
Mountbatten, Edwina, 217, 223, 225, 226
Mountbatten, Lord Louis, 31, 38, 213–18, 222–7
Mudd, Norman, 85
Mussolini, Benito, 80, 85

Nagasaki, 213
Nagichot, 30
Nairn, Ian, 45
Naples, 82
National Council for Civil Liberties, 202
National Union of Journalists, 151
Negrín, Dr Juan, 117
New Delhi, 4
New Statesman, 88, 198
New York, 58, 62, 167; Madison Square Gardens, 167; Yorkville, 167–8
New York Times, 169
New York World-Telegram, 99
New York World's Fair, 121–3
Newcastle, 163

News Chronicle, 115, 225
News of the World, 47, 81, 132
Nick, 245, 246
Nicolson, Harold, 146, 233–4
Nicolson, Nigel, 234
Niemoeller, Pastor, 120
Nijinsky, Romola, 66
Nijinsky, Vaslav, 66
Norfolk, Duke of, 107
Norman, Dr, 22
Northcliffe, Lord, 225
Norton, Jean, 224–5
Nunn May, Alan, 237

Ogilvie-Grant, Mark, 72
Ohn, Maung, 216
Olive, Father, 42
Ora, S. P., 95
Osborne, Charles, 61
Osborne, Dorothy, 9
Oslo, 99
Osterley Park, 147
Owen, Frank, 106, 132, 186, 213, 224, 251
Oxford, 126
Oxford Group, 98
Oxford Movement (Tractarian Revival), 3, 44, 45
Oxford Playhouse, 67
Oxford Poetry, 62
Oxford University, Christ Church, 52, 54–73, 87; Hertford College, 30; Musical Union, 68–70; Pusey House, 73; University Church, 59

P., Derek, 12, 13, 14
Paddy, 90–2, 93
Paget, Reggie, 188–9
Palestine, 113–14
Paris, 85
Parker, Dorothy, 95, 170
Parker, John, 198
Parker, Ralph, 232
Parkstone, St Osmund's, 55
Parliament, *see* House of Commons

INDEX

Peake Pasha, 113
Pearl Harbour, 168, 176
Pearson, Colin, 52, 54
Peckard Feast, 126–7
Peña, 117
Penang, 218
Petra, 113
Pevsner, Nikolaus, 45
Philip, Prince, 227
Phillimore, Lord, 126
Picasso, Pablo, 66
Pius XI, Pope, 110
Pius XII, Pope, 110, 111–13
Plomer, William, *The Dorking Thigh*, 222
Plummer, Leslie (Dick), 152
Poetry Festival, 1973, 60
Polignac, Prince Melchior de, 152–3
Polish Armed Forces, 202–3
Pollitt, Harry, 150
Ponsonby, Sir Frederick, 141
Pontecorvo, 237
Pope, Alexander, *Dunciad*, 149
Potsdam Conference, 213, 214
Pound, Reginald, 94
Powell, Enoch, 188–9
Powell, Sir Francis, 20
Prague, 118
Prestwick, 177
Priestley, J. B., 183
Prince of Wales, 176
Princess Josephine Charlotte, 204
Pritt, D. N., 193
Private Eye, 238
Pytchley Hunt, 189

Queensberry, Duchess of, 19
Quennell, Peter, 81, 102, 195
Quinton, Harold, 184
Quiroga, José María, 116

R., J. K., 131–41
Ramos, Francisco, 115
Ramsay, Captain, 169, 190
Rangoon, Orient Club, 215
Rapallo, 78–81, 93

Rathbone, Eleanor, 202
Rawlinson, A. E. J., 98
Rayner, John, 81, 195
Red Cross, 214
Reed, Austin, 98–9
Rees, Goronwy, 233
Repulse, 176
Reynolds News, T.D. as war correspondent, 27, 204–9, 214–26; T. D. writes column for, 197–8, 254; T.D. interviews Khrushchev, 239–45; changes to *Sunday Citizen*, 198
Rhodesia, 57, 190
Ribbentrop, Joachim, 103, 108, 153
Rice, 12
Richardson, James, 24
Richardson, Sir William, 197
Riding, Laura, 62–5, 255–6
Rio de Janeiro, 35–8
The Ritual Reason Why, 45
Roach, E. Keith, 114
Roberts, Alan, 222
Roberts, Wilfrid, 108
Robertson, E. J., 133, 151–2
Robertson, Mr, 123
Robeson, Paul, 98
Rome, 110–13
Roosevelt, Franklin D., 121, 168
Rootham, Helen, 93
Rothermere, Lord, 225
Roxburgh, J. F., 49, 55, 65
Royal Air Force College, Cranwell, 95, 96
Royal Commission on the Press, First, 97–8
Ruggles-Brise, Edward, 180
Ruggles-Brise, Sir John, 180
Rumbold, Sir Horace, 102
Runciman, Lord, 118

S., 156, 180, 185
Sackville-West, Vita, 234
Saigon, 225–6
Salisbury, Lord, 231

Sam, 212
Sampson, George, 197
San Bernardino, 170
San Diego, 169, 174
San Francisco, 123
Sauguet, 66
Sayers, Dorothy L., 183, 209
SEAC, 213
Searle, Ronald, 222
Secker, Miss, 94, 96, 100
Secker & Warburg, 99
Selfridge, Gordon, 96–7
Selfridge's, 96–7
Sen, Bireswir, 4
Sévigné, Mme de, 155
Sewell, Percy, 96, 101–2, 103
Seyzinger, Edmund, 25
Shaw, Bernard, 50, 154, 183, 201
Shaw, Bobbie, 132
Shaw, Tim, 57
Shawcross, Sir Hartley, 187
Shinwell, Lord, 193
Silver End, 184
Simon, André, 56
Simon, Sir John, 108, 109
Simpson, Cuthbert, 59
Simpson, Mrs, 106
Singapore, 38, 214, 217, 218
Sitwell, Edith, T.D. meets, 81;
    encourages T.D. to write
    poetry, 87; tea-parties, 92–3;
    finds T.D. job at *Daily Express*,
    93, 94; *Wheels*, 65, 82
Sitwell, Sir George, 82
Sitwell, Osbert, 57, 63, 81, 82, 93
Sitwell, Sacheverell, 81, 82, 93,
    94; *Southern Baroque Art*, 57,
    82
Slim, General, 217–18
Someren, Mrs Van, 101
Southampton, 204
Soviet Union, 228–49
Spanish Civil War, 80, 110,
    115–18, 147
Spanish Socialist Workers'
    Party, 118
Sparrow, Mr, 126

Spender, Matthew, 61
Spender, Natasha, 61
Spender, Stephen, 61–2
Springball, Dave, 150
Squire, J. C., 65
Stalin, Josef, 213, 244–5
Stanley, Lady Maureen, 102
Staveley, 162
Steer, Wilson, 183
Stein, Gertrude, 68
Stevenson, Melford, 201
Stewart, Bob, 71
Stowe, 49
Strachey, John, 103, 105
Stravinsky, Igor, 66, 102
Streeter, Dr, 98
Strindberg, August, *Spook
    Sonata*, 67
Stroud, 17
Stuartstar, 39
Suck, 59
Sudan, 30, 81
Sudetenland, 118
Suez crisis, 231, 249
Sullivan, J. W. N., 85
Sunday Citizen, 198
Sunday Mirror, 216
Sunday People, 233
Sunday Times, 82, 152
Sunday Worker, 74–5
Swaffer, Hannen, 94, 183, 184
Swan Lake, 232
Sykes, Christopher, 102
Symon, Dudley, 45
Symons, A. J. A., 56, 81, 164,
    195; *The Quest for Corvo*, 101
Sysonby, Lord, 141

Tate, Mavis, 212
Tate, Mrs, 108
Taylor, A. J. P., 224, 225
Tchekov, Anton, *The Cherry
    Orchard*, 67
Tchelitchev, 66
Tennant, Stephen, 102
Tenterden, 94
Thame, Spreadeagle, 55–6

Thomas, Dylan, 213
Thomson, Admiral, 238–9
Tickerage Mill, 81, 195
Time, 104
The Times, 72, 110, 132, 152, 154, 188, 232
Tobruk, 184, 201
Tolleshunt D'Arcy, 183
Tolya, 235
Tomalin, Nicholas, 152
Tommy, 90–2, 93
Toulouse, 118
Tractarian revival, 3, 44, 45
Trades Union Congress (T.U.C.), 70, 71
Tree, Ronald, 186
Truman, Harry S., 213, 214
Tunbridge Wells, 15, 16; St Augustine's, 16; St Barnabas, 16
Turville-Petre, Francis, 57

Uganda, 30
Ukraine, 243
Ulanova, 232
United States 58, 99, 119–23, 166–77
Uzbekistan, 241

Val, Marquis Merry del, 126
Vansittart, Sir Robert, 161
Vaughan Williams, Ralph, 48
Vayo, Alvarez del, 116
Vic-Wells Ballet, 163
Victoria, Princess, 223
Vietnam, 225–6
Vladimir, 235

W., 174
Wagner, Michel, 99
Wagner, Richard, 58
Walden, Brian, 4
Walker, H. E., 35–7
Wallasey, 156
Walpole, Hugh, 111–13; *Roman Fountain*, 111, 112–13
Walsh, Walter, 45

Walska, Ganna, 103
Walton, Sir William, 59, 60, 81
Wardlaw-Milne, Sir John, 188
Washington, D. C., 168–9
Watson, E. J. (Jimmy), 87, 95–6
Wauchope, Sir Arthur, 113–14
Waugh, Evelyn, at Lancing, 49, 65; at Oxford, 55, 72; influence on T.D.'s literary interests, 65; works for *Daily Express*, 93–4; T.D. writes about in 'The Talk of London' column, 102; on Brian Howard, 212; *Decline and Fall*, 56; *A Little Learning*, 49; *The Ordeal of Gilbert Pinfold*, 49; *Scoop*, 94
Weizmann, Dr, 113
Wells, H. G., 93
Westlake, Bert, 41, 131, 139
Westminster Bank, 7
Whitaker, Mary (Aunt M.), 19, 20, 21, 43
Whitby, Humphrey, 149
White, Dr, 74
White, Eric Walter, 69
White Army, 205–6
Whiteley's, 22
Wichita, Kansas, 169
Wilde, Oscar, 81
Wilkinson, Ellen, 198
Wilson, Father H. A., 155–6
Wilson, Harold, 190, 198
Wilson, J. B., 94, 100
Wilson, Leonard, Bishop of Singapore, 218–21
Winchell, Walter, 127, 167
Wine and Food Society, 56
Wintringham, Tom, 144, 146–7; *English Captain*, 147
Witham, 183, 184
Woking, 32
Wood, Jack, 222
Woolf, Virginia, 68
Woollcott, Alexander, 194
Workers' Weekly, 50
World Council of Churches, 99–100

World War II, bombing of
London, 56, 155–6, 157–61;
T.D. as war correspondent,
152–3, 204–9, 214–26; phoney
war, 152; Battle of Britain,
155; bombing in other towns,
156–7; 'Baedeker raids', 157;
Pearl Harbour, 168, 176;
U.S. enter, 168–9; T.D.
reports from Western Front,
204–9; Belgian Resistance
organisation catch
collaborators, 205–6; Arnhem,
207, 209; treatment of German
prisoners, 208; Buchenwald,
209–13; Burma and Malaya,
213–27
World's Press News, 142
Worley, Chief Justice, 221
Worthing, 46; St Andrew's, 16
Wright, Eric, 198
Wyatt, Woodrow, 215–16
Wykeham-Barnes, Peter, 183
Wyndham, Richard (Dick), 81,
164, 195

Young, Wilf, 200–1

If you would like a complete catalogue
of Quartet's publications
please write to us at
27/29 Goodge Street, London W1P 1FD

PENTIMENTO
Lillian Hellman

'An irresistibly readable book' – *Cosmopolitan*

'All in all, a beautiful book' *Daily Mirror*

Includes the story JULIA now filmed staring Jane Fonda and Vanessa Redgrave who won an Oscar for her performance in the film.

Autobiography 95p

AN UNFINISHED WOMAN
Lillian Hellman

'Throughout this memoir flit the years of the thirties, forties and fifties in kaleidoscopic fashion shifting page by page . . . lost decades beautifully recalled' – *Contemporary Review*

'This is a fine, important book' – Sandy Wilson, *Sunday Telegraph*

Autobiography £1.50

HONS AND REBELS
Jessica Mitford

This is the first volume of her world-famous autobiography. It is a wise, witty and incisive portrait of a vanished era of English country life and the devastating effects it produced in one remarkable family.

The second volume of the autobiography, *A Fine Old Conflict*, is also published as a Quartet paperback.

Autobiography £1.95

THE WORLD THE FLESH AND MYSELF
Michael Davidson
With a foreword by James Cameron

Now available again – this classic autobiography.

'The courageous and lovable story of a brilliant journalist's struggles' – Arthur Koestler

Autobiography £1.25

MOSCOW FAREWELL
George Feifer

'Deeply erotic . . . profoundly compelling' – *Los Angeles Times*

An unforgettable, very enjoyable, personal picture of the real flesh-and-blood of Russia – the world that four British Airways flights per week never reach.

Autobiography £2.95

CHILD OF A SYSTEM
Noel Arden

Foreword by *Anthony Storr*

'A testimony to the heights to which the human spirit can rise . . . the story of a woman of courage who relives her early life so that we may know what is done to our maimed brothers in our name' – Tom Hart, *New Society*

Autobiography £1.50

ALONE OF ALL HER SEX
The Myth and Cult of the Virgin Mary
Marina Warner

In this extraordinary book, at once, a feat of scholarship and a literary achievement of great beauty, Marina Warner penetrates the layers of Mariology to bring us something remarkable: a biography of the Virgin that reveals her in all her guises from human woman to Queen of Heaven.

'This is a most interesting and beautifully written book' – *The Times*

Mythology/Religion   £3.95   Illustrated

SAMUEL TAYLOR COLERIDGE
A Bondage of Opium
Molly Lefebure

'The first absorbing, original, convincing book about Coleridge to have been written for many years' – Geoffrey Grigson, *Country Life*

'For several days I was as hooked as any junkie on this stunning biography' – Jilly Cooper, *Sunday Times*

Biography   £3.95   Illustrated